COCKADOODLEDOO

CATHY WATERHOUSE

Copyright © 2020 by Samantha May

All rights reserved. No part of this publication may be reproduced, stored in any form of retrieval system or transmitted in any form or by any means without prior permission in writing from the publishers except for the use of brief quotations in a book review.

DEDICATION

To all the randy men in the world, without whom this book would not have been possible.

CONTENTS

DEDICATION iii

Part One 5

   CHAPTER ONE Straight from the Cow 6

   CHAPTER TWO A Vinegar Sandwich Please 18

   CHAPTER THREE They Strolled Down the Lane Together 36

   CHAPTER FOUR "Fuckin' ell Waddid You 'Av Fur Breakfast?!" 57

   CHAPTER FIVE One Day Through Ancient, Noiseless Woods 75

   CHAPTER SIX Can She Do 'Owt Wit Sheep? 93

   CHAPTER SEVEN Counting Testicles 110

   CHAPTER EIGHT A Milking Song 131

   CHAPTER NINE "No-One Sucks Cock Like a Man." 147

   CHAPTER TEN The Friendly Cow All Red and White 168

   CHAPTER ELEVEN She Is Not Any Common Earth 186

COCKADOODLEDOO Part Two A Ghastly Business 206

Part One

CHAPTER ONE

Straight from the Cow

August 2020

Six years ago, innocent as a day old duckling when it came to the impossible world of book publishing, and no one apart from myself ever having seen the manuscript, I sent the opening chapter of this book to the first literary agent that came up on a Google search, the Andrew Lownie Literary Agency. They were clearly a much respected company with excellent credentials and listed on the second page of the 2014 Writers Handbook.

This was the email response and subsequent phone call. It is entirely genuine. I haven't fluffed things up for effect.

'Dear Cathy,

Thank you for submitting your sample chapter. This has commercial and possibly filmic potential. Please send us the completed manuscript at your earliest convenience.'

I confess to having wee'd myself a little, such was my joy at this response. Later that day, Mr Lownie himself rang me. The conversation ran thus:

"You will have to meet with one of our agency people here in London."

(Shit, this is all happening a bit quick).

"Ah, no that's no good I'm afraid. It's very important I remain anonymous. The book contains delicate subject matter."

"That's not a problem, it would just be one of our representatives. We like to meet face to face with potential new authors, for promotional purposes." (I can sense a dark cloud gathering on the horizon).

"I see. Well, please don't expect a tiny blonde, I'm in my late forties and a size 24."

"I'm sorry, what size did you say you were?,"

"24."

"I'm very sorry but that is going to be a problem regarding promotion, but many thanks for your enquiry."

(And fuck you too Mr Lownie).'

A fantastically unfair world; I had the carrot of potential success dangling there for all of eight hours. It was a tough notion to get my head around, literary rejection on account of my waistline and for a few weeks after the telephone conversation I considered lying through my teeth and re-submitting the book to agencies, posing as a luscious, petite cutie. I changed my mind, I will always love food more than the expectations of the general public. My humour and physical appearance are more Jo Brand than Bridget Jones, and that's where I'm staying.

I gritted my teeth and sent the same chapter to dozens of agents, none of whom responded. In a dejected huff and stuffing the manuscript in a drawer where it hovered about at the back of my mind for years, I finally made the decision to self publish. If I only sell enough copies to fill the pick-up truck with diesel, well that's just fine and dandy.

As regards a polished book, I had to sell my pancreas to pay the publishing costs, never mind the £1700 editing/proof-reading fee quoted to me by most companies. Hence the grammar, punctuation and structure of the book is all mine, and pretty good too I reckon for a hatchling writer.

I am 53, a farmer and praise be to DNA, a woman. In 2005, aged 38 and in dire financial straits, I spent a year as the world's most disastrously qualified escort in order to buy a new Hereford bull and reduce the enormous overdraft which my sheep were, in the main, responsible for. It was a terrifying decision for a country girl whose raunchiest moment was giving the local farmer's son a hand job in his milking parlour.

For one year I juggled two professions, farming and escorting. Quite how I endured the sight of endless willies and the stress of preventing both occupations from overlapping, is well, bloody incredible. Added to that, I was going through an early menopause. And whilst genuinely thrilled at the prospect of no more wretched monthly haemorrhaging, I was still more thrilled at my rapidly declining sexual appetite as I had always found sex awkward and alien, a ghastly cocktail of biological smells, viscous leakages and morning breath.

Performing a shockingly unenthusiastic blow job for £30 with the stubborn remains of a ewe's afterbirth still up my forearms, was a definite first. Another was the local farm vet turning up, indeed, the owner of the veterinary practice!, he having seen my ample curves advertised online. I stood in the farmyard, numbed at the awfulness of the situation. Jesus what am I doing.

I'm sure there are women who bounce out of bed of a morning, happy as an Andrex puppy, overjoyed at the prospect of a day of paid sex with strangers ahead of them. I can safely say I was not an Andrex puppy. Performing lewd acts, stark bollock naked with a complete stranger who has just handed you £70 for the privilege, is about as erotically charged as having a smear test.

Here in 2020, my alarm clock is Michael the Dorking cockerel, crowing like his life depended on it at 5am. I'd never have the heart to put him in a casserole but truth be told, he's an evil little shit and launches himself vertically into the air to savage me with his beak and claws every morning, never tiring of the regular assault on my legs, which are now scarred and scratched. But his wives provide me with the most delicious brown eggs and as such I eat vast amounts of pancakes. The hens are to blame in part for my space-hopper shaped figure.

I am finally living my misanthropic dream in Cornwall in a remote and beautiful part of the North coast with five border collies; Meg, Sky, Floss, Lad and Jill. We all live in a small, rented stone cottage with an attached five acres of permanent pasture. I've never been married and have only had two long term relationships, both decades ago; Rupert was simply too nice. He bought me excessive quantities of flowers, saw to my every need and was a thoroughly all round good bloke. So I dumped him. The other bloke, Ryan, I'm sure had some form of undiagnosed epilepsy and would explode with rage, throwing domestic appliances about the place if he so much as burnt the toast.

I'm pretty much self sufficient in food and have a milking Jersey cow named Dulcie and a big white goat called Goatee. They provide milk, cheese, yogurt, ice-cream and butter. Plus creamy fudge and milk soap when I'm feeling industrious. I also have a small flock of ten ewes who lamb each Spring, a veggie patch and an orchard. Late Summer is spent making jam, lots of it, which I'm extremely possessive about so rarely give any away. By June the following year I will have consumed all 60 jars and still not be diabetic, I am a marvel of nature.

Milking and making all the associated products takes up a good chunk of the day. By 6am I've downed three cups of tea and have brought the portable milking machine to life with lights, a vacuum pump and the radio, all combined with much bleating and mooing. Dulcie is nearing the end of her annual ten month lactation. She'll have a few weeks off after that to blob about before getting flirty again with Chutney the Galloway bull. It's a good life, even the bloody awful days of lame sheep, mastitis and broken fences. I generate a small income from the sales of surplus farm produce, plus a few shillings from candle-making, not average sized candles mind, but bloody great things; two foot high by six inches wide with enough wicks to illuminate the Vatican.

Had I been of sound mind from approximately the age of five upwards, I believe I would have achieved the dream of a small farm of my own many years ago. But unfortunate childhood events resulted in a battle of lifelong depression and severe self esteem issues, both now completely under control with the aid of chocolate and Citalopram.

By 2004 I had managed to rent some land from Archibald and Henrietta Whitbread who owned Gallows farm on Silsden Moor in Yorkshire. I was also employed by them to milk their 80 cow Friesian herd. On my rented acres I kept a breeding flock of sheep and a few suckler cows. I needed a decent young bull and I needed a shearing machine and I needed them quickly. Pulling on bovine titties twice a day and mending Archie's dry-stone walls were barely enough to keep me in turnips for supper. Alas, no City and Guilds in money laundering or pension fraud existed, and so in a moment of madness and desperation I decided to give escorting a try.

In the second half of this book, the filthy half, I have included some of the many hundreds of texts and emails received from men during that mind broadening year, which are deserving of a publication all to themselves. Every communication is genuine and as received, with obviously the senders' names changed, the poor randy little buggars.

I am not a writer, nor am I a keeper of a personal diary. But after approximately three months of escorting, a seed of an idea began to germinate: I was writing the occasional blog on my escorting profile in order to try and attract customers, each one a step closer to a handsome new bull. The blog writing I found difficult, as having checked out other girls' blogs, they were all without exception highly descriptive passages of the gory goings on of their nether regions and those of their male customers. I decided to buck the trend and treated my readers to a weekly update of life on the farm. To my pleasant surprise, an awful lot of men commented on how entertaining they were and how I should write a book. I brushed aside most of these comments until a guy messaged me to say he'd read my blog whilst on the train to work and was, he said, 'laughing so hard he had to move seats to somewhere quieter,' and added that, 'I should write a book.' I began the diary that day, with a far far away idea that one day I may attempt to have it published. A smattering of knowledge regarding country matters may well enhance the readers enjoyment, but a devout townie will still derive much merriment I would hope, from listening to the lamentations of a woman who though being paid for sex, found it as palatable as a bowl of tripe.

A box of tissues plus a computer within easy reach are recommended. The former to dry the tears of laughter/pity and the latter with which to email me letters of hate for wrecking countless relationships.

Now the last time I was aware, in order to enjoy sex, one has to be in some way aroused by the person they are looking at. Given the number of fully sexually aroused men in the world at any one time, as against non aroused men going about their daily business, the likelihood of me, or anyone in fact, finding a random visiting stranger, attractive enough to want to exchange bodily fluids with, is, let's face it, pretty low. There's a much greater probability of stumbling blindfolded down the paint aisle in Homebase and picking out the perfect colour for your living room than meeting a client who you actually fancy. But I have distilled my reasons for having done it into one sentence: rams tup ewes to make money for the farmer. I tupped men to make money for the ewes. Something like that anyway.

Blundering about, completely clueless as to where to begin, I created a profile of myself consisting of some semi-clad, 'come hither' photographs (omitting my face should anyone recognise me) and a brief description of my sexual enjoyments and preferences, which were a long list of lies because I had nothing to put on it. Those interested would contact me via the website or ring me directly, and if he sounded pleasant enough and most importantly, normal, we would arrange a booking.

Escorting is a cash transaction and though the income it provided was a lifesaver, I cannot say I wholeheartedly approve of the activity. A single man visiting an escort is harming no one, assuming she is providing the service of her own volition. But a man visiting escorts who is in a relationship or married, is behaving very deviously indeed. If he is not happy with his wife/girlfriend, then they need to discuss the matter and see if something can be done to remedy the situation.

As for the escort, I believe it is damaging to the mind and spirit. The fact I was able to do it for a year and still remain relatively sane today must make me a pretty sturdy individual. I would say however that the alternatives for men; no-strings sex, affairs and one night stands are potentially littered with far more problems than simply paying for some relief. The aforementioned activities are often carried out without condoms and with the added complication of possible emotional attachment. Personally, I would far rather discover a partner of mine had seen fifty escorts than had a drawn out affair with someone. But then the thought of a partner appeals like a bowl of gravy and bullock's testicles....I prefer sheep, they are affectionate, constant and are not programmed to be devious. You can really talk to a sheep.

For twenty years prior to escorting I combed dating sites searching for impossibly handsome men that I was convinced would save me from myself and provide the happy ever after I craved; but all to no avail. The fact I was mentally unhinged during those twenty years and was gaining weight with the speed and efficiency of a barley-fed bull didn't help matters. However whilst escorting I was often visited by attractive men who having sweated over pictures of my enticing folds, were madly keen to meet me. About half a dozen clients were genuinely keen on taking me out for a meal and doing the whole dating thing, the drawback being they were generally all over sixty years of age with evil breath. Listerine should be a legal requirement in every bathroom, the original diesel coloured one that's as strong as creosote and anaesthetises your taste buds for two hours.

Like most women over a certain age I need to know a man is attracted to my vibrant, laugh-a-minute personality, not my vast and pendulous tribal breasts, before I can begin to feel any mutual attraction, even if the courting process is as brief as a hazelnut latte in Costa. But the men that book an escort naturally assume, quite rightly I suppose, that because the woman in question is offering her secret parts up for sale, she's as rampant as a March hare 24:7. Happily, they are unaware that she is saving for a £600 sheep footbath and has a £400 vet bill. During 2005 I estimate to have manhandled approximately 800 willies which I had no desire to manhandle. A figure that for some fantastical reason my mind was and is able to deal with. The year of the willy began thus...

In December 2004 I was sat on a wooden milking stool in a traditional old gypsy caravan; accommodation that had been provided for me by Archibald and Henrietta. Gallows farm was as cheery a place as the name suggests. The 12 foot x 5 foot 'hut' as I called it, sat on wooden wheels and contained a wood-burning stove and a small bed, built high above the floor with a little window at pillow level. When the ravages of a Yorkshire winter arrived, it was intensely cosy. The hut was situated on a stretch of moorland next to a solid stone barn where the sheep took shelter in winter and lambed in spring. A made up track some two miles long stretched from Gorse-head Lane further down the fell and finished at Archie's farmhouse which sat about 200 foot away from me. I sat in my hut that night with Moss, the farm collie asleep on the bed and two very small pink piglets, born two hours ago to an unenthusiastic sow. Winter winds had blown snow up against the wheels in drifts so that they were no longer visible, yet Moss and the piglets slept on, despite the gusts of a storm that rocked the hut from side to side. It was a wild and remote farm which I loved despite its bleakness. Thankfully there was an electricity supply to the hut powered by an old diesel generator but I sat by candlelight most evenings to save money and read books with endless cups of tea and ginger nuts. Water was fetched in buckets from the trough in the barn and boiled in a big kettle on the stove, in which I regularly baked bread and fruit cake, it was a bit of an uneven cook despite turning them, but they were super tasty.

This was all very Wuthering Heights and romantic but the fact remained I was horribly overdrawn and was absolutely bloody determined to make a go of my little flock of breeding ewes and cattle. I sat there with a mug of hot chocolate and a hunk of onion bread, wondering how the hell I was going to pay for anything for the next month on a 14th century turnip diggers wage. Initially, normal ideas entered my head such as evening pub work, repairing stone walls for neighbouring farmers and extra shepherding, all in addition to the 60 hour week I was doing at Gallows Farm. I calculated that were I to work twenty hours per day for the next six months, aside from being dead, I would still be low on earnings. It then occurred to me I might be able to take on the domestic demands of a farmer, any farmer, and get the old buggar to marry me, I'd then have a permanent roof over my head forever. This was easier said than done. My female contemporaries at the time were marrying the most delectable farming specimens and posing for their wedding photos in floaty dresses on big, green John Deere tractors. I however, drifting further and further away from an ordinary life realised that marriage to a farmer was never going to happen. The tractor driver here at Gallows farm quoted a gem one day, 'if you can't carry it don't marry it.' Christ, that's me out of the race then, I thought. Anyway, any eligible farmers/farmer's sons, all seemed to sense my dodgy mental state. Marrying into farming was not on the menu.

The word 'prostitution' kept bounding across my sight line like a demented rabbit holding a calling card as I sat there deep in thought. I tried pushing it away but it kept coming back. A battle of morals followed between good and evil. Evil won and I decided I was going to give it a bash. I mean how difficult could it be, it's only a willy after all, just more than your average number. Having sat with furrowed brow deliberating on which horrid pseudonym I should give myself, I decided on 'Delilah,' placed a naïvely worded advert in a local paper and awaited phone calls with the enthusiasm of Anne Boleyn mounting the scaffold. I cannot remember the exact wording but the ad ran something along the lines of:

'Delilah, buxom 37 year old, offers friendly massage, outcalls only.'

I knocked a few months off my age for good measure and decided on outcalls only because the hut was always filled with essential farming miscellanea, a collie and very often lambs. Detached sex with countless men is not what the hardworking, traditional gypsies of old England had in mind when they constructed their caravans. I didn't have the foresight to have two separate mobiles back then and anyway, on the day of the advert publication I wasn't expecting much of a response. Mine was very mild and innocent in comparison to other escorting ads. What on earth do 'cream-pie' and 'bukake' mean?!.

To my astonishment and horror the phone started ringing at 7.30am and didn't stop for days and days. I was too terrified to answer it having no idea what to say. Of the one call I did have the courage to take, I chortled merrily away to a dead silence on the other end, with the jolly tone of a Butlins rep taking panto bookings. After a week the need for money overtook my dread of the phone ringing and I returned one of the many missed calls,

"Hello, I'm returning your call."

"Oh yeah who's that?,"

"It's Delilah."

"Oh right yeah, you the one with the big tits?."

"Er yes, I suppose so."

"So what joo get for 30 quid?."

"Well..um, what sort of thing were you looking for?,"

"Blow-job n sex, joo do bareback n anal?,"

At this point I hung up, horrified. Bareback? Do men get turned on by riding a woman piggyback round the bedroom? I had clearly led a very sheltered life.

CHAPTER TWO

A Vinegar Sandwich Please

I won't go into any great detail on my early life/childhood as not having been a child prodigy on the violin, shut in an attic and fed Pot Noodles for ten years or been born the secret love child of Mick Jagger, it would be pretty dull to relate. Born at 3pm on April 12th 1967, to the great disappointment of my mother who had set her heart on the name Alfred, my parents subsequently divorced when I was seven years old. My brother, three years my junior, was cheery and normal and forged a successful career in aviation.

I cannot continue this book without including a brief passage on my negative experiences as a child. If I don't mention them, much of my behaviour over the next forty years are merely the workings of an idle misfit.

From the ages of about 11 to 16 I experienced trauma which has coloured my life. As a consequence I developed an overwhelming lack of confidence in my abilities and an ingrained self-hatred. 'Hatred' is a strong word but it's how I felt. I cannot go into detail on the nature of the trauma in order to protect living relatives and I'm certainly not blaming my every balls up, foible and character trait on childhood experiences. But there are significant issues, namely: self esteem, trichotillomania, abandonment anxiety and the crippling depression that resulted from them, which a child would not normally acquire unless early traumatic experiences had brought them about.

Abandonment Anxiety sounds such an innocuous and pathetic term. But the recurring deep depressions that resulted from it brought me closer to a suicide attempt than I had ever thought possible and has been responsible for the loss of nearly every job I've ever had. The trigger for the downward slide was the end of sexual and/or romantic involvements. Completely irrespective of who the man was; his job, looks, age, length of relationship: from two hours to a year; if he lost interest and his attachment to me began to wane, a panic would set in. The best way I can accurately describe it, is a feeling of horror. A cold dread that literally felt like the end of my world; I didn't want to live. And this happened each and every time. Once I'd crashed I couldn't function; couldn't get out of bed, work, wash, dress or eat properly for weeks or sometimes months. As you will read, escorting completely cured me of this massive brain problem, may the good Lord bless all men and their insatiable needs.

Trichotillomania began when I was around seven years old and according to Google, is a result of trauma, giving the sufferer a feeling of control. The condition ruled me for decades and was the cause of such misery that it is impossible to express in words. I'm not going into any more detail about my childhood but it's almost certainly the reason for my never wanting children. I remember being about twelve years of age and standing in my bedroom, a newbie on the menstruating scene with a ludicrously bulky and freshly applied sanitary towel wedged in my pants for the very first time. I stood there and knew that I would never want a family, I was never going to risk a duplicate of me and have them go through the darkness I went through. That said, I completely love my selfish singleton lifestyle now. I see children driving their parents to despair in Tesco, the miserable, harassed expressions of mothers with attached whining offspring clustered around them and often wonder if she wished she'd used birth control. My collies also find small humans odd and irritating, and were my pack of canines not within the safe confines of this farm, would doubtless be found terrorising children in urban areas.

My earliest memory was sitting in the bath aged about six and making the sensible decision to exfoliate my face with a pan-scourer, the aim being to produce the softest complexion in the world. Sadly I discovered I was only a lot redder. Guddling around in the various bathroom cabinets that evening I was curious as to the properties of Anusol, and having read the instructions, smeared copious quantities in and around my bottom. Much discomfort followed, due in part I would have thought to the fact I didn't have a sore anus to begin with. I continued with my quest and decided to see what Lemsip tasted like. The box looked rather appealing with pictures of fresh lemons on it, so I tore open a sachet and gobbled it up like sherbet. Finding it to be rather moreish and identical to Space Dust (remember that?) I finished the box. Quite how I didn't die in my sleep that night I don't know.

At aged seven I became fascinated by Mrs Tosland who taught history at school. She was kind and caring and smelt of Dettol, altogether very calming and reassuring. The smell, I discovered, came from the lozenges she sucked constantly, I assume in order to sooth her voice box whilst trying to control a class of seven year olds. Sat in bed at night I would pretend to be Mrs Tosland, and would suck on little ceramic beads that lay in a dish next to my bed, my doll Tiny Tears sitting opposite me, patiently listening to my learned lectures on any subject that sprang to mind. And me all the while sucking earnestly and puffing out imaginary antiseptic vapours. Every night I would accidentally swallow at least two or three of these beads and eventually consumed the entire dish. I don't remember seeing any beads in my poo and I must have swallowed dozens. Maybe my digestive enzymes were gearing themselves up for some serious gymnastics in later life and even at that tender age my stomach acid was able to break down small pieces of pottery.

My love for wild flowers began around this time and I was memorising with no effort whatsoever the Latin for them all, so how the hell I managed to obtain 'Ungraded' in CSE Latin later in Secondary school, I've no idea. And now, aged 53, I love the sound and texture of the Latin religious pieces, especially the Catholic Requiem Mass quoted in Mozart's and Verdi's magnificent requiems. I think when things are forced upon you as a child you instinctively turn your head. Latin was the educational equivalent of cabbage, though now of course I love cabbage, but only if lathered in vast blobs of butter.

I would pack a notepad, pencil and a wild flower identification book and disappear for hours in the countryside, returning home to draw detailed studies of the plants I had found. On a slightly less grounded note, I would also search for fairies inside each flower, ah I was still a girlie at heart.

Little warnings signs were going off back then of a life ahead that was not going to be smooth; we were at a neighbour's house, having been invited over for tea and cakes. All the other kids were merrily playing in the garden and I sneaked into the kitchen and planted my head in the cupboard searching out the mothership of the cakes we'd just eaten. I found it. An enormous tupperware container which I prized open and gorged myself on the contents of like a delirious famine victim, cheeks bulging, eyes darting to and fro. I crept back out to the garden undiscovered.

I remember sitting bored on the loo as little girl, chewing a Blackjack, head hanging down and observing with alarm, black syrup flowing alien-like, down through my nostrils and out onto the floor; my first real-time experience that throat and nose are actually connected. And on another occasion, sitting in a big iron bathtub in our freezing cold bathroom, deciding that a piece of white bread soaked in vinegar would be a tasty treat. A quick Google nowadays lists vinegar as a most efficient remover of limescale and other undesirable domestic crud. It also adds an excellent bite and satisfying tang to chips. No suggestion is made of its sole inclusion in a sandwich. The Romans offered it up to poor old Jesus on his cross, and he didn't like it either. But Google didn't exist when I was ten so I returned to the bath with a piece of thick white bread, saturated in malt vinegar.

After about six mouthfuls, I was suddenly unable to inhale for what seemed like an eternity. Believing I was going to die, naked, as a child in the bath from vinegar asphyxiation, induced in me a blind panic and I took a gasp of air. I've never touched anything pickled since.

One morning, I was traveling to school on the ancient and spluttering Gastonia coach, the rather friendly, sweet looking ones that were rounded on all the corners, like an old fashioned cottage loaf. The drivers all drove very recklessly, I'm sure it was the part of their day they dreaded the most. I was sat, unusually, on the back seat, a seat normally reserved for the 'cool' kids, and watching the disappearing road behind me. There was a loud bang and something large, metal and important looking clattered out from under the chassis and bounced off into the distance. A couple of kids told the driver that his coach was falling apart, he grunted something about 'pile of old shit' and drove on. No idea what the part was but it looked relevant to the smooth running of an engine. That same day at school I'd brought my beautiful xylophone with all its different coloured plates. I loved my xylophone and took it upon myself to give an impromptu performance in the playground, with all the kids clustered around gazing wondrously at my performing skills; me whacking the gaily coloured metal plates with the (whatever you call the stick with a ball on the end for hitting a xylophone) and a crowd of enthralled children listening to the metallic din. Not exactly Adele at the O2 but it was a start.

Meanwhile my taste buds still craved strange foodstuffs. Whilst staying at a friend's house, I ate about twenty raw seed potatoes complete with their many tubers attached. They were laid in trays in the sun on the window-sill of the spare room I was sleeping in. Even I had a hunch at that tender age, that the chances of me ending up happily married with two perfect children and a successful career, were slim. But if you'd told me I'd be pulling lambs out of sheep and be on the game for 12 months aged 38 I'd have told you to pull the other one.

A peculiar thing happened to me during school assembly one morning. I was about twelve years old and it must have been Christmas time because the hymn we were singing was Once In Royal David's City. It was whilst singing the following words, 'and our eyes at last shall see Him through His own redeeming Love. For that child so dear and gentle is our Lord in Heaven above,' that I unexpectedly had to fight back tears. I found the words deeply moving. I'm the same now, I get all choked up at the last verse of 'Mary had a little lamb' for goodness sake.

School life from the ages of twelve to sixteen consisted of no notable academic achievements and was endured at a terrible comprehensive, Talmeath near Thetford in Norfolk with teachers that seemingly hated their jobs. I was painfully shy, terrified of fireworks, thunder, fairgrounds and big lorries, and still am, of all four things. Blissfully unaware as I was at the time of the decades of self inflicted anguish that lay before me and the catapulting between 10,000 and 500 calorie days, I plodded on. Saturdays would see me returning home from my mornings work of shelf-filling in the village store, having walked the two miles of country lanes with two bulging carrier bags, full to the brim with anything and everything that looked remotely tasty. And all of it stolen.

I played truant frequently and along with my brother would trill an innocent goodbye to our mum in the morning and then make straight for the old boy who owned the village sweetie shop. We'd then sit in a hedge all day stuffing toffee bonbons and sherbet DibDabs. We were caught of course and given a daily verbal lashing for two weeks with no pudding at supper time, disastrous. The truancy officer would occasionally call, asking to see our mother. I would expertly lie and say she was out, promising earnestly to give her the ominous brown envelope, then nip down the end of the long garden once the scary visitor had departed and burn it amongst the willow herb and nettles.

Mum worked hard to bring us both up as a single parent and worked for a while at an all-girls private school, Highfield Manor. The crotchety old head mistress, Miss Ursula Fairfax-Chumley, was the chief goblin who presided over this distinguished establishment. She didn't like me, this was clear, even to my then unworldly self. But she had been kind enough to make my mother the incredibly generous offer of free schooling for her daughter as she could see our family was struggling. We accepted the old lady's offer, I left Talmeath and began life at Highfield Manor, being placed in a class a year below my age which pissed me off verily as I was clearly considered to be slightly simple. I was about 13 years old when I joined Highfield and threw away a once-in-a-lifetime opportunity of a private education by disgracing myself and was booted out. Trivial things like stealing everyone's biscuits at break time and smuggling in Charlie eau de toilette and dousing myself and all my classmates. But I was a lonely, unhappy rebel back then and fought back at every offer of kindness and normality.

All the girls in my class, nee the whole school, were impossibly lithe, pretty, sporty and very very posh, with names such as Tryphena, Camilla and Harriet Starbuck, all presumably descended from distinguished lines of Earls and Lords, dating back to Henry VIII who'd handed out counties like cookies to people he liked.

With their thick, flowing manes of catwalk hair and slim brown legs, muddied hockey sticks and Range Rover driving mothers, I blended in like Lambrusco on an Egon Ronay wine list. Fairfax-Chumley swooped into my class one day in her tweeds, surrounded by a swarm of stern-looking assistants, and scowled at me, looking as mean and bad tempered as a constipated vulture, declaring in front of everyone,

"Miss Waterhouse, you are **not** a Highfield Manor girl!."

This was absolutely on the nail as I found the whole atmosphere restrictive and contrived with a touch of feudalism thrown in with me firmly at the bottom collecting faggots (the original meaning of faggots is 'kindling'). I also refused to perform the compulsory goodbye curtsey to the teacher who stood on leaving duty everyday in the enormous oak-panelled entrance hall. I felt this was cap-doffing in the extreme and they could kiss my ars.

Once back at secondary school, in the reassuring company of kids from families with incomes that didn't stretch to and above six figures, I could continue my steady plod towards the goalpost of obesity in relative anonymity.

I had one, and I mean one, devoted friend called Susan whilst at school. She was quite a fiery sort, all teeth and flashing eyes that she expertly daubed metallic blue crayon onto, producing a very alluring effect. A fleet of males were always in hot pursuit of her and she was constantly perplexed as to my complete inability to flirt with boys. I just didn't get it, the whole art of flirting, it all seemed a bit silly to me. I hung out with Susan but didn't actually like her very much as she was rather aggressive, scratching my face viciously one day, when my usually meek, supplicating character, broke out courageously and merely nodded in agreement when she said her mother was a 'fucking whore.' But who else was I to slope off with down to the village bakery every lunchtime for my daily fix of a foot long lardy cake? She meanwhile was very organised and methodical, ate a neatly packed lunch everyday, passed all her exams, and the last I heard was a highly respected accountant.

I have to skip forward about 22 years now, just briefly, because Susan popped up again in a most unexpected way. After I began escorting, I'd gone to do an outcall somewhere. I don't remember much about it other than the chap was, without sounding needlessly horrid, unbearably boring though extremely polite and nice and with the most appalling breath. His was a neat, clean semi-detached house and we went into his bedroom, me leaning back and sideways as subtly as I could to avoid the full onslaught of the poisonous fumes coming from his mouth. As always I made trivial chat about this and that, and noticed a photo frame on the dressing table. Being sharp as a sharp thing when it comes to facial recognition, I commented,

"What a lovely room! And what a nice photo!," an excuse to lean in, as the face was worryingly familiar.

"That's my significant other, she's a good girl."

(Not from what I remember I thought to myself.)

"What's her name?," I asked breezily in a 'I'm not that interested just making conversation' sort of way.

"Susan, bless her, we have our rows but I do love her."

(Jesus holy mother, don't come home early Susan)

At school she was a neat, organised and conscientious sort, the sort that hand washed the contents of her suitcase immediately upon arriving back from our week long holiday together in Corfu. Why the hell did I agree to go to Corfu aged sixteen? I've no idea, it certainly wasn't for the partying and drinking, having never had an interest in all that. I had saved up the money for the holiday from the proceeds of my shelf-filling job at the village shop. The holiday was ridiculously cheap; a return flight and a weeks full board at a decent hotel cost the equivalent of my monthly consumption of lardy cakes. I assume the holiday was Susan's idea as I have no recollection of enjoying it, only being forced into swimming topless in the sea. I emerged after five minutes to find a youth staring at my udders and his girlfriend scowling at me. I dressed immediately.

The food problem was up and galloping by now, and once, when invited to her family's summer barbecue, I began a solo feeding frenzy on a par with a Great White shark. I could consume remarkable quantities and not feel sick, still can. Not one to be beaten, Susan attempted to match my consumption, but was defeated by the fourth burger. After the barbecue we went for a waddle by the river that wound through the meadows; miles and miles of beautiful farmland. It was amongst these woods and fields, alone as a child, on one of my many meandering walks, that I had discovered the wild flower Moschatel, on my hands and knees searching for hidden plant gems. Discovering and identifying wild plants gave me a deep sense of relief and peace.

Anyway, Susan and I arrived at the river bank, along with a family pack of sponge trifle fingers I'd brought and a can of condensed milk to dip them in to complete my TRex sized barbecue lunch. We stood at the little wooden bridge that crossed the river and managed to lever our way into the can with a sharp stone, wolfing back the sponge fingers loaded with the sweet, gunky condensed milk. I was shovelling it down my throat like coal into a steam engine boiler. Susan however vomited over the bridge into the river after three sponge fingers.

She had a permanent build-up of tartar on her lower front teeth that I always imagined had a hint of green about them, plus a very sharp set of incisors; an alarming prospect for an aroused man stood before her with his trousers around his ankles. Which brings me to my over-riding memory of Susan, her promiscuity.

Blimey she was a goer. I wasn't. I was a virgin and balefully regarded men like the flight deck of a 747; very complicated and no idea which button to press so best leave well alone. Susan however was subjecting her cervix and tonsils to all manner of mens poking and pounding, proudly announcing one morning that she'd given Billy Greenfield a blow-job behind the travel agents the previous evening, and showed me the forensic evidence down her pink sparkly top to prove it. I wasn't sure which I was most offended by, the ghastly stain or the blouse itself.

As a 16 year old school girl, without a steady stream of crappy, sugary, bready type food, I became dull, listless and anxious. I borrowed money from our science teacher, Mr Withy, on a weekly basis. He was a harmless, hobbit-like man who was the brunt of constant taunts and jibes during science lessons. A certain pupil, Justin, was a particularly callous arshole and would wind the poor little man up so much that one day he roared at Justin to 'turn the bloody Bunsen Burner off and get the fire extinguisher!.' Justin had been overly creative in the 'let's make fire' part of the science lesson and responded to Mr Withy's reasonable request by punching him clean in the face. A riot began then with much hallooing and shouting and raucous laughter from the other students. And in the midst of it, Justin and the hobbit doing battle and throwing punches at one another. Ah me, I doubt Eton has to poke up with that sort of peasant mobbing.

One day, penniless as usual I hounded the poor man through the maze of school corridors,

"But Mr Withy it's only three pounds and I haven't got any lunch!," I wailed in the most piteous tone I could manage, turning my empty palms upwards in a St. NoMoney of Talmeath gesture. In exasperation he turned around in the corridor looking most helpless and turned his pockets full inside out in front of me,

"I haven't got any money! See?!."

I continued to plead and finally he said,

"Look I haven't got any money ok!, not that you need any more food anyway," and gave me a derisory look up and down. This silenced me, I didn't ask him for money again. Even now I feel bad, what a thing to have done, to hound the poor scientist everyday for cash, shame on me.

Food was never far from my mind. As a teenager, whilst out shopping alone for roomy t-shirts at C&A (the clothing equivalent of Lidl), I would lose all interest in the clothes pretty soon and made a swift detour to Budgen (the 80's equivalent of the Co-Op) My basket was soon spilling over with packs of Mothers Pride sultana pancakes, (god they were good) family size Battenbergs, Scotch eggs and CocaCola. Returning to C&A, I would grab any old piece of clothing in order to gain access to a changing room and sit behind the curtain, feasting away like a devious hobgoblin. One day, quite unexpectedly, a little boy snatched back the curtain, we stared at each other blankly for a few seconds, sultana pancakes spilling out of my mouth. He pulled the curtain closed again and dashed off, thrilled at his unusual discovery, to his mother who stood waiting in the queue.

'Mummy Mummy! There's a big lady eating lunch in the changing room!.'

At school, the subject that appalled me above all else was Physical Education. The mere sight of those slim, impossibly popular and sporty girls, filled me with a cold dread. The hockey stick was surely a tool of torture. It inflicted great pain and injury. Why would anyone want to aim it at anyone's ankles?! I just couldn't understand. Though I rather liked the 'fish n chips, fish n chips, fish n chips, salt!' rhyme. At the word 'salt' the ball was bashed with terrifying power and I would scurry away to the edges of the field in an effort to get as far away as possible from it for the duration of the game.

One day whilst stood in line waiting to bat in a game of rounders, the ball hit me hard in the back of the head with such force I felt instantly sick and thought I was going to die. The attention it brought me reduced me to such anxiety I had to lie and say I was fine in order to make everyone go away. I was far from fine however and felt sick for hours afterwards. Perceiving myself to be the target of a hitman, I resolved to hide in the toilets at all future rounders and hockey games.

Cross country running did produce one notably positive result; whilst limping along I discovered and identified snowberry, a white-berried winter shrub. Thus I decided thenceforth that plant identification was an altogether more productive activity than running. It seemed preposterous to me. What on earth was the point? Was there a burger van at the finish line? No there wasn't. So let's do something meaningful or stay inside in the warm.

Two sporting incidents occurred at Talmeath which irked me greatly. They both happened on the huge, green, short-turfed sports field. One day during long-jump, a pursuit best left to cheetahs and kangaroos as far as I was concerned, my brain underwent some sort of seizure and for no obvious reason I decided that when my turn arrived at the long sand-pit, I was going to show these sporty fuckers that I could leap as long and as far as Daley bloody Thompson.

It was a moment of assertiveness and confidence as rare and as fleeting as a solar eclipse. The PE teacher waved her hand vaguely in my direction, in a 'no earthly point you even attempting this but seeing as you're next in line, get it over with you lumbering buffoon,' manner. I leapt like a fucking gazelle on LSD. Three metres I believe it was. I was bloody thrilled. And?!!...no one reacted, no one, not a single goddamn response, no one even seemed to have seen me leap. They just continued on as if nothing had happened. Did I dream it? Was I wearing Harry Potter's invisibility cloak? I couldn't understand it.

The other sporty misnomer was at hurdles, running full tilt down a field and leaping every hurdle and winning the race. It was another solar eclipse. And again, no one bloody noticed! Was I cursed?

High jump terrified me. What on earth, pray tell me, was the point? How did jumping over a ludicrously high metal pole prepare one for adulthood? I stood in line awaiting my turn, watching the others leap the thing as if there were metal springs on the soles of their feet. It looked completely superhuman, I couldn't help but marvel at these people. Anyway, I stubbornly refused to even attempt jumping and would limp pathetically up to the apparatus, stop dead in my tracks and look blankly at the teacher hoping she would send me off to do something useful such as litter pick the playground.

The school canteen was my refuge in the midst of all this dreadful going to school business and my day would revolve around the blissful hour spent in it. Main meals, like most school dinners were pretty uninspired. Whichever cook or cooks allowed the nuclear fission of vegetables everyday should be hauled over coals, were these women not trained or meals monitored occasionally?

There were always two types of lunches on offer, a healthy 'meat n two veg' type meal, and a crap one, guaranteed to produce constipation and diabetes. There were two aisles and the children could make their own choice as to which queue they joined; as a result there was always a lot of meat pie, veg and cauliflower cheese etc left over. The 'crap' food queue offering was dreadful, Jamie Oliver would have thrown his hands up in despair. It was, quite literally, pizza, chips and jam doughnuts, which, had all three items been expertly produced, it at least would have been a tasty journey towards blocked arteries. However the pizzas were about six inches in diameter, deep-based in appearance, but possessing an interior that was in fact, completely hollow. The topping resembled a photograph of a cheese and tomato pizza, being so thin and miserly in quantity that it could be pulled away from its sad hollow base and shaken to and fro like a Polaroid picture. Even I, on most days, couldn't face these dehydrated, vitamin depleted discs masquerading as pizzas.

One pudding does stand out though, it was heavenly and I would devour it like a ravenous beast: Swiss Jumble Pudding. I've no idea what it was made of but I suspected a medley of the week's desserts; a jumble of syrup, oats, butter and other unidentifiable ingredients with nothing recognisably Swiss about it. I didn't care, the taste was sublime and upon finishing my serving I would move efficiently between the rows of tables, asking pupils 'have you finished?,' and whisk away the leftovers and pile it into my own bowl.

With the unenviable qualifications under my belt of a 'B' in O'Level English Language, a 'C' in Art, and CSE Maths and Latin both Ungraded, I followed my ever constant friend, Susan, around like a little duckling all the way to Mary-vale Technical College to enrol on a course in Hotel Administration. It was entirely inappropriate for a binge-eating misanthropist but seeing as I was directionless as a sky born kite minus its string, and had no idea what I was doing or where I was headed, I trotted along for the ride. Faking an interest in hotels only lasted a year and four memories from the period remain: never use bleach in toilets, it erodes the enamel and allows poo and wee to stain the surface, thereby necessitating a daily bleach application, and cleaning the lampshades in every room on all five floors of the Coburg Hotel in London, with a randy little Iranian waiter in hot pursuit. The third memory is of my mother attending an open evening at the college, and being greeted by the perfectly groomed course lecturer, who, sitting at her desk, exclaimed wide-eyed and rather seriously,

'Well, there's that hair!.'

The final memory was the loss of my virginity to a Libyan with Motown hair, called Ibrahim. The Libyans were enrolled on an English language course at the same technical college, and moved as one black-haired mass about the college, talking impossibly fast in Arabic. Susan had struck up a relationship with one of them, named Ali, whom she enjoyed frequent and noisy sex with whilst staying at the Libyans communal house. It was a three bedroomed property never containing less than fifteen occupants at any one time, with always about half a dozen in the kitchen chewing on raw chillies like lollipops. Regardless of the time of day or night, two Libyans were always to be found concocting vast vats of chilli, tomatoes and meat, hot enough to heat a swimming pool and consumed in silence with the occasional grunt between mouthfuls; the entire ensemble of Libyans being sat in a circle on the floor, the vat placed in the centre and surrounded by piles of pitta bread.

Ali was infatuated with Susan, and I, a little envious of their intense emotional connection, not to mention the endless humping which I found a tad scary, decided I ought to avail myself of a Libyan too. I wasn't too bothered which one. Turned out it was Ibrahim, probably the least attractive of the bunch. He wasn't particularly interested in me either, but I was determined to see what all the fuss was about regarding this humping business, and so he dutifully climbed aboard one night and poked his willy into my poor little hymen. It felt like having a large splinter removed with blunt tweezers and the sheets looked like a goat sacrifice had taken place. He then ordered me to go and wash them by hand in the bath, which I did, can you bloody believe it?! Any self respecting woman ordered to hand wash her own defiled sheets would tell the man in question to fuck off.

CHAPTER THREE

They Strolled Down the Lane Together

> They strolled down the lane together
> The sky was studded with stars
> They reached the gate in silence
> And he lifted down the bars.
> She neither smiled nor thanked him
> Because she knew not how
> For he was just a farmers boy
> And she a Jersey cow.
>
> — Anonymous

After leaving hotel college I made the momentous decision to enter farming, a career choice that would bring about destruction and mayhem to the agricultural community. My mother, raising an eyebrow at my inexplicable interest in peasantry, enlisted me on a course at the local agricultural college. This she was sure would snuff out the flame of interest and I would be begging for a job in TopShop by the following week. Susan was equally surprised at my decision to make the strange, disconnected leap from the warmth and hospitality of the hotel industry to castrating piglets and driving tractors. I surprised them both by thoroughly enjoying the first month and the months to follow. Why on earth I should have thought of farming was simply because I wanted to shun society, to live alone in a sprawling farmhouse at least ten miles from human habitation, and spend my days tending sheep and cattle.

I had a vision of my bonnie Bathsheba self, wafting about the hills and moors, crook in hand, linen shift and woollen cloak billowing in the wind, convinced Gabriel Oak would sweep me off my size 4 feet. These days I'd be lucky to get a second glance from a 25 stone out of work railway worker.

I have spent all day bent double in the sheep barn, weeing myself copiously with the exertion of turning over 70kg Dorset Down sheep, while I administer various treatments. Thighs and knees working to keep her from catapulting forwards, lethally sharp foot trimmers in my right hand, 10ml syringe and needle between teeth and a can of antibiotic spray in wellie.

My agricultural career began well enough. Meadowmeads college, where my mother had enrolled me, was a fantastic place of learning. A campus and a working 400 acre farm comprising of a 180 cow dairy, a pig unit, a calf rearing unit and a large breeding ewe flock, plus large buildings given over to the training of tractor driving and implement usage. Thirty years later the change is heartbreaking; the entire 400 acres having been converted to an equine training facility. About half a measly acre has been generously allocated to accommodate a few goats and a couple of pet sheep in order to train the handful of youngsters that are still keen to get into farming and ultimately feed you and I.

I was a student there for two years in 1985 aged 18, if my maths is correct, and for the first year I was under the auspices of the Youth Training Scheme which involved two days college attendance per week and a further three and a half days of piteously paid farm work on an assigned farm, Barleycorn Farm in West Sussex in my case. The pay was £26.25 per week but it seemed a good sum of money to me at the time. The second year at Meadowmeads College had me gain a Credit in Animal Production, no idea as to the significance of this but a Credit seemed an achievement compared to the pass rates of the other grunting, semi-literate agri students.

One day, sat in a Forage and Grassland lecture, we were told to put together a project on wild plants. I was ecstatic. Now here was something I really could do, and do well. I wish now I'd gone into a career in plant conservation, God knows we need it. And now with the toll man's greed and his invasive nature has taken on wildlife, I certainly missed my calling. After a month I presented my project, complete with pressed flowers, botanical drawings and medicinal, agricultural and folklore related information. I felt especially smug and was awarded top marks as I watched my classmates sheepishly hand over their Spar carrier bags full of weeds they'd yanked out of the verges on the way to college that morning.

Agriculture was a different game back then. If you could up-end a sheep, worm her, check her teeth and clip her toe-nails in less than a minute you were considered 'fit for the job' and would make jolly good progress along the path of peasantry. I was most definitely not in the 'less than a minute' category as it took me twenty minutes just to catch the bloody sheep. Half the lecturers thought I was hopeless and fat and suggested I take up horticulture. The other half, I say half, it was one lecturer; a tall blonde chap who taught Manure Management, who'd said, 'Cathy needs to be more confident, she hides her light under a bushel.'

Amazingly, I was told that I should lose some weight if I were to be employable, a damn cheek seeing as I was only about 10 and a half stone, hardly obese. Lecturers would never get away with that sort of behaviour nowadays thank goodness. A twenty stone vegan with a lanolin allergy would be welcomed with open arms onto a sheep shearing course these days.

I was horrified at the suggestion that I should take up horticulture instead of farming. The 'hortis' were a strange, ponytail wearing, lentil-eating group of students and the thought of harvesting lettuces and pruning for the next 60 years was appalling. I was determined to do something that was against the grain, something that didn't come naturally to me and hence was a challenge, as it gave me a feeling of worth and value. Farming seemed a good choice. Rising at 5am to deal with kicking Friesians gave me a tremendous sense of accomplishment. By choosing farming I could continue to take no interest in my appearance, daydream about Gabriel Oak and live in rent-free tied farm cottages.

My year at Barleycorn farm was to be the happiest year of the next twenty years. The wretchedness of abandonment anxiety had not yet kicked in, that monster was lying in wait. It was my first time away from home, I loved my new-found independence and was in heaven. It was a small, tenanted family farm, run by Old Ma Trickett who lived in the huge old farmhouse. Her two daughters, Mary and Elizabeth, dwelt in the other two smaller cottages with their respective husbands and children. Barleycorn Farm had been in the family for years and comprised of 200 acres, thirty dairy cows and sixteen horses at livery, plus three horses of their own.

I milked, reared calves, mucked out endless stables, cleaned tack, scrubbed the milking parlour, made hay, scythed nettles and cleaned out the hen-house; this was a very low, ancient, dark and many beamed outbuilding which necessitated the labourer therein to bend nearly double to go about his or her labours, me in this case. The 14th Century Luttrell Psalter, a beautiful book depicting numerous and often comical scenes of medieval rural life always springs to mind when I recall my work at Barleycorn Farm.

In the henhouse there were many hidden alcoves where the myriad of hens would perch, poo and lay eggs to their hearts' content. Over the central massive old beam hung a forlorn, cobweb festooned, bare electric bulb whose purpose it was to mimic the sun, dangling on a long length of baler twine. As the level of hen poo gradually built up over the weeks, the bulb in effect became lower and lower, until the hens would knock their little heads on it as they scratched about. The 'sun' was on a simple timer to mimic the longer, brighter days of spring and summer because traditional breeds of hen cease to lay eggs once the days become shorter. The modern hen's eggy hormones are not as dependant on the earths rotation around the Sun as the older breeds. She has been selectively bred to fire out one perfect little egg everyday even when there's two foot of snow on the ground.

The overpowering smell of ammonia whilst mucking out the henhouse would have felled a lesser mortal but no job thwarted me. I was mad keen for hard labour and powered through the farm day with boundless enthusiasm. My upper body strength increased at an alarming rate and within months I had grown myself a set of Fatima Whitbread arms and neck muscles. Despite the low wage I felt rich as a King and happy as a sparrow.

We took two young female work students on. They were terrified at the nature of the work, cried most of the time and were rescued after a week by their flapping, squawking mothers. One of the flapping hens stared at me in a mixture of astonishment and admiration as she observed my labour-toughened hands and generally neglected peasant demeanour. If you ever saw or ever do see, Cold Comfort Farm, a 1995 Thames Television film, adapted from the book by Stella Gibbons, take a look at Rennet, I wasn't too dissimilar. As the mother hen beheld my cheery and smiling countenance, she was, I'm sure, intrigued that the capability for seriously hard farm graft and happiness, could both reside in one person, particularly in a 19 year old female who's contemporaries would mostly be found giggling in Freeman Hardy and Willis or MacDonald's on a Saturday, instead of a henhouse. Flapping hen also remarked what lovely skin I had, remarkable given that soap and water were not top of my list of priorities.

The first time I was given sole responsibility for milking the cows, I was terrified. Mary and Elizabeth had taken themselves and their two horses, Monarch and Archie, to a horse show. I succeeded with no disasters but had to have an emergency poo, brought on by nerves, in the exit race at the back of the parlour, with six gentle bovine faces looking down at me curiously. With no loo paper to hand, it was chlorhexidine impregnated udder wipes. Once I was experienced in the milking routine and used to handling the cows, milking was a lovely job, particularly in the hotter months of the year when the coolness of the stone walls and the cold water afforded much relief from the labouring out of doors under the hot sun. The parlour was an old fashioned six-abreast type, which, as the name suggests, allowed for a maximum of six cows to be milked at a time. Each cow would enter through a sliding door which was opened and closed by the milker. It was a relaxed system of milking cows albeit a slow one but in the days of small herds, it didn't matter. Rarely if at all does anyone milk in these old style parlours now because herds are so huge. If farmers were paid a decent price per litre for their milk, we could see a return once more to fields of black and white cows. What I loved most about abreast parlours was the individual attention and handling. The cow entered at your level and once on the raised milking plinth, she could turn her head to look at you, and if nervous, reassure herself that she was in no danger.

I would begin milking after an afternoon nap, which Elizabeth insisted I take. It was a very sensible thing to do when you'd been up since 5.30am and the sleep recharged me sufficiently to keep going till the day's end. Milking machines, along with washing machines and central heating must surely be amongst the most welcome of mans' inventions. I can and do milk by hand, you have to sometimes if an animal has mastitis and needs stripping out in order to remove the infected milk. Sometimes a lamb/kid/calf needs extra attention and feeding via a bottle if it doesn't have the strength or wherewithal to locate it's mum's udder. In such cases the dam is milked and the resulting creamy goodness is then transferred to a teated bottle. Stomach tubing is something I have had to carry out many times on lambs and the occasional calf if the youngster is too weak to suckle.

A radio was always on at Barleycorn farm whilst I was milking, it seemed to keep the cows calm and helped to provide that essential sense of routine and familiarity which cattle thrive on. Most of the cows preferred certain places and were most put out if made to stand somewhere different, much the same as us humans prefer a certain place at the kitchen table or a specific chair. The only interruption to the smooth flow of the milking routine was when a fresh batch of heifers needed parlour training. This was when I discovered my character was not best suited to being a herds-woman. Nervous teenage cows crapping everywhere produced in me a very similar behaviour.

One afternoon I had finished milking and whilst walking across the farm track to the feed store, I fell straight into a three foot hole some silly bastard had dug, and slit my palm open on the journey down. Not one to make a fuss in those days, I bandaged it up with hoof wrap, silage tape and finished mixing up the hot bran mash for the horses.

Old Ma Trickett, the evil matriarch, was ancient and very scary. Every evening she would insist I change for dinner, an odd feudal custom which I didn't understand. I would reluctantly remove the baler twine from around my middle which held up the size 16 charity stay-press trousers, (I was only about a size 12, hence the baler twine) wash the cow dung from my hands and plonk myself down at the table in front of the old woman. Mealtimes were a very worrying affair; ancient and convoluted slices of home-killed pig that had sat in the fridge for weeks were fried up on the coughing Rayburn and served up at breakfast time. I remember charting the decaying process of one lonely rasher of pig in the fridge, noting its change in colour and shape over the ensuing weeks from a healthy pink to a deathly grey and finally to a ghoulish green. The morning came when I discovered to my horror that it had gone and far worse, the old lady announcing I was to be given bacon for breakfast. With her sat opposite me, I was far too scared to say anything, and as the putrefying flesh entered my mouth, I involuntarily spluttered the contents over the table.

'I did wonder if it was a little past it's best,' she croaked. The auld bitch knew full well it was 'past its best,' but was too mean to bin anything. She was a deadly combination of typical elderly frugalness and typical elderly forgetfulness and wasn't able to compute which foodstuffs were edible or in the latter stages of decomposition. Aged 93, she was stick-thin and always on the go. One afternoon I discovered her up a ladder painting the kitchen ceiling and every morning saw her sitting down to a bowl of porridge with plentiful quantities of cream on top and brown sugar. All of us, the two sisters and their families sat down to hearty, calorie dense meals; butter, cream and meat flowed freely and not one of us was a fattie. A life on the land kept us all in good health.

One of my daily jobs was to collect the eggs. The hens roamed freely and laid their eggs wheresoever they pleased in divers nooks and crannies around the farm, so the age of an individual egg could be anywhere between one hour to several months. We also had cockerels. Cockerels plus hens equals chicks, hence one morning Old Ma presented me with a hard-boiled egg for breakfast, the inside of which contained a fully developed, fluffy and hard-boiled chick. Yum.

The herd of 30 Friesian X Jerseys calved in the spring. We had names for all the cows; Bonnie, Boo, Boo2, Bo-Derek, Flower-Pot, Flower, Moira. Moira was a beautiful British Friesian, more white than black, very sweet natured and gave heaps of milk.

I was amazed how a delicate, fine-boned breed like the Jersey, of which half the herd was comprised, could give birth so easily to a Charolais, a huge Continental beef breed. I milked once per day and the sisters did the second one. Like all dairy farmers back then, we sold our milk to the Milk Marketing Board who collected the milk daily in little blue refrigerated tankers. I frequently cocked things up and would accidentally let colostrum flow through the pipeline and into the steel milk tank in our dairy. Colostrum is the rich, yellow, gunky stuff, similar to egg yolk in consistency, which the cow produces in her udder for a newborn calf. It is unlawful to put this in the tank for four days after a cow calves as it does not constitute normal milk. Average Joe sat in his flat in Croydon wouldn't appreciate this oozing into his morning cuppa. When having committed this balls-up, I would wait in nervous anticipation for the sound of the tanker rumbling down the farm track, praying he wasn't planning on taking a sample for bacteria levels, butterfat, protein and lactose, something he did on a weekly basis on randomly selected days. As he unwound the big suction pipe from his tanker I agitated the paddle in the tank furiously and hoped he didn't notice the slight hint of pink in the milk (colostrum often had a hint of pink about it if the cow in question was a first-time calver).

If I'd had a cow kick a milking cluster off her udder and it landed in a cow-pat, thereby vacuuming up liquid cow poo, though I'd snatch it away, hose it off and reattach it to her teats, the total bacteria count or TBC, would be horrendously high. I would try and intercept the postman each morning and open any MMB letters if I knew a cluster had fallen in muck to avoid a bollocking from the sisters. It was frustrating, they never seemed to get high TBC's and yet I tried so hard to keep everything as clean as possible. In the main though, the TBC's were pretty good.

The milk produced after calving, 'colostrum,' as previously mentioned, is very rich, thick and nutritious and intended by Mother Nature, amongst other things, to be an efficient laxative for the calf. At Barleycorn Farm, the calves were fed colostrum, also dogs, cats and myself. We had no choice in the matter. I carried it back to the farmhouse in three gallon buckets, each swinging from two hoary hands, the contents still warm from the freshly calved cow with bits of muck and hay floating on the surface. Old Ma poured it into deep earthenware pans, threw a handful of raisins in and baked it for two hours in the Rayburn. This bovine equivalent of Senokot was compulsory eating for days on end until even the deathly bacon in the fridge began to look appealing. In desperation I would sneak down late at night and steal food from her cupboard. Tinned chocolate pudding and jam roly-poly were boiled on the stove by candlelight so as not to be seen, and wolfed down in the hope it was a safer bet than the contents of the fridge the next day.

Old Ma possessed a huge, antiquated iron roller; a great rotating machine which the old corvid would sit at like Silas Marner at his loom, pressing piles and piles of sheets. She would also hold the occasional dinner party, held in the vast, oak-panelled dining room. Early one morning after milking, I poked my head around the dining-room door and saw about twenty starter portions of very neatly placed hard-boiled eggs, each halved and carefully topped with a spoonful of mayonnaise and sprinkled with paprika. It's funny how things stay with you, ie the image of green fur on the eggs. I was witnessing a living prophesy; the poisoning of twenty people in twelve hours time. It was early morning and the dinner party was at 8pm..eggs?, refrigeration?, come on this was rural Sussex.

One of Old Ma's elderly Labradors had its first ever poo in the house, an accident simply down to the poor thing's age. Without pausing for breath, she had the farmhand, Ollie, take it outside and shoot it, I was devastated. On another occasion, whilst sitting in the kitchen one morning, enjoying a well earned cuppa, I overheard the crow talking about me through the wooden partition,

"I don't like the girl, she creeps around like Jesus."

(I don't like you either, evil dog killer and purveyor of botulism)

My involvement with the opposite sex at this time was limited and quite pathetic. Having lost my virginity to Ibrahim, he of the Jackson Five hairdo; it was two years later at Barleycorn Farm when I met a chap at a Christmas party given by Elizabeth. He was fifteen years older than me, known to his friends as 'hatchet-face' and possessed a well defined paunch and tousled brown hair, odd that I should have been attracted to such a bloke. By devious means he managed to end up at the farm, in my bedroom and 'covered' me in the space of about 40 seconds. He apologised for his failed performance and sloped off home. I remembered nothing of the forty seconds, just the sensation of him having what seemed like a small seizure and a horrid smell afterwards (that would be the semen, oh god). I had no interest in males at this time, just a mild curiosity, such as one might have for raw oysters.

I was released from the farm for two days every week to return to Meadowmeads College to complete my training. We covered everything from castrating piglets, foot trimming the dairy cows to changing the oil in the tractors. One day we were shown how to kill a chicken as we all stood in a freezing barn in January, each with a doomed bird hanging upside down in our shaking, inexperienced hands,

"Now put two fingers either side of the neck and twist down and to the side," the lecturer had instructed.

"And if you can't finish the job, don't attempt it."

Needless to say I couldn't do it. I wanted to take my hen home and set her on the lawn and feed her corn and mealworms.

I do remember with much satisfaction the day when we were tested on our practical ability to reverse a tractor with an attached trailer. My turn arrived, with two dozen or so students all looking on and the dreadful male chauvinist instructor watching on in sneering amusement as I completely cocked it up. He awarded me nil points with a re-test booked for the following week.

When I returned to Barleycorn the next day, I decided in a rare moment of focus and drive that I was not to be beaten and resolved to spend every available spare moment reversing a trailer. I reversed bloody everywhere; up and down the farm track, round the fields and gradually reversed into tighter and tighter spaces, no mean feat with a very elderly tractor and trailer and no power steering. Mary exclaimed one afternoon,

"Bloody hell! How did you manage that?!," observing the tractor and trailer parked squarely between the combine harvester and the bale elevator with six inches either side to spare. On my return to college the following Monday, the same lecturer re-tested me;

"Ok," he muttered, nodding me in the direction of the test area. I reversed the tractor and trailer in one smooth, skilled movement with all the students smiling on as he weakly raised an eyebrow and said, "no problems there then."

One of the female students came up to me afterwards and said, "That showed him!." Damn right it did.

Hay-making at Barleycorn was wonderful, a traditional family event and a very important one because the glorious results of our hard labours kept the animals alive all winter. Back then, the seasons followed a more familiar cycle than we see today, with winters producing two foot of snow, blown up against the stable doors every morning. The daughters' husbands, Clive and John, would cut the grass with the old drum-mower behind our cab-less Massey Ferguson tractor. Once the grass lay in huge cut swathes, smelling unimaginably delicious and evocative, Mary, Elizabeth and myself would share the work of turning the hay with a tractor powered hay-tedder, until after about four days it was crisp, green and sweet and ready to bale. We never seemed to worry about not having enough unbroken sunshine to dry the grass in those days. Summers were real summers, long and hot. Once the hay was baled, John carted it up to us girls waiting in the stack. Clive drove the baler which gobbled up the flower-filled rows, belching them out as a perfect green rectangle every minute or so. An eight bale sledge was attached to the back. Clive would keep a steady eye behind him as he drove and as the eighth bale popped out, he would open the sledge, releasing them in a neat block. It requires considerable skill, a keen eye and quick reactions as balers block up regularly, ours did anyway. It's not a good idea to remain long in the company of a man who's baler or combine is blocked, best to go off and make yourself useful elsewhere.

Once enough bales had been produced, John would bomb round the field with an implement called a 'flat-8-grab,' attached to the front of a second tractor. It was a huge metal implement with sixteen big hooks under it which picked up the whole block of eight bales, John would layer these blocks up until the stack was six blocks high, thereby creating a 'flat-8-48' stack. On the front of another old tractor was attached a 'bale squeeze' which opened up on hydraulic arms and held the stack of 48 bales securely as it was driven up to us waiting girls. I loved this traditional system, because with three of us we would have 48 bales stacked quickly and could have a 15 minute breather whilst waiting for the next delivery.

I was fit and strong in those days, nothing like the puffing blob I now resemble. Mind you, I can still chuck a bale about with no problem, you don't lose that core strength, and I've never had a bad back in my life.

Hay bales were heavy and scratched your bare skin and my arms and legs were red and sore by the time hay-making was over. The baler was a stroppy bastard of a machine that produced either 2' or 5' bales depending on its mood and manoeuvring these around by hand, about 35kg a piece in a three foot space between growing stack and hot roof in 25 degrees was not for the faint hearted. The strings cut deeply into your palms and fingers but I always got through the discomfort barrier and loved it. It is unbelievably hot, hard and sweaty work and certainly wouldn't be for many people, particularly these days.

We had two young lads help us one summer, twins, about 17 years old, very dishy and very aware of their gorgeousness. After two hours they came up to us girls, who were tossing bales about like confetti high up on the stack,

"We can't do this anymore, our hands really hurt."

Old Ma Trickett would bring us out iced tea throughout the day which was very welcome and gave us a much needed hit of caffeine. Mary sneakily conceived twins during hay-making I was told. Nine months later she was washing cows' udders in the milking parlour and bent down to attach a milking cluster. The cantankerous old bovine kicked her in the back of the head, pushing her forward with a bang onto the glass milking jar. She looked a bit teary eyed and shaken but carried on in stoical farm-worker fashion. The next day she gave birth and within three days was milking again with the twins in their pram watching her, getting liberally splattered with cow shite for two hours.

I experienced my first animal death at this farm, a very poorly, three day old calf. I lay down next to it in the straw and willed it to live but it died. I sobbed and sobbed and just couldn't understand how nature could take such a young life after nine long months of being nourished inside it's mum. Thirty years later I'm obviously a lot more hardened to farm deaths but I regularly become very attached to certain animals and as a result they end up staying on the farm forever. I will never make any appreciable money from farming because I love the animals too much and dread the end of August when I have to take my annual batch of about ten lambs to the abattoir. It feels wrong to take the life of a six month old animal who I brought about the birth of so that some overweight townie can leave half of it on their plate and go back to watching TV. I generalise once more but you get my drift. In fact, last year was the first year I made the decision not to put the ram in with the ewes in order that no lambs would be born in the spring. My little flock are now permanently retired.

 I am in awe of horsey people, really I am. I look at them up there, perched on a huge, leggy and volatile beast, steering it around casually with the ease of a Mini Coupe and am dumbfounded. I had one riding lesson many years ago, just the one; The instructor plonked me on a pony a bit too small for me I would have said and it began walking of its own accord, with no word from me. The whole thing felt very unnatural, the girth was loose, the saddle slipped round and I slid straight off. I stayed off and decided to stick with the internal combustion engine for the purposes of getting from A to B. Barleycorn had sixteen horses and every one of them scared the living bejesus out of me. By far the worst job on the farm was attempting to get four, wet, miserable, very tall and highly strung horses, that were waiting to come in from behind an electric fence, back into their individual stables. With four lead ropes in one hand, I would clip one to each head collar and with the other hand I would grasp the electric fence's insulated handle and open back the single strand of pulsating live wire without letting it touch a horse or myself. The horses meanwhile, all desperate to come in, madly jostled about in their keenness to leave the muddy field. Dodging sixteen iron shod feet and with all of us sliding around in deep winter mud and ice, it certainly was a ridiculously difficult thing to expect me to do. Inevitably the wire would touch a horse and all four would break free and career wildly off round the farm, whinnying and bucking as they went, leaving me a sobbing wreck by the gate.

One cold, rainy afternoon in January, I trudged across to the milking parlour to set up ready for milking, replaced the bung in the bulk tank and got an electric shock, not a huge one but enough to know something was wrong. Telling Elizabeth, she waved her hand dismissively and said it would be fine. Not convinced, as milk and electricity didn't seem a good combination, I carried on as ordered. The cows came in and were most unhappy, kicking and misbehaving. It turned out the entire parlour was live!

We had a wonderful old cow named Flower, she was about fifteen years old and when she came on heat (bulling) which is every 21 days in cattle, she would become very enamoured with the milker, never her herd-mates. I learnt never to walk in front of Flower when she was bulling as she would rest her head on your shoulder with the intention of jumping on you, not good. 600kg of Friesian rising up onto its back legs is an alarming site. Similarly, I was feeding the heifers one morning and a young calf did the same thing; I was putting feed in their trough one minute and the next I was on my hands and knees with a hoof on each shoulder, pinned to the ground. She weighed about 150kg but after much effing and blinding on my part she thudded back onto all fours.

Barleycorn Farm..I loved it, wore handouts and baler twine and mooned about in a wistful Wuthering Heights cloud and thought I'd be there forever.

CHAPTER FOUR

"Fuckin' ell Waddid You 'Av Fur Breakfast?!"

My two years at the farm came to an end, it having been part of the Youth Training Scheme, which was, I think, viewed as providing basic skills for uneducated youths, however I thought they were a great idea. I managed to scramble up another seismic rung on my rickety career ladder and began work at Toad Farm in Worcestershire, run by Nobby Plowright and his wife Charlotte, daughter Sandy and son, Robert. The seven months I spent there were not a pleasant experience. Nobby was a bad tempered, cantankerous old farmer who originally haled from Yorkshire. An excellent example of his acerbic nature follows;

I was instructed to knapsack spray the entire 140 acres in order to kill the nettles, docks and thistles. There's no way I would agree to do anything of the sort nowadays as these plants are essential for wildlife, but thirty years ago there wasn't the awareness of the importance of conservation as there is now.

Devising a system that my physique could cope with, I would place the empty 20 litre sprayer on a stack of four bales, as once full it was an impossible task to bend down to the ground, insert both arms into the arm bands and stand up. By filling the container with water and chemical on top of the bales I could heave it on to my back and stagger off to murder the enemy plants. 'Stagger' is the word. 20 litres on your back is quite a weight unless your previous career was a coal delivery man, and as it sloshed from side to side, I too would be sloshed from side to side, swerving around like a drunkard. I wore no mask, goggles or gloves. Health and Safety didn't seem to be much of an issue back then and I spent weeks absorbing lungfuls of toxic spray.

The spraying was endless as anyone who has covered 140 acres on foot will know. On this particular day I had refilled and lurched once more up the farm track to spray the final field which entailed bending down under a live electric wire. This was hard but I managed it, and just as I started to crank myself into a vertical position once more, with the sloshing knapsack strapped to my back, I received an almighty electric shock as the fence power travelled through the water in the knapsack. The situation worsened, clouds rolled in, the sky grew darker and thunder began to rumble. Within ten minutes there was fork lightning filling the sky and there I was, the perfect electricity conductor complete with a metre long metal spray nozzle. As the rain grew increasingly heavy, spraying was clearly a waste of time so I made my journey back to the farm buildings. Nobby roared at me...

"Hast thee sprayed everything?!,"

"Yes I have," I replied weakly,

"So what's that then?!," he shouted, jabbing a crooked finger in the direction of a plant on the far horizon. I must point out that although Nobby was a renowned nightmare to work for, he was also a bloody good farmer, no one could deny that. And just as well, he had no other positive attributes, the grumpy old fucker.

Aforementioned plant in distance looked to all intents and purposes like a nettle. Nobby had been keeping a close eye on this plant since I began spraying several days previously, and had been winding himself up into a fury, convinced I had missed it because the chemical kills plants within 48 hours. With a heavy heart I trudged up the farm track and saw immediately that the plant in question was White Deadnettle, which though very similar looking to the common stinging nettle, belongs to a completely different genus of flowering plants and one which the chemical wasn't effective against. It felt bloody good telling Nobby this, as he had no idea it wasn't a nettle, and it shut him up for once.

Robert, Nobby's son, fancied me and asked me out constantly. I refused his advances. The only thing I found attractive about Robert were his hairy and muscly forearms but I figured that wasn't sufficient relationship material. His sister Sandy, was not quite the full shilling and of dubious personal hygiene. But she did bring us an all-milk sweet coffee every morning, something I really looked forward to on those bitter winter mornings. The weather has definitely warmed up over the last 30 years, my fringe would regularly freeze solid as it poked out from under my hat, something that has never happened since.

I think Robert must have decided that the best form of revenge at my not agreeing to date him was to have me stack ten tonnes of sugar beet nuts. The huge, fully laden lorry arrived after the morning milking on a freezing day in February, complete with a jolly driver that I was to unload the sugar beet with. An existing stack of approx 800 bags was already in the barn, Nobby always kept well stocked up for winter and sugar beet is an excellent source of energy for livestock.

The driver expertly reversed up as close as he could to the stack with his ten tonne cargo. Ten tonnes is equal to 400 bags, each weighing 25kg. No mean feat for a woman. I was stood on the stack waving him back and once the lorry was positioned alongside me, there was a two foot gap between myself and the loaded lorry with a fifteen foot drop to the ground below. The plan was to have me pass each bag across to him from the lorry, so obviously we needed to swap places. Thing is the lorry was about three foot higher than the stack. I looked worryingly at the gap between us and the long drop to the concrete yard,

"Ee ar luv give us yur and an arl pull yerrup," he offered casually.

"Er, ok but you should know I've got no footing here," I tried to explain, "you'll be pulling up a dead weight."

"Nar you're all roit, there's nuthin of yer, give us yur and."

So I gave him my 'and' and he gallantly attempted to haul ten stone vertically with one arm. Both of us fell like Tom and Jerry characters in straight lines to meet the concrete below with a hard 'smack.' He actually landed on a sack of sugar beet, saving him from the concrete. I however dropped like a lead balloon and landed flat on my back on the ground. His response remained with me to this day,

"Fuckin 'ell! Waddid **you** have fer breakfast?!."

The laughter that ensued was instant and I was unscathed, amazing really. We completed the stacking with regular attacks of helpless giggles. This infuriated Robert who passed us now and then carrying out his daily chores, all the time scowling up at us, assuming my girlish behaviour was of a flirtatious nature. The giggling came to an abrupt halt when Robert called out in a raised voice,

"Well you've really gone and beggared it up this time!." (He would never ever swear, 'beggar' was strong stuff for Robert). It turned out I had unknowingly broken an 'invisible' electric fence whilst driving the tractor along the one mile farm track that divided the neat fields on either side with their different groups of cattle in. And grouped for good reason; feed levels, breeding, stages of pregnancy, bulls, heifers; about six fields in all divided up with electric fencing. Now Charlotte, Nobby's wife, told me one morning that she regularly watched me from the farmhouse with her binoculars as I drove up the track everyday to feed the calves in the end field,

"Thee needs to look tut left un tut right un check olt cows in olt fields," she had said to me.

For Christ's sake, I thought to myself, I can't even take a breather from the relentless manual work, sit on a tractor for twenty minutes and pick my nose in privacy and comfort.

So, horribly conscious now of being watched whilst driving, I would turn my head to the left and right in a strangely exaggerated fashion, in fact so much to the left and right to please the old woman on birdwatch duties, that I wasn't looking ahead enough and had driven, completely unaware, through a single strand of electric wire that stretched across the track to redirect a group of cattle. The wire had nothing attached to it, a plastic feed bag for example, to alert drivers to its presence, and so it was invisible from the tractor cab. It was also noiseless and I drove on, unaware of the impending balls up.

Whilst giggling and stacking sugar beet, two different groups of Friesians were now mingling happily. Robert was apoplectic with fury and was hopping up and down in an effort to contain his rage, which must surely have been bursting to get out and yell 'fuck!' and 'shit!.' Fortunately, Nobby had gone out that day so I was only subject to the fury of one whip-cracker. They must have cursed me that evening as they sat down for supper.

I developed back, arm and shoulder muscles like an Olympian champion at Toad Farm and was exhibited like a freak circus act by Susan, who for some unknown reason was still on the scene. She would drag me around to various pubs and clubs, bundling me into a chair and have me challenge numerous strapping young men to arm wrestling contests, most of which I won. I remember a Saturday night at the White Rabbit nightclub in Kidderminster. I was shuffling and swaying self consciously on my chosen spot on the dance floor in a poor attempt to mimic Chaka Khan's feminine moves, when Susan shouted in my ear above the raucous tones of 'Ain't Nobody,'

"Your arms and chest are lit up!."

I'd been painting the dairy at Toad farm that day, in a special parlour paint to give a highly durable, plasticised coating to the walls, that enabled them to be pressure washed hundreds of times after being crapped on by hundreds of Friesians. It was brilliant white, thick as molten metal and tough as a space shuttle's entry shield. Nothing got the stuff off your skin, only time and endless abrasive chores. Apparently it became florescent when exposed to bright light, in the White Rabbit nightclub.

Nobby Plowright rose at 4am everyday of his life and ignored the putting forward and back of the clocks as it 'upset the cows.' His only break in the grinding routine was on Christmas Day, when Robert would milk in the morning and Nobby would have a lie in until 6am and celebrate the birth of the baby Jesus by enjoying a microwave meal for supper with the family instead of the traditional meat and two veg they had the rest of the year. He had an excellent system for ensuring every single cow had her full ration of feed everyday and didn't lose out nutritionally through herd bullying. As each group of five cows left the parlour, waiting for them in five neat piles, was a shovelful of moist brewers grains (a by-product of the brewing industry) delicious smelling, warm and lovely to work with, I did love shovelling the grains. On top of each pile was a small scoop of phosphorus and calcium and a big scoop of sugar beet nuts. Each cow would calmly feed at her own pile. The system was effective but labour intensive and I doubt any dairy farmer would devote such time to individual cows these days.

One day I was given the job of treating the herd for warble fly. This notifiable disease has now been eradicated thank goodness as it is a horrid condition of cattle, reminding me a bit of the film Alien; the warble fly would lay it's egg on the beast and eventually after much wheedling around under the unfortunate cow's skin, the by then enormous grub would burst out through the skin of the animal's back, thereby reducing the value of the hide, ugh ugh ugh. Treatment was the application of an organophosphate liquid, poured along the cows back. A quick Google of OP reveals its nasty and potentially devastating effects on the user, particularly if one is exposed to the chemical over a number of years. No mention was made of this to me at the time and I got on with the job of treating the cows. Standing in the exit race of the milking parlour, as each batch of five milked cows trundled out, I would pour a measured amount of OP along their backs. Dressed in a woolly jumper, trousers and wellies and wearing no waterproofs, the liquid would run down my hands, arms, front and occasionally splash onto my face and hair. By the time the job was complete, I was well and truly dosed for warble fly.

A job I hated was cutting back the black plastic sheeting on the silage clamp. This was a huge pile of damp grass cuttings, tonnes and tonnes of the stuff, collected during the months of May and June. The grass sits inside an enormous bay of railway sleepers or concrete. It is rolled by driving a tractor backwards and forwards over it whilst the forage harvester and trailers continue to bring in the grass. Rolling is vital because any air left within the grass causes it to rot, resulting in a great big compost heap, great for growing veggies, no good for feeding to cows. By removing the air you end up with pickled grass which is highly nutritious, the distinctive, lingering odour of which, permanently clung to my hair, clothes and skin. Once rolled it is then covered in thick plastic sheeting to keep the air out and the sheet weighted down with hundreds of tyres, all butted up next to one another. The clamp sits undisturbed until the winter arrives or when the cattle run out of grass in the fields. This is where I enter, trusty penknife in hand, unenthusiastically stumping towards the vast heap of silage which measured about 150 foot long, 50 foot wide and 15 foot high. Somehow I used to find a way to scramble up the sheer face of icy cold, pickled grass by grasping at lumps and outcrops until I eventually hauled myself onto the top, hurled off some tyres, thereby exposing the plastic, which I then removed about three foot of with my knife. Thus a fresh section of grass was available for the herd to chomp away at. On a par with milking a batch of kicking heifers, flinging tyres off the silage clamp was my most dreaded job. No matter how the tyres were flung, violently or in a serene sweeping motion, the contents would always splatter me from face to foot in ice cold, stagnant rain water.

During the making of silage that summer at Toad Farm, teams of young drivers working for local agricultural contractors, would hurtle back and forth from field to clamp in enormous tractors, their mission to complete the job and move onto the next farm. Contract silaging is a high speed operation because pretty much every farmer wants his grass cut and ensiled at the same time. It was most unfortunate for me that the silaging here coincided with my knapsack spraying...

One particular young tractor driver took a shine to my crouched form going about its business of nettle killing, and would bring his enormous tractor to a steady creep alongside and attempt to chat me up as I sprayed. This made me very nervous as it was a sure fire thing that Nobby was watching the very much one-sided chatting-up process through his poxy binoculars, complete with the now stationary tractor and me looking helplessly up at the driver. I would heave a huge sigh of relief once he'd driven off, laden with tonnes of grass, towards the clamp. Minutes later he would return, hurtling along the farm track towards the forage harvester, stopping by me for some rustic wooing and then speeding off again. I was becoming more and more agitated and prayed he would just lose interest and buggar off, which he didn't. In the end I agreed to give him my phone number just to shut him up, then proceeded to stumble as fast as I could to Starvall, a ten acre field well out of the eyesight of the contractors where I hoped there would be some nettles in need of spraying.

Nobby of course roared at me for holding up the contractors by being 'winsome.' Winsome, I ask you, wearing a knapsack sprayer and overalls.

Another job at Toad Farm was to flush milk-stone remover through the parlour pipes. Milk-stone is similar to limescale but caused by milk not water and though the parlour-cleaning system was very effective, a deposit would remain which gradually built up inside the pipes. The solution was to use phosphoric acid, also contained in CocaCola. It was a delicious looking, pinky-orangey coloured liquid, a foolish choice of colour as it was a dead ringer for Lucozade. Having filled two, three gallon buckets with diluted acid, I stepped up into the parlour from the dairy and tripped. I'm not exaggerating when I say that a full six gallons of the stuff drenched my face and entire front. I immediately plunged myself headfirst into a water trough and emerged with all my body parts intact. Thank god phosphoric acid, diluted for use, is not evil enough to dissolve facial features.

Another wonderful memory at this farm was the enduring of a terrible bout of thrush. I'd never heard of the word before then, only that it was the name given to an attractive little songbird. It caused the most excruciating itching and felt like full blown sheep scab between my legs. I would drive the tractor deliberately into every pot-hole I saw, craving the relief of the jolting about of my backside on the seat. Natural yogurt gave some relief but made my crotch smell of curdled milk. Eventually I could bear it no longer and went to the doctor where I was given pessaries. Oh the bliss. It was during the thrush outbreak that Robert decided to have me paint the roof of a field shelter. I climbed a precariously placed ladder and spent three hours, fifteen foot above the ground, daubing thick, black gunk onto corrugated metal and indulging in furtive scratching of my lady parts. Lunchtime arrived and Robert, having whisked the ladder away, found it highly amusing to walk away calling, 'jump it's not far down!,' leaving me sat on the edge of the roof on the last unpainted bit. Frantic to get to my lunch, the only nice bit of the entire day, I remained there on the roof for twenty minutes until the vision of my untouched lunch lured me off. I closed my eyes and dropped like a stone.

'Robert's hairy arms'

After seven joyous months, my work placement at the Plowright's came to an end. I had decided by then to make my way to Fendown agricultural college in Lancashire to enrol on a course in dairy farming. This was as solid and sensible a decision as entering farming in the first place: Sat in class at Meadowmeads listening to the lecturer spout forth the many benefits of cattle slurry, the lad next to me had asked,

"So what you doin' after this course ends?,"

" I don't really know," I replied, which was an honest answer if nothing else.

"Oim off to Lancashire to learn dairy farmin'," he informed me. And that was it, my imagination had been fired up once more and a vision of Cathy Waterhouse as a besmocked milkmaid carrying buckets of warm milk, filled my poetical head.

Attending full time college was my first grown up experience, in that I was surrounded by people of my own age or older, and not the cows and chickens I had thus far had the sole companionship of. This required me to interact, something I found incredibly difficult, although I did manage after a year, to be awarded the Top Student prize and a Distinction in Dairy Farming, a ridiculous thing when I couldn't get out of bed much before 8am and was genuinely scared of milking cows. A bad tempered Friesian can render you a permanent simpleton with one well aimed kick at your skull. My cowardice during milking was notable; ropes, kick-bars and tasty food to keep the cows occupied were all used to prevent my arm/hand/head, being crushed. It was all rather sad really, as my milking experience at Barleycorn farm had been lovely, but somehow the modern style parlours produced a much more nervous cow.

The seven people on the course comprised of myself, Stella Thomas, Catherine Childs and Lizzie Hall, amongst others. All went well for the first few weeks until the three females decided a spot of bullying would liven up the drab routine of college life. This was something I hadn't encountered before during my school education, so I was ill equipped to deal with it. I remember thinking at the time, weren't we all a bit too old for such childish stuff, that said it was upsetting, and the fact I had no friends to confide in, blessed as I was with the social skills of a Hebridean sheep, meant there was no choice but to confront the dealer in the pack, Stella. As I walked back to the student accommodation one evening after supper, I could see a silhouette in the top floor communal bathroom window. It was dark and the window was of course a frosted privacy glass but I could see the distinct shape of someone engaged in a stabbing motion. I made my way up the stairs, into the bathroom and after a quick peer around the room, discovered my own soap bar had been mutilated with something like a compass. In an instant I'd had enough and walked straight into the room of the pack leader without knocking,

"So what was the point of the soap stabbing thing Stella?!,"

I looked on with much satisfaction as she backed away into the corner looking suitably terrified and denied all knowledge of the violated bar of soap.

After that there was no more bullying, in fact, a welcome change occurred; prior to the soap finale, all three girls were so consumed with 'coolness' and other vital teenage pursuits, that their grades began to slide ever downwards. We were all tested weekly on various subjects, and I, along with a jolly nice Ugandan student named Evaristo, would generally come out top. It was my academic superiority and loner status that fuelled her fire I imagine, ha! After the confrontation, the other two girls disowned her almost overnight, apologised for their behaviour towards me and blamed their involvement for their disappointing marks in the weekly tests. After that the problem disappeared.

A poor diet resulted in evil flatulence in my room most mornings. So overpowering in fact for the poor cleaner that when returning later from lectures, I would find the previously locked window flung open, as she'd gasped for air presumably and my athletes foot treatment, liberally sprayed about the place to try and douse the smell. They were the type of intestinal gases that can only be produced by the scoffing of abnormal amounts of carbs and sweets; I would walk the half mile journey to Fine Fare most days and stock up on white sliced loaves, cheap spread and chocolate bars. Once safely back in my cramped den of learning I would feast continuously, and then at meal times, would waddle off to the college canteen. Having to queue and then walk around with a tray of food, looking for a space to sit, was excruciatingly embarrassing as I was convinced the entire canteen was deriding my fatness and weirdness. They weren't of course but I was weird and I was becoming fatter. At one point I made a real effort to stop buying crap from the shop. After two days I ate an entire tin of Marvel, a powdered milk replacer, that was sat in my room, the only item containing calories I could find. During another phase of attempted calorie reduction, I'd managed a week on salad and Ryvita before succumbing to the calf milk-mixing machine. It was an expensive piece of kit, which mixed up huge quantities of milk automatically according to the demands of the calves. I ladled out a litre and drank it down; warm, sweet and delicious, with my fellow students looking on in disgust.

Men didn't feature at all apart from a chap called Christopher Jackson, who was on the NDA Course (National Diploma in

Agriculture). He was attractive with a nice smile and I felt sure that one lunchtime, whilst queuing, he shot me an appreciative look. For many weeks I pondered on that look, though it could well have been a look of curiosity as I was a devotee of self tanning lotion at that time and was permanently orange.

We had two dairy herds at the college that were run as two separate businesses and us students were entrusted with the 'pretend' management of both herds. One herd was small, about 80 Friesians and was looked after by Arthur. Herd two, was 260 Friesians and was milked by Ivor, a single, 40 something Lothario with a fine set of false teeth of the traditional glued in variety and a tousled mop of sandy coloured hair. He seemed to me then to be a craggy looking bloke but at one time, I suspected, probably quite attractive. By the early 1980's however he had definitely reached the craggy stage and was regularly inseminating our course tutor, Rachel, unhappily married to an insignificant other and whom I'm sure had a jolly good time in Ivor's farm cottage most evenings.

After three months had elapsed I was taken aside by Rachel, who suggested I switch courses and enrol on the Diploma in Agriculture as she said the current course was a bit too easy for me. I however was too scared and pathetic to accept the offer which would have involved joining a new class of all-male students who were already three months into the academic year. In hindsight it was foolish not to have taken up this offer, it was a very generous one.

Our student fees allowed for a couple of trips per year away from the college to expand our farming minds. One such trip was to France which seemed very exotic to me then, still does really, but mingling socially with people made me very anxious. I was convinced no one liked me and found it all very difficult. Bloody typical then that when boarding the coach at college, I realised in a complete panic that I'd left my passport at home, 200 miles away. Thankfully my father drove it up to me in the nick of time. The lost passport episode caused me so much stress that within two days I'd erupted in what looked like ORF on my face. This little beaut goes by the proper name of Contagious Pustular Dermatitis, caught from infected sheep. It transpired it was a small patch of psoriasis.

The trip itself was pretty dull, involving numerous excursions to medieval dairy goat farms, where we would all huddle around an elderly French peasant who sat crouched on a milking stool, pulling rhythmically on a goat's udder and not looking too enthused about the job either.

Once back in the UK, we were treated to a day spent on a veal unit. When I think back, this really was an awful thing to have witnessed; about fifty calves chained in individual pens. I found it upsetting and completely unnecessary. Mercifully, veal, though still unpopular because of the stigma associated with the crate system, is now produced in big straw-filled barns, the veal crate having been banned. The resulting meat is now a rose colour because the muscles have been allowed to work. It is a great shame that veal is not more popular in the UK as it would lend real value to those calves born into the herd that are not needed as dairy replacements.

Back then, the chaining of the poor things in their crates only allowed for very restricted movement in order to produce a white meat. Will mans vanity and greed ever end? Anyway, us students were there to de-horn all the calves. I surprised myself at my speed and efficiency at this task and whilst many other students struggled, I cracked on, injecting anaesthetic into the groove located above the eye, thereby numbing the corneal branch of the lachrymal nerve which supplies the horn bud area. Once I'd injected ten calves I moved back to the first one, by which time the drug had taken effect, the area was numb and I could use the gas heated dis-budding irons (like a Stone Age set of curling tongs) to painlessly remove the tiny horn. This procedure was carried out to prevent the animals harming each other with their horns once they were released from their crates and moved on to whatever the next phase of calf rearing was in France all those years ago.

Why does it take us humans so long to figure out that something is a crap idea? I mean, who the hell decided that pulling out thousands of miles of hedges was a good thing? At last though, during recent years and especially in the present, we seem to have realised the carnage we have brought about and a good percentage of people are passionate about reversing the plight of our wildlife. I laid awake late last night, my mind flitting to and fro between the theology and evolution debate. Were we ultimately derived from single cell proteins or is there a Designer? a Creator? Stephen Hawking admits 'the creation of the Universe does have religious overtones.' Personally, I hope he is right and someone is out there, probably pondering on the wisdom of his decision to have ever created us.

So...to return to the subject of agri college; the course came to its official end and I wore my look of 'look at me, I'm the smartest student out of forty people,' badge, with great pride. The National Certificate in Agriculture course had thirty three students on it plus our little bunch. Academic achievements were totted up from each individual and I was awarded first place, plus top overall for studies in farm records and book keeping, what the hell?, I'd got a CSE maths grade 5 whilst at school, which meant I'd only just managed to fathom the abacus. Anyway I left with a Distinction and a scholarship nomination. I didn't understand what that meant, possibly a very posh college placement somewhere, but I do recall journeying to London to meet the Duke of Westminster and giving him my reasons for wanting to be at the forefront of the dairy industry. The student who gave the best speech, chosen from amongst others around the country, was to be awarded the scholarship. I've no idea what I said to the Duke, being unable to tear my gaze away from his absolutely enormous eyebrows. I think I waffled on about enjoying getting up early and therefore was perfectly suited to a life of milking at dawn and dusk forevermore, an outright lie. Thankfully I wasn't chosen and so packed my spotted neckerchief, tied it to a stick and set off for Shod Lane farm in Norfolk, a 500 acre arable and dairy farm.

CHAPTER FIVE

One Day Through Ancient, Noiseless Woods

> *One day through ancient, noiseless woods,*
> *A calf walked home as good calves should.*
> *He made a trail all bent askew,*
> *A crooked trail as all calves do.*
>
> — Sam Walter Foss

Shod Lane, with its fields of swaying, golden wheat and black and white cows, was the first job where I was permanently situated away from home and oh boy did the Royal Mail do some good trade during the two years I spent there. I was completely hooked on buying stuff from mail order catalogues and there being no internet back then, would scour the classifieds of the glossy magazines such as Country Living and order dozens of catalogues containing impossibly pretty and ridiculously overpriced nonsense. It was a form of addiction and the thrill I experienced when another catalogue arrived gave me a high of intense pleasure. It was short lived though, my mum paid off my horrendous overdraft and wisely said she would never repeat the generous offer. It was at Shod Lane that my love of all things eclectic began. Anything odd, original, unique and unusual and I would go without proper food for two weeks in order to buy it.

The novelty of manual farm work had long since worn off by the time I began working in Norfolk; milking the cows twice a day, feeding the calves and general parlour maintenance, were more than enough for me. I was far more interested in my new hobby; calligraphy, and mooning about to Clannad in my cosy cottage. Mind you, compared to other 'normal' jobs it was probably bloody hard work.

The calves, and there are always a lot of calves on a dairy farm, were born in the dairy buildings where the milking cows lived. Once they were about 72 hours old, they were moved to the calf-rearing barn having suckled plenty of colostrum from their mothers. There was a distance of some half a mile between these two premises. Before I continue and for those of you who are not clear as to how milk is produced, here is a brief description:

All the bovine milk we drink comes from a cow that has calved, this means she cannot produce milk unless she has given birth. The potentially controversial bit comes when the calf has to be removed from its mother, permanently, at around 72 hours of age. Now the staunch vegan will expound a powerful and lucid argument based on the welfare implications of this practice. Surprisingly, for someone who has worked on several dairy farms and drinks about two litres of the stuff per day, I agree with them entirely. Cows are pregnant for nine months and when the calf is removed, she will bellow for her offspring for days. I find it sad and upsetting at having been responsible for this over the years, and I am still perpetuating the practice by drinking milk. But change comes at a price: if farmers left the calf to suckle on it's mother and still continued to milk her, probably only once per day until a natural weaning took place at around nine months, the dam's milk yield available to the farmer would be greatly reduced and the price of milk would be a great deal more. Additionally, we would need many many more dairy farms to supply the nations milk. Well, I think for one that this is a fantastic idea, and would very happily pay 3x the current retail price for milk were this system to be adopted. And if this book sells enough copies, this is precisely what I intend to do, to set up a dairy farm where calves are not removed from their mothers and the grazing fields are not intensively sown with two or three grass species, but are sown and managed as traditional wild flower meadows. Let's take certain land management practices back by a hundred years or so, armed with modern technology and science. That is a formidable combination. The planet would start to recover due to the tremendous increase in wildlife biodiversity that results from these traditional farming practices, such as managed hay meadows. Wildlife is decreasing at a truly alarming rate mainly down to two reasons; modern farming methods and building development. I can't do much about the second one, but I will do everything I possibly can, however small, to help with the first. I'm a bit on the fence with this latest re-wilding thing though; I mean if you stopped farming a farm and left nature to go it alone, it would revert to scrub and eventually to forest. The best biodiversity is achieved by carefully managed farmland; wetlands, meadows, woodland, marsh, arable headlands left for annual flowers etc.

 Back to the calf-rearing; when the dairy building had about four new-born calves in it, I would have to walk them across the yard, one hand under the calf's head directing it, and the other hand using the tail as a rudder. Burly herdsman simply scoop calves up and carry them but with an average Friesian calf weighing around 40kg, it wasn't an option. This is why the majority of herdsman are male, it is a heavy job, bollocks to this sexual equality nonsense; men and women are completely different. We need them and they need us.

I then had to bundle the calf, protesting loudly at this point, into the dilapidated back of an old Austin Maxi which had had the back seats removed to facilitate the comfort of its bovine passengers. The farm track was on private land so the Maxi wasn't taxed or MOT'ed, was far from roadworthy and sorely abused. The calf would continue it's immensely loud bellowing inches from my ears as I drove, smearing quantities of evil liquid poo, which in the young milk-fed calf has an appallingly savage smell (think babies nappies but ten times the ferocity), over the windows, floor, and on several occasions, down my back and head. Conversely, or would that be perversely? the manure of adult cattle I love the smell of and find very comforting. The combination of silage, cow dung and milk is a wonderfully nostalgic cocktail.

Myself and calf bounced and slid our way to the farmyard in the Maxi, banging into slurry-filled pot-holes and scraping the chassis on the uneven, rough track. Once at the calf-rearing barn I would once again steer my little charge with his or her tail to join its' mates. The barn was made draught proof and cosy by the positioning of enormous, rectangular straw bales, moved into place with the aid of a tractor, to create many pens of differing sizes according to the number of calves therein. The bit that was really heavy going was carrying and lifting 25 litre drums, dozens of them everyday, of warm, reconstituted milk powder over the five foot high bales to reach the greedy little blighters. The calves were on an adlib milk system and fed through teats attached to pipes which were submerged in big blue 500 litre drums into which I would tip the 25 litre containers of milk. The calves, once used to this strange looking blue cow, were very content.

Providing good hygiene is practised, calf rearing is an enjoyable occupation, preferable to milking cows I found. I remember one day going to check on the down calvers (due to calve) and walking into the field to find mum had wandered off to graze while her newborn slept peacefully in the grass. I approached quietly to check all was well. The calf opened a languid, long lashed eye and shot up onto its feet. To this day I've never seen such a young beast move so fast. It took off from a standing position, Usain Bolt fashion and didn't stop, careering across several fields and leaving me bent double, puffing like an old steam train. The farmer managed to corner it hours later but it died from exhaustion. It was very sad but then farming is sometimes. Unless the entire world happily consumes a diet solely comprised of soya milk, Linda McCartney sausages and vegetables, I'm afraid these unfortunate things will happen.

One of the many aspects of milking cows that really didn't enthral me, come to think of it, any dairy herd of any species, but particularly cows because they produce on average, 64 litres of dung and urine over a 24 hour period, is the length of time you end up chained to the milking parlour, up to five hours per day on average. Getting up early is and never has been my thing. Heaving myself to a vertical position before dawn and wading through mud and slurry on cold, dark mornings was bad enough. And then onwards to spend hours in a frozen milking parlour, being shat and pissed on from a great height was the stuff of nightmares. On winter mornings I often had to blowtorch the frozen pipes to be able to milk at all. And if there was a power cut it meant connecting the tractor power-takeoff shaft to the vacuum pump. There were always mechanical problems with milk pumps, pulsators, filters, sanitary traps, boilers, drains, refrigeration, belts and pulleys, plate coolers, milk lines, vacuum lines, clusters, claw-pieces, teat cup liners, it was never ending. The invention of the robot milker must surely have been the brain child of a farmer at 4am in January.

Kicking cows caused me many sleepless nights and for good reason; the owner's son, Matt, had been kicked in the face whilst milking and wore a big scar across his face to prove it, so Willy, his father, installed an extra rump rail so cows couldn't kick out so far into the milking pit. I wasn't reassured by this rail as when you reached between her back legs to attach the milking cluster, the cow could very easily smash your hand and arm against the rail that ran along the bottom, if she felt so inclined. I used kick bars on the worst culprits. This is a curved, adjustable metal bar which was placed securely over the cow's hips, with one end under the top of the back leg; it was rubberised at both ends so caused no discomfort but meant that she couldn't move her leg forward to kick. I had loved the old-fashioned abreast milking parlour at Barleycorn farm, but this one was a 10:10 herringbone, far more efficient because many more cows could be milked per hour. It's very difficult to describe a milking parlour to the uninitiated without using an odd mix of space module type terminology alongside perverse words such as sucking and blowing and pulsating. Anyway let me paint a picture of myself in this pulsating building: the cows stood in two lines at 50 degrees either side of a rectangular 'pit.' This then positioned the herds-person at udder level and at the perfect height for sustaining kicks to the milker's upper body. A row of five clusters hung along each side and these were attached to the udder. It was old, badly lit and festooned with cobwebs but as I was stuck with it, I took great pride in keeping it spotless.

For your info, cows have four stomachs and are super efficient at extracting every last nutrient from grass/hay/silage. When you look at the size of a cow, on average about 450-600kg, the fact they can maintain body condition and produce up to about 20 litres of milk per day from forage alone is really quite incredible. (Dairy guys please feel free to contact and correct me if my milk volumes are not up to date).

Willy, though affable and pleasant, was not very efficient and instead of disbudding his calves at around three weeks of age when they are easy to handle and the horn buds are quick to remove, would wait until the calf was two years old and going through the parlour twice per day, as training for the day she calved and would be milked. This was unacceptable because it meant a proportion of the herd had long and pointed horns and the rest did not, resulting in some dangerous bullying. One day, Emma, a particularly fine heifer, had one of her hornless herd mates pinned against a wall, bellowing in panic. I'd had enough and insisted Willy book the vet immediately to de-horn them all.

The day arrived and each horned cow was bundled by the farmer, myself and an unimpressed vet (who was wondering I'm sure why the hell we hadn't done this two years ago) into the cattle crush (this doesn't 'crush' cattle as the name suggests, it restrains them for the safety of cow and operator).

I don't remember the exact method of horn removal but it involved an awful lot of blood and a big cheese wire but I was much relieved at the now safe environment for the cows. The vet had worn a white coat and looked dressed for keyhole surgery rather than big pointy horn removal. We all three looked fresh off the film set of a horror movie afterwards. I had a big soft spot for Emma the bully, she was beautiful with her perfectly proportioned black and white markings, so I kept one of her horns as a souvenir, boiled it and oiled it and put it on my mantelpiece, as you do.

A huge Limousin bull called Alfred (pronounced 'lim-oh-zun' and completely unrelated to the fancy car) was kept at Shod Lane farm in order to impregnate his many bovine girlfriends. He was amiable and would stand in the collecting yard every morning and afternoon whilst his ladies were being milked and then meander into the parlour, his enormous testicles swaying between his legs. Willy would often scratch Alfred's woolly head and I would pipe up from the pit,

"Don't make him friendly!."

Never trust a bull or a ram and never turn your back on them regardless of their temperament. In fact a tame bull or ram is far more dangerous, much better to keep them wary of people. My city-dwelling brother visited me at the farm one weekend and was confidently striding about the fields, helping to get the herd in for milking with commanding calls of, 'geddon up there girls' and 'move along ladies,' encouraging them towards the milking parlour.

"There's the bull, isn't he a beauty?!," I called out above the noise of mooing cows and wind. Upon hearing this my brother had left the field and cleared a five bar gate within thirty seconds.

Alfred went lame one day, so Willy booked the vet and gawd knows how but we managed to persuade the bull into the crush, however the vet refused to treat him unless he was sedated. Bloody sensible I thought, no time for fearless bull-handling. He was so enormous, even a tiny tantrum whilst confined in a crush would have had all three of us on the front page of the papers; 'tragedy down on the farm as three people puréed by Limousin bull.'

Willy kept a certain number of the male calves that were born to the cows and chose not to castrate them. One drawback of keeping male cattle entire (not castrated) is the potential for dangerous situations to arise. You may well be thinking 'so why leave their bollocks attached if it's so dangerous?.' The reason is the animal gains a lot more muscle when kept as a bull and therefore produces many more burgers. But the simple task of bedding them up every morning with fresh straw could see you plonked down at the nearest A&E which was why I happily left the job to Willy, fok dat for a cream soda. He used electrified scaffolding pipes to keep these truck-sized occupants contained, however I didn't know about the live pipework in the barn until he asked me, casually as was his way, to straw them up one morning. I agreed just this once. I don't suppose a group of bulls was ever bedded up as quickly as they were that day, such was my eagerness to get out, but as I ducked under the pipework, I made contact with it and genuinely thought the barn roof had collapsed on my head. It was the biggest bolt of electricity I've ever had. Undeterred I continued with my labours, utter hero that I was.

I was permanently penniless at Willy's farm, no idea what I spent it on but it was mostly unnecessary nonsense such as a two foot resin sculpture of the witch from Terry Pratchett's Discworld and a set of six pewter goblets depicting the Arthurian Legends, certainly different from nail extensions and spray tanning sessions which most other 22 year olds were spending their money on. My budget shaped my diet which consisted of the cattle variety of corn-on-the-cob which I cut from the towering crop of forage-maize we grew for the dairy cows. Forage-maize has been specifically developed for cattle and possesses none of the sweet, golden nibblity tenderness of its cousin, the Jolly Green Giant. This stuff was as tough as a witch's broom and had to be boiled for half an hour and slathered in butter, even then it took a decent set of teeth to grind through it. I also boiled up fodder beet on a daily basis, otherwise known as mangold-wurzel, an extremely high-energy winter feed for the cows. The mangold-wurzel root was huge and I would march out to the fields, bucket and fork in hand and dig up what would be my supper for the next three days. Milk was free of course, thousands of litres of the stuff. I always kept a bottle of Camp Coffee in the dairy and when I'd finished milking I would ladle warm milk into a calf feeding bottle, add some Camp Coffee and guzzle it down, delicious. At home, I kept my milk in empty glass Calcium Borogluconate bottles, an injectable medicine which we treated hypocalcaemic cows with. Unsuspecting visitors to my cottage would widen their eyes in alarm as I sloshed the raw milk with bits of silage in it out of an ominous looking brown bottle into their tea. Hypocalcaemia is a metabolic disorder of dairy cows, seen mostly in high yielders from their third lactation onwards. Basically everything shuts down and they stop eating, pooing and calving and eventually lapse into a coma and die. It is the cow's inability to absorb enough calcium and is more prevalent in cows giving large amounts of milk, another man-made problem. To prevent the condition, every cow, immediately after giving birth to their third calf, ie the third lactation, was given one bottle of warmed calcium, injected slowly under the skin using a flutter valve. It is amazing to see a recumbent cow and then watch her spring to life within minutes as the calcium takes effect.

We are certainly a peculiar species are we not, expert at fucking Mother Nature around and bringing about the extinction of many animal and plant species. Then all at once, utterly brilliant at inventing and creating products and strategies to reverse and counteract the problem we created.

I managed to cancel loo rolls off my shopping list completely by using rolls of udder wipes from the milking parlour. My giant loo-roll would hang on a giant loo-roll holder made of baler twine, and wasn't, I should add, a powdery scented, quilted roll of puppy softness. It was a two foot wide roll of coarse blue paper and did the job but was quite rough on my backside.

One cold morning after milking, I set to work cleaning the bulk tank, and bending down to get chemical from the rows of drums that were sat against the wall, my head with its woolly hat attached had brushed against the vacuum pipe which is where I used to hang cloths, scouring pads etc. Many hours later, having been to the shop for groceries, organised the Artificial Insemination man and greeted the Health and Safety inspector, who'd come to look at our slurry pit's safety features (there weren't any), I was preparing for the afternoon milking. Willy casually stepped into the dairy to check all was well. He took one glance at me and remarked in his customary, dead pan manner,

"You got a pan scourer on your head," like it was your average daily farm occurrence. And indeed I had. I can't believe even now, 25 years later, I had walked around town and into shops with a fecking scourer on my head.

Earlier that same day, the besuited young man who'd come to check out the safety of the farm was not impressed by the slurry pit. It was basically an enormous hole that simply dropped away next to the concrete track outside the parlour. It was several metres deep and was full of liquid cow shite. A thick crust had formed on the surface over the two years since it was last emptied and Willy, being of a decidedly devil-may-care nature, would drive over this crust with his tractor whilst scraping the yards. One morning the crust gave way and I watched in horror as one about to witness another farm fatality statistic. The old tractor began to sink down on one side but somehow he managed to get enough grip on the broken crust to enable him to lurch out onto the concrete. Completely non fazed he carried on scraping. Drowning in slurry, what an awful death that would have been.

We had a particular Friesian cow, number 135, whose behaviour in the parlour gradually became more and more erratic until her incessant kicking made it impossible for me to apply the milking cluster to her. I put a kick-bar over her but her nervousness worsened over a matter of weeks until she really was unmanageably mad. I don't mind admitting that she scared the hell out of me. A half tonne cow can snap an arm like a marmite Twiglet.

One afternoon she was standing in the parlour awaiting milking and began kicking with extra ferocity, lashing out at the metal rail which held the cows safely in their stall. I left the parlour when she began to draw blood from her leg and could still hear the 'bang bang' of her kicking as I drove away to the farmhouse to tell Willy,

"If you want 135 milked, you can do it yourself."

With much tutting he drove back with me to the parlour and somehow managed to get a milking unit on her, a waste of time as she was so maddened by now, not a drop of milk was forthcoming. The next morning as 135 stood in the yard, she turned her head, saw me, panicked and in her effort to get away she fell and never managed to get back up again. We moved her with the aid of a tractor to a cosy pen but after two days she was still unable to stand and we had no choice but to have her put down. A post mortem revealed BSE. Poor old 135.

Tractor driving had always appealed to me and when I mentioned this to Willy during my first summer, he had pointed to a huge blue Ford tractor and said,

"We need silage carted to the clamp, off you go."

With no training whatsoever, I clambered into the enormous cab, whose first step up was about three foot from the ground, found a gear amongst the endless sticks, levers and knobs, and lurched off,

"Which gear for this job?!," I yelled at him over the 300hp engine noise,

"2, high ratio, you'll be fine."

I was slightly panicking by now as I was clearly expected to match the pace of the young lads carting silage, who were all roaring around at furious speeds. The job involved me driving alongside the forage harvester in the field, which cut and blew the grass through a tall spout into the huge trailer which was attached to the back of my tractor. I had to keep my speed just right, too slow or fast and the precious winter feed would miss the trailer and shoot onto the ground. We used an evil product called Sylade, which was sulphuric acid and ensured the grass would 'ensile' and not just compost and rot. With no air conditioning and every window broken or missing, my face stung as it was pelted with acidified grass for hours on end. At one point I thought I was going to be pushing up the daisies; with no experience at all of driving down a hill whilst towing a heavy load, I simply trundled on as before, at full tilt in second gear as instructed. After a few minutes I realised by the movements of the tractor that I wasn't in control and the trailer was pushing me down the hill faster and faster, it was bloody terrifying. Instinctively I didn't brake thank goodness and as the track levelled out, the engine took over. Cheers Willy.

I was given the job of rolling one autumn which I was thrilled about, anything was better than milking and despite my near death experience during silage carting, I couldn't wait.

"Keep going anticlockwise, not too slow or you won't break up the clods."

Off I went with three ring-rollers attached to the back of the tractor and Willy's instructions in my ears. There were 100 acres to be rolled so not your average cricket pitch but after three hours of diligent driving and regular checking behind me to see that all was progressing as it should, I started to become a little bored and stared hypnotically ahead for long spells, daydreaming of supper and my calligraphy projects. An hour later, I looked behind me and discovered I'd been rolling with no roller as the bloody thing had detached itself about five acres ago. I drove mournfully back to my abandoned implement, managed somehow to wrestle successfully with big metal rods and couplings and continued on.

Shopping for groceries was not a case of nipping out to the village stores on my bicycle; the nearest shop was Thetford, some five miles away and I didn't have a driving licence at that point. Not fancying cycling or walking down a dual carriageway with a weeks worth of bread and baked beans, I had a bright idea, I would take the calf transport, namely the Austin Maxi and drive it across our farmland in the rough direction of Thetford and as far as I could get across the fields, before having to stop at the fence. I would then climb over and walk the remainder of the distance. It was a good (ish) idea in theory.

I got as far as the third field from the farm, about 150 acres in and still three miles from the town, before having to stumble across a heavily ploughed field on foot, climb through barbed wire and continue my journey. I had a cat at the time called Nettle, and so ended up hauling endless cans of Kitekat across rough terrain in the dark with no torch. It wasn't one of my brightest ideas. Subsequently I booked ten driving lessons, passed first time and thereafter took the old David Brown tractor to Tesco.

We had a small flock of geese in the yard that would hiss and flap thunderously towards any human being, be it a stranger, Willy or myself. They didn't bother me, and sometimes, when thoroughly hacked off with their aggressive antics, I would grab the pack leader warmly by the neck and hiss 'no!' as our beak and noses touched. It made no difference.

My romantic involvements at the farm were fairly pathetic, the last three years having been spent in blissful celibacy. I loved being shut away from the stir of society. That said, I did feel at such a young age I really ought to at least make some effort to socialise, so I joined the local Young Farmers Club, and much to my surprise was descended upon by the sons of two local farmers. One offered to pick me up the following week in his sporty motor, presumably having spotted the forlorn old tractor I'd rolled up in. The other chap was the aforementioned Jeremy Whitbread, the son of a wealthy local farmer. The first candidate did indeed pick me up in his sporty motor the following week and took me to my second evening at the YFC. I hated it, was chronically shy and couldn't wait to get home to my cat and Clannad. The blow job I'd performed on Jeremy he'd evidently enjoyed and we somehow ended up in my bed with me wearing my new, size 10 ivory, satin chemise from Next. I have no idea what possessed me to buy the thing as it was a very feminine and delicate piece of nightwear, far more suited to Marilyn Monroe than a herds-woman. Clambering into bed, there was an audible snap as the thin shoulder straps gave way. Jeremy ejaculated before I'd even laid hands on him so based on that single incident, I didn't contact him again.

Just Google-stalked him, damn, the man has a 500 acre arable farm in Northamptonshire and endless converted outbuildings for BnB's and holiday rentals, oh and a very slim and smiling wife called Penelope. Fuck. There are treatments for premature ejaculation aren't there?.

CHAPTER SIX

Can She Do 'Owt Wit Sheep?

After a year of being shat on at 5am and kicked, I decided I couldn't handle milking anymore and placed an advert in the Farmers Weekly;

'Female seeks position on farm, accommodation required.'

I was back living at home by then and my poor mum was subject to the calls that came in..

"Ellaw I war ringin abart ad int Farmers Wickly, is this yon lass?,"

"Hello, no I'm very sorry she's not here at the moment, could I leave Cathy a message for you?,"

"Ay, can she do owt wit sheeep?."

"I believe she can, it's best you speak to her yourself though."

Another time, I picked the phone up and a dull, nervous sounding male mumbled, 'a position you're looking for is it? What sort of 'position' would you like?,' I hung up.

Eventually I accepted a months trial on a dairy goat farm in Wiltshire. The job as herd manager, herd manager!, came with a gorgeous farm cottage/granny annexe which I couldn't wait to settle into. Unfortunately the owner, Mrs Whyteman, was still very much attached to 'granny' who had been dead for over ten years and whose ghostly presence, she assured me sternly, still enjoyed twitching the net curtains and enjoying her tea and cake every afternoon. I'd been told therefore, that I was on no account to use the sitting room, which was all beautifully laid out as per the day granny had died, complete with Royal Albert cups and saucers and a fire laid ready in the grate. Occasionally when idling away a few minutes, I'd open the sitting room door and have a nervous glance around, half expecting to see granny rocking away in her chair, cramming a French Fancy into her mouth.

I was to share the cottage with my farm assistant, Sarah, a lovely lady similar in age to me and who I got on exceedingly well with. The goat farm, called Meadow Bank Farm comprised of 200 milking Saanen goats. The Saanen is a breed of goat equivalent to the Friesian cow in terms of milkiness and produces between 3 and 4.5 litres per day over a ten month lactation. The most noticeable and utterly tremendous thing about milking goats was the complete absence of liquid cow shit. At the end of two hours spent milking 200 cows, it required a jet washer and several thousand litres of water to clean the parlour and yards, plus a tractor and scraper afterwards. After milking 200 goats however, I used a dustpan and brush to sweep up their ladylike little droppings, it was heaven. When it came to parlour training the new influx of goatlings (first time milkers), their delicate kicking and capering about was not a problem at all. I would hold two legs together with one hand and hold the unit firmly on the udder with the other, probably not an easy feat by most people's standards, but for a woman who'd been used to the mighty blows of 135 the Friesian, this was as easy and as pleasant as making fairy cakes. The relief milker who helped us with the goats every Saturday had once spent three hours trying to control 35 naughty little goatlings and in exasperation had said to Sarah,

"How the hell does Cathy do this on her own?!."

The other huge advantage of goats over cows is that mastitis was rare, probably because of the cleaner surroundings due to their producing currant-like poo instead of liquid poo. The parlour had only been installed three years ago, it was a hygienic blue and white colour, with a built in radio, tea and coffee making facilities and a shower!, heaven, that and the fact that goats are friendly, lovable little things too, all made for a very soft job.

We had a team of electricians in one day and I offered them all tea;

"Yea great thanks, but we don't want that goat stuff in it," pointing to the row of Saanens that were shooting milk into the glass jars under each milking point. I handed out the mugs of tea and they all guzzled it down gratefully whilst I waited till they'd finished before telling them that they'd drank fresh goats milk. Much theatrical gagging and choking followed. Similarly I had goat sausages made from some cull males and people would rarely accept one. But if I said they were pork sausages, they'd eat and enjoy them, remarking on how lean and delicious they were and then proceed as normal with the affected nauseous coughing when told it was actually goat sausage they had eaten.

Someone remarked one day that eating goats cheese is like 'sucking a billy goat's foot,' not something many can claim to have done, but quite an accurate simile if the cheese is of the mature variety. I love goats cheese, and when eaten fresh it has absolutely no goat tang at all.

We had three big Saanen billy goats and every 17 days (the oestrus cycle of a goat and sheep) I had to 'change the raddle.' A raddle is a tough, webbing harness that the billy goat wears during the mating season. It has a metal slot in it which holds a coloured block of crayon, thus every nanny that is mated by the billy will be smeared well and truly about the rump area with orange, green or blue crayon and will hopefully give birth in five months time. This makes kidding and lambing very efficient and by changing the crayon to a different colour every 16 days, a farmer can control batches of births in order to organise breeding management.

For the crayon changing at Meadow Bank Farm, I used to have to get togged up like a deep sea fisherman with every part of me covered in waterproofs; wellies, plastic leggings, a sou'wester hat and coat and rubber gloves, otherwise the smell would persist in my skin for days. One of the billy goats, Mickey, was exceptionally pungent and would indulge regularly in the endearing billy-goat habit of performing oral sex on himself. I'm assuming those of a more delicate disposition are currently reading Jane Austen and other similar works by equally accomplished writers, and as such are as disconnected and distanced from such peasant scribblings as these, as I am from the works of Plato. Therefore I need not worry over the possibility of offending the reader.

Mickey would crouch himself up, pop his willy into his mouth and then when suitably aroused, would spray all surrounding victims with a potent mixture of urine and semen. An important part of the ritual is also spraying their own beards and as a result, a billy-goat's beard is permanently dripping with unmentionable bodily fluids. Therefore their heads are to be avoided, unless you're a nanny goat, then this foul cocktail is as exciting and delicious as Lynx Africa. In fact for the purposes of individual mating, a piece of cloth, thoroughly soaked in billy goat fluid, is stored in a lidded glass jar in order to ascertain exactly when the nanny is on heat, as the receptive time period is quite short. The owner wafts the cloth under the nanny's nose everyday, making sure to return the cloth to the jar each time and tighten the lid to retain its pungency. The nanny will dismiss the offending article with an imperious turn of the head and continue in her munching of hay or whatever her occupation is at the time, until that is, the day arrives when she is on heat: instant Beatle Mania; her ovaries will be galvanised into action by the smell of the cloth, and she will morph into an uncontrollable sex machine on a mission to find the owner of the cloth's smell.

Whilst working at this farm, my odd relationship with food must surely have been noted by Rupert, my boyfriend at the time. He was endlessly patient and would arrive every weekend with flowers, having arranged an evening out for us. I was perfectly horrid to him and wasn't capable of appreciating at the time his thoroughly good nature. He was normal and grounded being an agricultural mechanic and could fix any combine harvester or tractor that was put his way, he must surely have loved me very much indeed to put up with my weirdness. We did healthy, rural things together, such as ploughing matches and restoring gypsy caravans. Sadly I didn't fancy him and I didn't love him, not that I had any idea what love meant, I still don't, only that I didn't missed him between visits, and having moved in with him I would relish his nights down the pub so I could play my beloved folk music. Rupert, as a die hard Meat Loaf fan couldn't get his head around these odd rustic tunes.

One Saturday morning, awaiting the arrival of a smiling, flower-laden Rupert, I suffered an attack of the food madness, wolfing down whole packs of laxatives before running away across the fields with a bulging Spar carrier-bag and purging my tortured soul on ginger snaps and iced buns. The diarrhoea that resulted from these sessions was unprecedented. With the farm dog, Twig, suffering from some form of canine IBS, our little farm cottage smelt permanently of the dysentery wing of a Delhi hospital.

Though I am able to jest with the wonderful benefit of hindsight, I was actually a seriously mentally ill woman, and suffered almost constantly with intolerable levels of anxiety, self hatred, depression and general wretchedness. These feelings had been ever present since I was very young. I clearly recall, aged about 12, lying in bed, staring at the wall and drawing an imaginary red button on the wall that I wished with all my heart I could press, so as never to wake up in the morning. I never actually attempted suicide but the thought of dying was a welcome one. The really bad times saw me bed-ridden for weeks and the depression cost me many jobs. But in the way that is often typical of a depressive, I could be disarmingly funny and deeply self-deprecating, something that comes very naturally and is a big pick-me-up.

Where was I? Ah yes, diarrhoea. I was now a regular at the local country pub and after a long day of kidding goats, (assisting them to give birth) making yogurt and mucking out, I would sit myself at the bar and sink several Bacardis and endless bags of Doritos. I'd then make the sensible decision to drive home, cursing the car with its 'broken' steering column that stubbornly refused to stay on the left hand side of the road. Whilst at the pub one night I spied a lone male, he was seriously gorgeous, black hair and green eyes, a deadly combination. I decided within minutes he was going to be dragged back to our sulphurous lair, so being completely pissed by that stage, I managed to seduce the poor lad and he accompanied me home. I zigzagged my way up the stairs with him trotting up behind.

It was most unfortunate timing because once again I was suffering from self inflicted diarrhoea. Oh my fucking Christ, has anyone other than me tried keeping their vagina open during sex whilst simultaneously keeping their rectum firmly shut? when all it _really really_ wants to do is to open and evacuate four packs of liquid Jaffa Cakes and Doritos. I was hugely relieved when he left, literally.

Sarah and I shared all the work between us at Meadow Barn and there was an awful lot of it. We did everything from changing billy raddles, pulling kids out of nannies in difficulty, baling hay in the summer, making 200 gallons of fruited yogurt every week for sale to Holland and Barrett and packaging never ending quantities of milk for sale to Waitrose, using the utter bastard invention known as the 'milk-packing machine.' Regardless of how kindly and even-tempered a person you were, after two hours alone with piece of equipment, you would be capable of serial murder in an old peoples home. It would behave perfectly for thirty minutes, popping out neat little sealed cartons full of chilled, health-giving goats milk. Then it would crunch a full carton, with a spectacular firework display of milk all over the dairy. With one carton completely mangled in the machinery, all the other cartons followed from behind, backed up, squashed and exploded too. You became pretty quick at legging it to the big red button on the wall to cut the power supply.

We both took our turns at each of the varied jobs, and when it was Sarah's day to milk-package and I was strawing up the goats, I could hear the familiar 'dum dum clunk ker-plick, dum dum clunk ker-plick,' as it behaved itself. And then an almighty roar of, "you fucking mother fucker!!," I generally hung out in the safety of the barn till she'd finished packaging.

Yogurt making was even more unpredictable than cartoning the milk. Medieval alchemists I'm sure were more successful at creating gold than we were at making yogurt. Yogurt making involves a precise interplay of bacteria for it to be successful and bacteria have a penchant for a 'do as you likey' attitude at times.

It was always an early start on a yogurt day if you wanted to be in and collapsed in front of the TV by 10pm. We would both be in the dairy by 5.30am with one of us starting work in the parlour and milking the goats whilst the other would set up the dairy in preparation for yogurt making. Even at that early hour I could feel the slow build up of tension, with familiar thoughts of 'will it or won't it.' By this I mean, will the yogurt set and thicken properly, or will it stubbornly remain in its original milk form?. If the bacteria decided they didn't want to play ball and the milk remained as milk, it meant a phone call to Holland and Barrett to explain once again, our embarrassing predicament. Inevitably, on the fifth occasion of ringing them, they cancelled the contract.

It was a great shame though because we were so fastidious. Everything was immaculate and every stage followed to the letter, from the warming of the milk in the huge steel vat to the actual potting off of the cultured milk. At the end of a long yogurt day I would fall into bed and then wake as if from a bad dream at 3am, go to the warm incubating room, where the hundreds of pots were hopefully thickening, only to discover on peeling back a lid that it was still liquid milk, another failed batch. It was very stressful indeed.

One early morning, and still dark outside, unbeknownst to us, a huge moth had landed in the milk hopper that sat above the potting machine. A week later a terse letter and a wrapped pot of yogurt arrived from the health store, informing us that a customer was 'shocked and distressed to find an animal in her yogurt.' Not as bloody stressed as I'd been making the stuff.

When yet another entire batch had failed, I pulled off the lids of every pot of strawberry, raspberry, black cherry and natural yogurt and fed it all back to the goats, they loved it. Unfortunately for the business turnover, I also loved it and would eat a tray of six black cherry yogurts in one hit, it was delicious. I believe my record was three trays in one hour.

Once, whilst mucking out the goat sheds one Sunday, Terence Whitcombe-Thomas who lived in a palatial manor house some half a mile away, strode into the barn and requested that I didn't muck out on a Sunday as he usually entertained family that day. I in turn asked him if he could refrain from shooting pheasants on Sundays as I too needed to relax, and in damn sight more need of it than he was. Knob.

We had a young Glaswegian lad who helped us out a couple of times per month, called Dave. Dave decided he really rather fancied me and would drive the tractor slowly up and down the enormous shed as I forked the inaccessible edges out by hand. He would leer at me from the cab, making suggestive remarks in such a strong Scottish dialect I couldn't actually make out what he was saying. I do remember him, exasperated as he was by then at his failed attempts at winning me over, fairly spitting out the words,

"Jee wanna come oot fur thee evenin?!." I declined.

A lifetime's problem with carpal tunnel syndrome began at this farm because there were so many goats to foot-trim. I usually did about ten every day, it was knackering and my wrists never forgave me.

The tale of Meadow Barn farm ends sadly. I had been working there for about two years when the owner decided to purchase some new goats and unknowingly introduced Johnes disease into the herd, a viral nightmare that causes wasting and arthritis. It wiped out over half the herd and the owner decided to call it a day and sell up. It was a very sad day when the buildings lay completely empty.

'Mickey the exceedingly smelly billy goat'

We are now in the UK, one of the most wildlife depleted countries in Europe. Having encouraged farmers to pull up millions of miles of hedges after the Second World War, the numbers of birds have declined drastically and are still declining. Hedges have been replanted since then, we have tried to make amends. We have lost 97% of our wild flower meadows, this is indeed a tragic situation.

Without going into endless ramblings and spouting statistics; in a nutshell, it all starts at ground level: if you have plants in abundance, and more importantly, in abundant variety, you get the insects that feed off the plant sugar and you get the seeds that the plants produce. And what do birds eat? Seeds and insects. In addition these insects lay their eggs on plants which hatch into grubs which the birds feed to their young. It's simple. The number and variety of birds are the most accurate indicator of the biodiversity of an area of countryside. It starts on the ground.

So...I am endeavouring to establish a wild flower meadow on an elderly neighbour's 30 acre field here in Cornwall and a return to traditional hay making methods, that is to say, cutting hay *after* the grasses and flowers have seeded. Modern haylage and silage making is largely responsible for the disappearance of these beautiful meadows because both these grass crops are cut early, before most things have seeded. But my neighbour has very little money, doesn't own a tractor and as such I cannot get this wild flower meadow up and running. I have wracked my brain for ways to be able to do it, but it all comes down to finance. Having emailed countless organisations including Natural England, Plantlife and the Princes Trust, enquiring as to where I could get some financial help in order to establish a meadow, none of them could offer any assistance. Natural England responded with an email that radiated as much warmth and understanding as a Dalek. Indeed I responded with, 'are you an actual person?.' I doubt the author of said email could identify a sodding blackbird, let alone direct me to a source of meadow funding. Another wildlife organisation sent me a link to a potential source of help that made leaving the EU look simple. All these organisations bang on about how tragic it is that we have lost 97% of meadows, a voice calls out, 'I want to give 30 acres back,' and no-one can help.

How do we turn this around? The people with the serious money; the rich landowners and wealthy Londoners who buy up once productive farms and fill them with horses, a playground at weekends. These are the people who have the funds to make a BIG difference. And this is coming from someone who has farmed, and who has witnessed first hand, the neglect and bad management by moneyed landowners. I was chatting to a local farmer who delivered straw here last week,

"Alright Steve, how's it going?,"

"Ok thanks, I've got Natural England coming round this week to discuss a possible move up to Higher Level Stewardship but if it's ridiculously complicated I won't bother, I'm too busy."

Higher Level Stewardship is something a farmer can opt into. There are different tiers of 'care' that a farmer can choose to give to wildlife. He is under no obligation but if he does, he gets paid a bit do it. It's a crappy and ineffective system. And if you need proof, look at the wildlife statistics. Farming in sympathy with wildlife should be compulsory. Likewise, if you are an investment banker and you use your bonus to buy a three million pound country house and land, then you should be legally bound to manage a percentage of your land for wildlife, along with whatever else your personal intentions for the land are.

A 150 acre farm near me was bought by a well known musician. He loved the house and had it renovated beautifully, however the land was completely neglected. I had a visit a few months ago from the old boy who used to work that farm by hand; digging ditches, trimming hedges and coppicing the 80 acres of sweet chestnut. The musician has no interest in any of it, and so rents it out to cattle and sheep farmers. This rental arrangement so common over much of UK farmland, serves to exacerbate the neglect, the tenants having little or no interest in the long term management of land that does not belong to them.

Rant over. Onwards then with the story of Paco, a harmless and unsuspecting young man who I'd met online one evening whilst collapsed over the computer, having done battle with the milk-packing machine for three hours. He was a classical musician who should have known better than to meddle with a goat-woman. I exchanged about a dozen messages with him on the site and obsessed as usual, the same old obsession I was crippled with, with virtually every man that had ever shown me even the slightest romantic/sexual interest.

Paco, on a scale of 1-10 on the attractiveness scale, was about a 3. But you see I was in the clutches of Abandonment Anxiety and it was only the truly plain looking individuals that escaped my obsessiveness. Or if there was a hint of attractiveness there but they were boring as hell, they too would escape my dreadful tentacles. Unfortunately for Paco, he wasn't sufficiently ugly and I became fixated on him.

Dear me, this poor guy. I think he'd twigged I was a sausage short, and after both agreeing to meet for the first time in London after a musical recital he was giving, he then cancelled our date via a computer message. I was disappointed to say the least, and my tortured mind went into the by now familiar whirlwind of frenzied panic as I searched for ways to win back his attention. I had remembered which church he was performing at and set off for London, undaunted by the fact he'd cancelled the date and I had no A-Z of the Capital.

I found the venue and settled myself in the second row from the front, looking as pouty and seductive as possible. Halfway through the performance he recognised me from my internet profile, and began to look a little scared. I'm not surprised, I'd have been crapping myself. After the performance I raced backstage and asked for him. 'He's already left,' they said.

Bloody hell, he must have shifted it double time because although I ran across London looking for him, the last I saw was a dark, cloaked figure carrying a wind instrument case, hot footing it away from the church as if he'd seen the AntiChrist. Truly, I had Mad Cow Disease.

On a slightly more serious note, the psychologist who'd first diagnosed me with Abandonment Anxiety had said to me in that initial session;

"When you go out there, on dates, opening yourself up emotionally to men, remember you are a child, a ten-year-old terrified child, looking for a loving parent, don't do it." It seems she was right. And that is why I am happy to remain overweight and unkempt, safe in my Wurzel garb. Men no longer look at me and I in turn do not look at them as I know there is no point, unless the man is registered blind. I'm sure it must sound very sad but honestly, it was a conscious decision. I cannot risk ever becoming attracted to anyone, because when the man in question starts to cool down, which he will, I am laid out cold and I have too much at stake now; a farm for starters. Yet I am happier than I've ever been. I can honestly say, hand on heart, that since living here in Cornwall, I have never felt lonely. I just don't particularly enjoy the company of people. We are a horrid species, we kill each other for no good reason, we lie, we invented plastic and then fill the earth with it.

CHAPTER SEVEN

Counting Testicles

After I'd left the goat farm in Wiltshire, I worked freelance for what seemed an eternity, scrambling from one farm to the next. I finally decided the heady heights of travel were my destiny so I boarded a ferry and began work on a farm in the Loire Valley in France, making goats cheese and castrating piglets whilst cruelly underfed by the stern old woman that owned the place, well, not strictly underfed but stingy with her helpings. So off to Sully sur Loire I would pedal, on an old French onion-sellers bike every morning in my quest for 'flan,' an ambrosial confection, worthy of the Gods. I have never found its likeness here in the UK. Our egg custard tart is a poor relation of this understated masterpiece of smooth crème patisserie contained within a crisp and sweet pastry shell, I'd kill for six slices of it now. Oh how I loved flan, such a small insignificant word for something so heavenly. Home I would pedal along the banks of the Loire and into my room to devour my pastry in privacy. Most days as I returned home, there was a masturbating Frenchman by the river with an enormous erection. Being young and innocent, sort of, I was shocked at this public display of pornography and decided to inform the authorities. I enlisted the help of a bilingual friend of my employer to accompany me to the Gendarmerie. The Chief Gendarme, though trying his best to look very concerned, obviously couldn't have given a hoot and I had the impression that the wanker by the river was probably quite a familiar sight, and given no more attention than the postman.

The old lady had a daughter, Carolyn, who ran the farm, and it was she who decided that a 6am trip to an abattoir would be a jolly nice day out for me. We arrived in Orlean at a huge abattoir that killed 3500 pigs per week and I found myself surrounded by a group of flat-capped French farmers all looking morosely on at the proceedings. This was pig-killing on an industrial scale, and though horrid, it was very efficient; 15 minutes from live pig to suspended refrigerated carcass. The building was as big as an aircraft hangar and the system for moving the pigs throughout was impressive. Pigs are not the easiest of livestock to move, they don't always group like sheep and cattle, and due to their intelligence can become stressed very easily so a system of overhead warm water sprinklers would come on at set intervals. As the pigs became agitated, the warm water instantly calmed them.

In order to encourage the animals to move up a gently sloping ramp towards the stunning area, there was a long elevator with a circulating floor and cushioned sides, thus the pig was moved along with no effort required by either itself or employee and as such there was no noise or stress. I stood with the group of farmers and fixed my gaze on the pig at the front of the queue. It's expression was one of curiosity but calmness. The stun pads were located within the walls of the padded sides of the elevator which sloped up hill, and as the pig approached the top of the belt, it was stunned and dropped off the end. A man in a white boiler suit, not the best choice of colour, stood waiting and as each stunned pig dropped off, he drew a knife along its throat, placed a huge hook under its head and the pig was hauled up by a complicated system of chains and pulleys that circuited the entire hangar. It would then bleed into the gridded floor beneath. The pig, along with hundreds of others, moved in a regimental fashion along the overhead chains and was submersed in hot water, bristles scraped off, gutted and through to the refrigerator.

Up until visiting the abattoir I hadn't thought of myself as being overly squeamish but it was seeing the face of a very much alive and curious pig, to then see it dangling and gushing out blood, whilst below me, rivers of blood flowed through the metal gridded floors on which we were standing, that had me realise in an instant I was about to pass out. Panicking at the thought of the attention this would draw and a vision of myself sprawled on the ground with a team of confused French farmers peering down at me, I looked up at the ceiling and forced myself to think of the loveliest thing I could bring to mind. It happened to be a piece of music by Enya, called Watermark. It worked thank goodness. Fortunately, I don't now associate this lovely song with the slaughter of pigs, something Enya would be jolly appreciative of too I would imagine.

The next morning was to be spent castrating piglets, a procedure carried out in France at that time to prevent 'boar-taint,' which produces a strong piggy-tasting meat as the male animal develops sexually..ugh, I'll have the cheese on toast please. The piglets were approximately two weeks old and you would imagine then that they would be fairly easy to restrain. Not so. I took hold of each piglet in turn, turned it upside down and held it against the front of my left shoulder by its back legs. Carolyn injected a little anaesthetic into each testicle, waited a while for it to take effect and then carefully removed their wee little balls. As I released each piglet after castration, they scooted off and began play-fighting with their mates and generally enjoying themselves, none the worse for their operation. I was pretty damn strong in those days but the strength required to restrain a piglet was huge, they are solid little power packs of muscle and catching hold of one is like trying to catch a self-propelled, squealing bar of soap. It took a lot of arm power and I had to wear ear protection because the decibels produced were so loud. My official job, other than piglet restrainer was to count the testicles afterwards. An uneven number was bad news as it meant that somewhere Carolyn had left a potential future father to unwanted piglets, capable of at least half inseminating sows.

The nice part of my job in France was milking the goats and helping to produce the Crottin de Chavignol cheese, little round concentrated nuggets of intense goatiness that one either loved or detested. I loved them, with warm baguette, tomatoes and olive oil, delicious. Milking the goats was a labour intensive system but one which I loved. In an old stone barn, there was a tether attached to the wall at spaced intervals, one for each of the goats. Half an hour before the afternoon milking I would straw the barn up, put out their hay and water and open the small sliding door. In they all trooped and always to the same spot. The only naughty one was the billy, a gorgeous, black and glossy, horned chap called Adam, who would dart about, daring you to catch him and prancing around between the girlie goats, stealing their food and knocking the milk churn over. He was bloody annoying but very lovable. I used a portable milking machine on a trolley, complete with a small generator, milking cluster, pulsator and milk churn. Each day I would carry the milk over to Carolyn, into the cool stone dairy opposite the milking shed and she would magically turn the milk into Crottins.

My long suffering boyfriend, Rupert, visited me during my four month stay and took a shine to Carolyn. I stood in the haystack one sunny afternoon, watching them chat amiably to one another and sincerely wished he would take up with her instead of me. I found the whole relationship thing exceedingly dull and wearisome, compulsory efforts to smarten myself up for example and look vaguely feminine, were intensely arduous compared to the satisfying occupation of eating. One night whilst Rupert was staying in France with me, Carolyn's mother had made an enormous dish of cauliflower cheese. It was bloody delicious and would have been a perfect meal apart from the depressingly normal sized portion which left me hungry within thirty minutes of eating it. Subsequently I planned a raid on the fridge that evening and waited for everyone to go to bed and for Rupert to nod off so I could sneak back into the kitchen and scoff the lot. She had cooked two whole cauliflowers for four people and about four pints of thick cheese sauce so there was plenty left. All went to plan although I felt as bloated as a bloaty thing after my midnight pig-out and was worried as to how I could maintain a look of innocence when questioned as to where it had all gone, strangely it was never mentioned. Now I'm not writing this next bit down just to get a laugh, but the wind all that cauliflower produced in me was well, bloody appalling. It was a real challenge keeping sufficient distance between myself and Rupert the next day whilst my poor intestines aggressively drove out the gas. Seriously folks, do not overdose on cauliflower.

We had a little black ram, only about two foot high, called Norman. He was a Ouessant, a French breed of sheep, a compact woolly ball of bristling meanness with an impressive set of horns that wouldn't look out of place on a buffalo and which caught me many a time on the back of my knees. I learnt to dodge Norman after the third smack in the patella. We also had an immensely tall goat called Aggie, a castrated male, his head was up to my chest but he was friendly and very affectionate. One day I was aware of unfamiliar noises from behind the goat shed which I discovered later, were the sounds of the travelling slaughter man. It was very disturbing to find dozens of containers labelled 'Aggie curry,' in the freezer the next day and I was horrified to think that Carolyn could have been so heartless as to kill him. Needless to say I refused to eat any unidentifiable meat based meal I was given from then on whilst in France.

Rupert visited me a second time and arrived bearing Cadburys chocolate and a kilo of Farleys rusks, for though I was 24 years old at the time, fully weaned and with no milk-teeth, I did miss my rusks terribly, confined as I was to a French farm with 100 pigs, 25 goats and Norman.

He was curious as to why I'd used newspaper in order to completely cover the full length mirror in my bedroom. Somewhat embarrassed, I explained that I would only pull my lashes and brows out if I could see them. So far this idea had worked and they were growing back, not for long though,

"It's a bit strange to cover a mirror in newspaper," he politely remarked. Damn right it was strange, but trichotillomania had and continued to affect my life hugely. I was convinced for decades that once cured of the problem, happiness would return, forever.

He also went on to remark,

"It makes you look like a field without hedges."

Cheers for that Rupes, but then he was right. Without black eye pencil I looked terminally ill because I wasn't just pulling a few out, I'd removed the lot. If I'd been as determined in my career as I was in facial hair annihilation I'd have done extremely well in life. Bald eyes gave me a permanently washed out look and staying an entire night with any man I happen to date (Rupert was the only bloke I'd ever owned up to about my problem) was very stressful indeed, as I had to sneak out of the bedroom post rumpy-pumpy, apply make up and return to bed. Trichotillomania totally controlled my life along with dieting and was the governing factor in my mental state. After 3-4 weeks of not pulling and eating very little, I unarguably started to look a lot prettier. I would be happy and funny and social and super productive. But when the eyelash demon arrived unannounced, I would hurtle headfirst into an abyss of depression. Living with myself was like scaling Everest 24/7. The summit was a visible, tantalising object, the reaching of which would change my world. But I was stuck on the lower slopes, and for every 100 foot I climbed, I slid 100 back.

Returning to the subject of animals in France, there was also a big hound-like dog at the gite called Val de Loire, who regularly exercised his evolutionary right to kill cats. I had taken all the neglected farm cats under my wing within a week of arriving and fed and sheltered them in my room at night. One day I was high up in the haystack, throwing down bales for the goats, and a snoozing cat welcomed me with a contented miaow. Val, upon hearing the sound, scaled the twenty foot sheer-sided stack in seconds, teeth bared, snarling and barking ferociously, intent on a serious mutilating spree. I was genuinely terrified for the safety of the poor cat and so standing between him and it and with no time to put any thought behind my getting rid of mad dog tactics, roared at him,

"Fuck off Val you fucking fucker!!," as I noticed a holidaying couple in the yard below me, chatting politely away to Carolyn and glancing awkwardly up at the blaspheming haystack.

That same day I was guddling around ineffectually in the flower beds pretending to weed and unearthed a foot long, black metal dagger. For years I used it as a candle wax remover from tables etc. About a year ago I made some enquiries as to its actual identity. It's a late Medieval dagger, woo hoo!

'On the pretty banks of the Loire there lived a masturbating Frenchman'

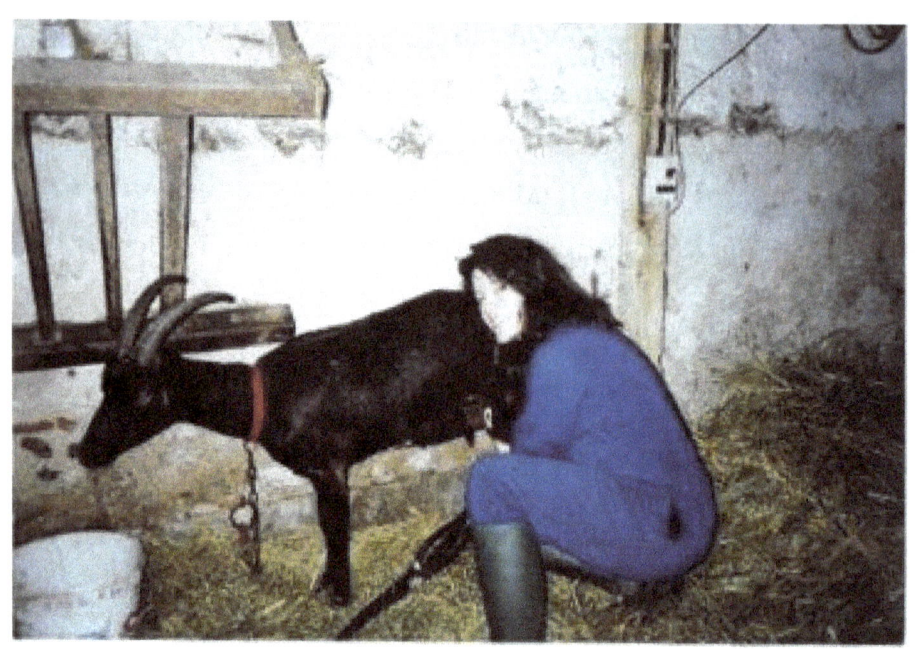

Back from France and living with Rupert in Ascot, Berkshire, I began once more the tedious hunt for farm jobs up and down the UK, always being drawn to the remote and wild areas of Yorkshire and Scotland, never Wales though for some reason. Could be something to do with the dating experience I'd had with the Welsh dairy farmer who'd put me to work like an oxen every time we met.

My most shaming farmy moment in all this sporadic peasant labouring was running away at 3am from a dairy farm in West Cumberland. I'd loaded up my car literally to the roof and left a pathetic, apologetic note to the farmer, James. No idea what it said, something along the lines of,

'Can't cope any longer, having mental breakdown, might have BSE,' then drove away silently in the small hours. Quite why I left in this manner is beyond me. Rupert was horrified, he was such a decent, conscientious chap, hard working and punctual, a thoroughly good egg. For some inexplicable reason he happened to glance up a little side road as he was leaving for work in his van, and there I was, hiding in my Peugeot 205 between rows of parked cars having just driven the eight hours from Cumbria. He insisted I return to the farm immediately and apologise to the old git, which wild horses wouldn't have made me do. Why on earth I didn't simply hand my notice in like a normal human being I don't know. I am by nature an ornery, contrary creature who opposes authority and hates routine. Still, it was an awfully irresponsible and cowardly thing to have done and it shames me to think of it now. James promptly stopped my pay cheque, I can hardly blame him.

I began working in West Cumberland two months after returning from France. The farm comprised of 50 Friesian and Jersey cows and was set in a stunning part of Cumbria. What the hell was I doing? Hadn't I experienced ladylike goat dairying and a glimpse of a life free from cow slurry? Still, off I went and settled into my gorgeous, rent-free cottage. Most of the time I was pretty good at the job and it was really rather sad that the farmer took a genuine dislike to me. He was extremely well spoken with shoulder length brown curls that he tossed about as he worked, for James had made enough money in the city to buy 130 acres and indulge his farming dream. One very cold winters morning I'd come in for a well deserved breakfast, having milked and washed down, fed the calves and farm cats, bedded up the cow cubicles with fresh straw and scraped the yards free of slurry with the little grey Fergie tractor. I was feeling rather proud of my mornings work when the old fucker walked unannounced into my kitchen, threw back his curls and bellowed;

"Wart the bleddy hell have you done todair?!."

Another time whilst I was milking in the morning, radio on, cows all behaving themselves, he strode into the milking parlour and roared at me, purple faced with rage,

"Well yoove rillair gawn and fucked theddup havun choo!."

Apparently, so he told me, I'd driven the tractor whilst one of the tyres was flat. I simply hadn't noticed and had been driving on the metal rim which was now dented and going to cost him a lot more than a flat tyre.

There were two farm cats, Lizzie-Lea and Rumple. One morning I was awoken by a miaowing beneath my bed and discovered Lizzie had had kittens. James drowned them all. I was horrified and insisted he take both cats to be spayed, it was inhumane to allow them to keep breeding and then kill their young. To my amazement he did indeed have them spayed, I was so relieved.

He and his wife, Elizabeth, had a daughter called Lettice, pronounced 'Le Teese.' It didn't matter how hard I tried to pronounce it, the word would propel itself from my mouth as the well known salad vegetable.

One of the cows, number 138, a gentle, quiet creature, became unpredictable and would occasionally launch a big hoof towards you as you went to milk her. Cows are big animals but generally even tempered by nature, unlike horses which left me a terrified, weeping wreck. Poor 138, it began with kicking in the parlour, then her being picked on by other herd members who by this time had sussed out that there was something decidedly un-cowlike about their herd mate. She then began to fall over in the yard, but would regain her footing fairly quickly, however this worsened and eventually she had fallen over so many times that a leg had become infected. The vet was booked, whereupon she fell over once more, her pus-filled leg went pop and I had a litre of foul smelling infectious fluid running down my face and neck. The vet looked up and gave me a wry smile, "you'd better get that washed off." Of course, she should never have been allowed to reach this stage, as James should have separated her, called the vet and made her life comfortable much earlier on in her illness. The diagnosis was once again BSE.

James was, if you hadn't gathered already, a miserable old toad. I remember standing in the farmyard and seeing him in the distance moving sheep, the far off little white shapes moving in response to the black collie behind them. I watched in amazement as he picked the dog up and hurled it through the air. Obviously the poor dog hadn't put the sheep where James had wanted them, which is almost always the handlers fault, not the dog's. May his seeds, both arable and testicular, wither and die.

The farm was situated near Blake Fell in West Cumberland. It nestled in a valley and as such was too steep for the milk tanker to climb out of had he even managed to get to the farm in the first place. So a labour intensive system had been devised to get the fresh milk to the top of the hill everyday. It involved me milking the cows, pumping the milk through into the big steel vat in the dairy which chilled the milk down to six degrees, it having left the cow at body temperature. The chilled milk was then pumped into two smaller portable insulated tanks which were towed behind the Land-rover, taken to the top of the farm, unhitched and left for the milk tanker to collect. It was a hell of a lot of tank cleaning for a small dairy herd, three tanks on a daily basis. The winter was a challenge with the Landy at full throttle in first gear, crawling it's way up a hill that was sheeted over with ice, and pulling two attached trailers containing 1000 litres of milk, all sloshing around behind you. I was made of sterner stuff back then, these days I need to sit down and fully recover with a cuppa on a regular basis. One morning I hadn't checked that the outlet caps on the tanks were fully tightened and driving up the hill I looked behind me to see milk pouring down the farm track. Leaping out and screwing the caps tight, I don't remember being caught out for this.

We had an ancient tractor, the old grey Fergie I mentioned, as familiar a piece of farm machinery as the fields they worked. It was a compact, spluttering beast with no cab and no safety roll bar, so if the old girl went over on her side you were either crushed to death or badly winded. Complaining yet dependable, it could only be persuaded to fire up its engine by the driver climbing aboard, knocking it into neutral and freewheeling it down the steep hill. Upon its rapid and alarming descent it would splutter into life, having bounced the poor driver up and down mercilessly on the metal seat. As it hurtled and gained momentum down the hill, the driver had to stand up and lean round to squirt EasiStart into its belly. Once in full chugging mode it would career off down the hill whereupon an impressive U turn was executed and both driver and elderly tractor would make their way back up the hill to scrape out the cubicle sheds.

My love of wild flowers was still apparent and whilst gathering the cows for the afternoon milking on day, I happened upon a wild plant which in nearly every respect resembled the deadly poisonous Hemlock Water Dropwort, that is apart from the petals, which were composed of a double ring instead of a single. To this day, I'm almost certain this was an unrecorded subspecies, because it was listed in none of my botanical books. I really should have had a botanist out to look at the plant.

One exceptionally lowly task involved me climbing inside the muck spreader. It was a huge, cylindrical metal tank, with a wide opening running the fifteen foot length of the spreader. Inside was a medieval looking arrangement of chains which were flung about violently when the machine was in motion. My unenviable job was the disentangling and removal of endless metres of baler twine that were tangled up in the chains. I suspect the farmer believed this to be a deserving task as I was bound to have been responsible for leaving the string in the muck and straw bedding in the first place, which would then have all been scraped up by a tractor during the winter muck out. In fact, I was and am very tidy in many respects, (though conversely filthy in others) and am fastidious in never leaving string lying about.

One day I was thrilled to be asked to muck-spread. This was a definite rung up the career ladder, and made a bloody change from milking and washing down the parlour. So I motored about the yard on the old tractor as quick as I could, getting the morning chores done and out of the way, pushing the slurry up the ramp where it would slop satisfyingly down into the muck spreader, its jaws open and waiting. I leapt off the Fergie and climbed inside the luxuriously cabbed, bright red Massey Ferguson that pulled the muck spreader, having only been given a ten minute lesson in the use of it the previous day. Selecting a gear from a confusing array of knobs and levers, I set off. At the point in the field that James had said to engage 'Power Take Off,' I did so, but was frantically scrabbling around to try and find first gear in high ratio in order to drive forward. Meanwhile the shit was flinging wildly about and after ten minutes of sitting stationary, still frantically searching for the right gear and swearing like a stone-picker, I had managed to deposit a thick layer of dung over a large area. James was livid as usual as I would have burnt the grass beneath the dung.

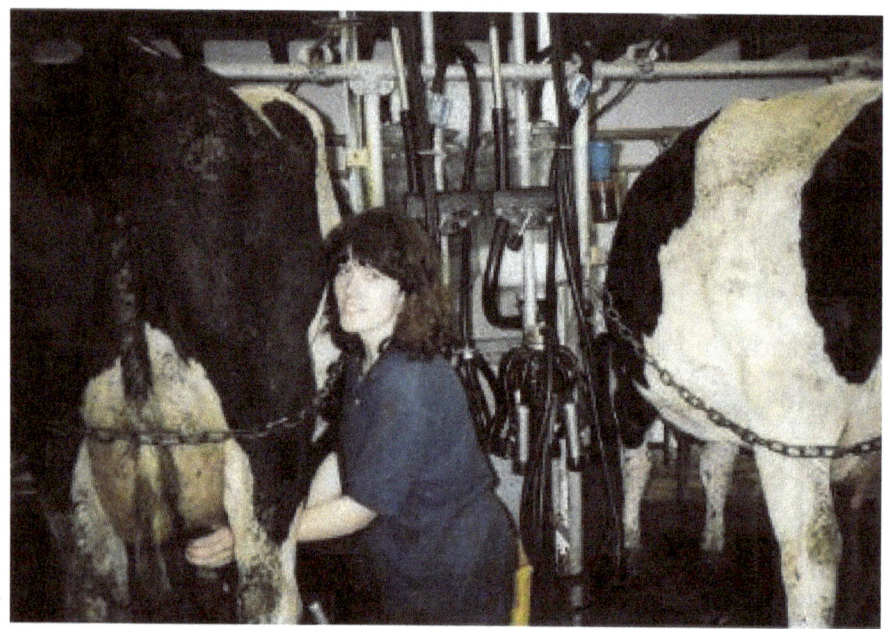

Having run away from Cumbria and the cantankerous James, I returned to live with Rupert once more and decided something a little lighter maybe a better choice for me job-wise. Possibly they were right all along at Meadowmeads college in that I should consider a career in onion-growing or truffle-hunting.

I was sat flicking longingly through the glossy pages of Country Living one day and saw an advert for a company looking for animal/home sitters. So off to the sprawling farmhouse of the company's owner I journeyed, complete with a couple of references; one from my mother posing as the owner of a 500 head of Aberdeen Angus cattle in Perthshire, and another entirely made up reference from a Mrs Jilly Pitt-Hawkins, who owned an 800 acre estate in Cheshire and for whom I ran the entire place, comprising of 100 acres of vineyards, a flock of 300 Southdown sheep, three bed and breakfast cottages and a ten acre asparagus crop. Excellent stuff, I was very proud of my comprehensive work of fiction. As luck would have it, the owner of the house-sitting company didn't need to speak Mrs Pitt-Hawkins, just as well as it would have entailed some serious voice-over acting on my part.

And so my career as a home/pet sitter began. It appealed because though on average I only earned £35 for a 24 hour stay, the 'work' mostly involved me watching daytime TV all day. As mentioned before, I rarely watch TV now as it makes me feel a little guilty when I have so much else to be getting on with. If TV is combined with heaven forbid, a takeaway, that surely is decadence on a par with solid gold bathroom fittings and a crystal encrusted loo seat.

My first job with the company was looking after five Dandy Dinmont terriers in Buckinghamshire. This didn't involve watching TV all day, it involved keeping the little feckers separated so they didn't draw blood from one another. They were Crufts show dogs and the modest little house was full of photographs displaying the much loved Dinmonts, preened and fluffy and covered in rosettes. Consequently the pressure was on to do a good job and sure enough, a split second of me looking away and a scuffle commenced of gladiatorial proportions. I prized them apart by roaring obscenities and banging saucepans together. Upon her return home, the owner was politely unimpressed as she was now down to three unscathed Crufts entrants. The remaining two had inflicted a couple of bite wounds on one another, not good for the show ring.

Another house-sitting job was in Hertfordshire. I arrived 24 hours before the start of the job to be shown the daily routine, which read like the assembly instructions for an underfloor heating system, it involved looking after one dog and three cats. The third assignment was a gorgeous old farmhouse in West Sussex, once a farm, now completely horseyfied, with the old milking shed an outside drinks bar complete with heated pool, the design equivalent of spoilers on a Rolls Royce as far as I was concerned.

My long established mental problems were rapidly gaining momentum at this time and one evening saw the beginning of a strange and tumultuous period in my life as I sat down at the computer which the owners had given me permission to use. Having Googled homemade potpourri ingredients and the fairy music of Co.Donegal, I somehow ended up on a dating website called UDate.com. Within the space of ten minutes I'd gone from purchasing The Complete Encyclopaedia of Faeries, Hobgoblins and Brownies by Katherine Briggs, to flirtatious messaging with Holland's equivalent of Robbie Williams: Xander de Buisonje.

He was tall, dark, musical and famous. I was instantly smitten and completely obsessed. It fucked up everything; my head, my job and my heart for nearly a year. Was he real or some sad little man impersonating him? I'll never know, but after several months of messaging and telling me he loved me, (I know I know what the fuck?!..) he rang me. Sure enough, a sultry, sexy voice sounded in my ear with a strong Dutch accent and a Dutch prefix to the mobile number. It even got as far as me waiting at Waterloo station, passport clutched in my hand, for a text to arrive from him saying he was waiting for me in Schiphol and to give me the go ahead to board a plane. The text never arrived. The whole sorry experience was utterly surreal and looking back, it was clear I was very ill to have even allowed the situation to continue.

The possibility of actually meeting with a real pop star had catapulted me into a deranged state of eating virtually nothing and working out in a gym for three hours every evening. My profile picture looked gorgeous and it was this that had enticed him in the first place. I was incredibly skilled at making my face and hair look stunning in selfie photographs, with glued in hair extensions and three sets of false eyelashes, the sad reality being I was completely unrecognisable in everyday life.

The crooning Dutchman texted me at one point saying,

"I hope you haven't got a big bum, I don't like big bums."

Shit, I thought, and spent an hour every night thereafter walking on my buttocks round the bedroom to the Village People's 'YMCA' courtesy of Felicity Kendal's workout LP.

After the hoax trip I'd made to Waterloo, I decided I'd had enough and called the asshole's bluff, Googling Dutch chat magazines to see if any of them would be interested in my story.

If this guy was for real, a full page spread would bring his producers and record company out of the woodwork, or at least I hoped it would. Well, it worked, in so much as a magazine emailed me back requesting an interview. Holy smoke! It was all bizarre, but honestly, it was terribly sad in reality because the core reason behind my behaviour was Abandonment Anxiety. The Dutch reporter flew over from Holland to meet me at a coffee shop in Guildford and said he thought there was a good chance that it really was this pop star guy as he was well known for being a womaniser and was currently in a long term relationship. He took photos of me and my mobile phone with 'Xander's' text messages on it, all lending some credence to the story, pointed his professional journalists camera at me and told me to look as woebegone and broken-hearted as possible, which I did, no acting necessary, hazelnut latte in one hand and passport in the other.

The magazine was printed, a centre spread, the reporter kindly posted a copy to me, all in Dutch of course and to this day I've no idea what it actually says but I vaguely got the gist of Dutch for womanising, sex addiction and breasts.

One week later I received a phone call from a man with a Dutch accent, introducing himself as the 'singers manager,'

"Now that the magazine has been printed, do you intend to proceed any further?,"

I replied with 'no I didn't.' At that moment, 'Xander', walked through the manager's office,

"He said to say hi to you," the manager said.

The whole episode was one of the most bizarre and unsettling periods in my life. If it had happened to let's face it, any other well adjusted woman, she'd have brushed him off months ago as a fake, who ensnared and deceived women for his own distorted ends.

The country house in West Sussex where I'd met the Dutchman online, was owned by a successful, middle-aged couple who'd left me in charge of a lurcher, a basset hound and three cats. There was a neat, square hole in the utility room wall which served as a cat flap. I came down one morning and thought I'd dreamt the following events as I recalled them later; a cushioned, comfy bench that sat against the wall next to the kitchen table by the warm Aga, contained both dogs and a fox, all curled up happily. The fox took one look at me and shot out through the hole in the wall, leaving me to clear up the devastation. The fox (I assumed it was him, not the dogs) had emptied bins, torn open bags of flour and biscuits and crapped **everywhere**. As anyone who is familiar with the smell of fox poo will know, this was not your average clearing up session. I had no idea where to begin and I was now late for my day job on a local farm. Unluckily for me, the wife was a skilled clairvoyant, having gained quite a reputation in her witchy woo craft and as such was in high demand for 'seeing' situations that had occurred during animals' lives, sensing their troubled minds and interpreting their behaviour. She was obviously pretty damn good at her job because a week after I'd left the property, she rang the agency to say she was not happy about my house-sitting capabilities. I think she must have been genuinely telepathic because her Mystic Meg skills had located the hot chocolate stain on the cream sitting room carpet which I thought I'd concealed, Agatha Christie style, underneath the rug. And I've no doubt she'd 'seen' the fox and dog party in the kitchen.

CHAPTER EIGHT

A Milking Song

> I shall never hear her more
> By the reedy Lindis shore,
> "Cusha cusha cusha," calling,
> Ere the early dews be falling.
> "Come up Jetty, rise and follow,
> From the clovers lift your head.
> Come up Lightfoot, come up Whitefoot,
> Follow follow Jetty to the milking shed."
>
> -- Jean Ingelow

It heralded the beginning of a very expensive decade when I first saw an advert in a glossy mag which read 'long luscious hair forever!' I rang the number.

'Glue-in hair extensions, Kensington Church Street, £300 for a full head.' I was beside myself with joy, having had no idea such things were possible, labouring away as I was on a farm in the middle of nowhere, blissfully unaware that hurricane Katrina was causing havoc in America, Daniel Craig was the new James Bond and for £300 you could be transformed from Christine Walkden to Cheryl Cole. I was desperate to get to Kensington even if it meant selling 100 bales of hay. The news of this revolutionary hair treatment produced the same effect in me as a bandage swathed, limbless individual seeing an advert for a permanent cure for leprosy. Happiness was mine! With two foot long tresses, the world was my oyster.

With the hay sold and the money in my wallet I boarded a train to London. How the hell do millions of people do this everyday? Winding through the long, convoluted tubes, a rabbit warren of stations with strange sounding names. Where exactly was the Elephant and Castle? London appeared to be distinctly lacking in both. I arrived at the impossibly fashionable hairdressers, filled with impossibly petite young women and men, possessing legs the width of my arms and wreathed with levels of confidence, perfume and gorgeousness I could only dream of. Ushered into a padded leather chair, fed milky coffee and those delicious biscuits you're always given with coffee in posh places, the uplifting classical harmonies of 50cent in my ears, I watched the two hairdressers work their magic. Three hours later, a Medusa-like vision stared back at me from the mirror. Damn I looked good! From the neck up I was fanciable!

One week later I had pulled out every single hair extension, yep, all gone. This was the trichotillomania and self harm rampaging through my system. I had worked out that if I rolled the little pea sized pieces of glue between my fingers until sufficiently softened, I could pull the extensions away from my own hair shafts. The thing is, it wasn't just the extensions, a proportion of my own hair would come out too. So, ever resourceful, I rang the hairdressers and explained in my best confused and disappointed voice that the extensions had all worked loose;

"We are terribly sorry, that's most unusual, please do rebook and we'll replace them all free of charge."

I returned and they reapplied them, only with a lot more glue this time. As a consequence my head felt extremely heavy, and it was impossible to wash my scalp properly. They looked nice for about 24 hours and then gradually became more and more matted, no matter how hard I tried to maintain them. After ten days my head was one big felted mass of acrylic fibre, lending me a wild, Neolithic appearance. I could stand it no more and cut them out with a pair of sheep shears. Funnily enough, after my first visit to the salon, I emerged knowing with absolute certainty, that I would be bedded by a male within two weeks, men are attracted to long hair. I was bloody right too; a young Lancashire lad working as a lambing assistant on a nearby farm, bundled me into his Pringles and lager filled caravan and did the deed, still in his farm boiler-suit. Long, Pre-Raphaelite tresses have the same effect on men as dried liver treats offered to a dog. Neither can resist.

Situated as I am, in the Cornish countryside, there is hopeless mobile signal and broadband is unheard of. So finally, after a year of screaming obscenities at my iPhone, hurling it across the room and once on a particularly bad day, stamping on it, which was very silly of me and very childish, not to mention pointless because it is the topography's fault, not Steve Jobs, I have decided on the company "3" with which to connect to the outside world. It works! It bloody well works! I turn on a little white plastic thing called a dongle and dangle it from the bird feeder by the back door of my cottage, whereupon it weaves its mysterious invisible waves between the hundreds of acres of woodland, mountains and thick stone walls of the farm outbuildings and connects with a mobile mast somewhere. I am a happier woman and have for the first time watched Uptown Funk in its entirety, free from endless buffering and loading, and marvelled at Bruno's kissable lips and mocha coloured skin. I had no idea he was so little.

Sat here with a cup of vanilla chai, my mind travels back several years, when I trundled up to London to see Michael Flatley in his theatre production of Dangerous Games. Honestly? Two out of ten. Lord of the Dance was fantastic, so why drag it back kicking and screaming. It was awful, a wailing ex girl-band member slotted oddly between robots with LED lights on their heads doing Irish dancing. The highlight however was being seated next to a rather attractive young man in his twenties who I'd initially clapped eyes on when he leapt, gazelle-like, from the row in front of me to the seat next to mine. Why oh why didn't I change out of my farm boots. They warmed up during the performance and by the time the teary eyed, sequin clad Irish pixie had lost her sparkly flute to the giant Irish robocop, my dung encrusted boots were perfuming the atmosphere around me and my dishy little toy-boy. Who knows, maybe if I'd changed my pants, worn normal shoes and eyeliner and not proudly showed off my screensaver of a Swaledale ram, he may have been blinded by the 22 years between us and sprinted across London after the performance to find me.

To return to the house sitting phase, the company must have been either very short of sitters or very forgiving of my misdemeanours because they rang me again;

"We have a job in London for you,"

"But..I've never driven in London, I'd never find the house, let alone find my way out again!."

"Buy an A to Z, you'll be fine!," which I did. But on my first job which was in Hampstead, I completely bottled it and took the train in with Bod, my border collie at the time, who I'd initially rescued from a horrid farm when she was a youngster. I adored Bod, she was perfect in every way, except the day we trained to London. At Waterloo station, she produced copious diarrhoea at the top of the main escalators. It was one of the few situations in my life where I have felt genuinely helpless; hundreds upon hundreds of poe faced commuters hurried by, with fleeting, cursory glances at myself and the hunched collie, whose explosive poo seemed to be endless. I had no choice but to remain at the crime scene until help arrived, which it did, in the form of a foreign rail staff member who gallantly said, although rather seriously,

"Is ok I do it,"

"Are you sure?,"

"Is fine I do it."

I've since felt guilty about not giving him £10 or something at the time, as that really was above and beyond the call and all that.

The house in Hampstead was the perfect antidote to the dog and escalator experience, a lovely Victorian house in Thurlow Street, with a dog called Denzel and a fridge full of chocolate. The owners were both Harley Street doctors and the wife said to me, as I tactfully commented on the fridge contents,

"We always start the day with some good quality chocolate." (I always start the day with two Wispa bars but I'm not sure this qualifies). I returned to the Denzel job six times over the next few months. I loved the contrast between the ostentatious rural retreats, masquerading as farmhouses and the London houses, who weren't faking anything, they were London houses occupied by Londoners. The contrast of a peaceful rural idyll and the hustle and bustle of the city was jolly nice. I walked Bod and Denzel on Hampstead Heath every day when in London, enjoying the magnificent views of the City whilst surrounded by the lakes and sweeping grandeur of the heath. My innocence took a bit of a knock when one day, walking through a small thicket of shrub and birch trees, I noticed a number of silent, motionless men, standing like stone sentinels amongst the trees, occasionally walking a few feet then stopping. Were they counting bird species? or maybe it was an outing for the inmates of Bedlam. Back on Hampstead Heath High Street, sat outside a café, enjoying a Black Forest hot chocolate and sharing the marshmallows with Bod and Denzel, I began chatting to a chap sat at the next table, who told me the odd men were basically selling their wares to one another, the 'wares' being their willies. I was disappointed at this news, it sullied the beauty of the heath.

The agency rang me again when I was back in Ascot with Rupert and said they had a job for me in Finchley looking after a Bichon Frise for three weeks. I agreed, only this time I would take my chances in a car, tackling the jumbled mass of tagliatelle that was the road network of London. It took me four hours to navigate my way from Ascot to Finchley. On the return journey, three weeks later, I was a heap of jangling anxiety and heart palpitations, in part because my bladder was filling rapidly and where the hell was I going to pee? It occurred to me that I would never find my way out and would have to ring Rupert to be rescued. I stopped outside an Indian restaurant and dashed in, only to be told the toilet was for restaurant users only. Being desperate by then, I went next door to a Halal butchers. The men all leered at me but agreed I could use their loo thank god.

The three weeks at Finchley had been lovely. They had a grand piano and an enormous walk-in larder filled with every kind of delicious food. By the end of my stay I had managed to teach myself the music from The Piano by Michael Nyman and was a stone heavier. The Bichon Frise had been given the unfortunate name of Fluffy, which made walks on the heath rather embarrassing as Fluffy would wander off, necessitating my calling his ridiculous name for all to hear.

Back home I was becoming ever more restless. Rupert was such a perfect boyfriend, too perfect, with an immaculate three bedroomed semi and manicured rose beds. I must have had a deep seated need to be beaten and raped daily instead of making his tuna sandwiches every morning and hoovering. Rupert had an extremely bad tempered black cat called Nutloaf. One morning I arose to discover the entire house was covered in oily, black paw prints. This was no exaggeration. Nutloaf had obviously trodden in a lot of engine oil in his nightly travels before returning home. In fact, judging by the quantity and distribution of the paw prints, it looked like he'd plotted his route around the house very carefully. During the night he'd made a full circuit of every room, walked across every piece of upholstered furniture, leaving perfectly prints all over the salmon coloured three piece suite, the pale beige carpets, the white, broderie anglaise guest room bedspread, in the bath and on the toilet lid. The little black fucker had done a top notch job in redecorating the entire house.

Oddly enough, I remained calm at the discovery of Nutloaf's stencilling project. I hired a Vax and blitzed the house in a day.

Treading on the scales one morning and seeing the dial bounce its way to 14 stone, I decided it was time to transform myself to an 8 stone vision of gorgeousness, dump Rupert and live happily ever after with an impossibly handsome, utter bastard of a man, much more exciting. My weight dropped at an impressive rate and upon my third weekly attendance at Weight Watchers slimming club, I'd lost 4 pounds in seven days. Another two weeks and I was down to just under 13 stone. However the minuscule calorie intake, barely enough to keep a shrew in good health, could only last for so long and within six weeks I was back on the pork pies, ginger cake and pizza.

Returning to WeightWatchers that week, I stood sheepishly in the weighing-in queue, listening to the other ladies who were chattering away over their 'naughty week of a sneaky custard cream on Thursday.' My turn arrived and I stepped onto the scales. The WW lady-in-command threw a puzzled look at the scales and asked me to step off and on again,

"Well! That's incredible!," she exclaimed, "the scales say you've gained 9lbs!."

I smiled inwardly at my record-breaking weight gain.

I have always had an obsessive love of the washing machine and tumble drier. I love them in equal measure, they are my favourite appliances. If the garment label reads 'hand wash only,' in the washing machine it goes. I like the freedom of experimentation it gives me, and I await the results with trepidation, similar to my putting a Herdwick ram on a Dorset Down ewe. So when I put Rupert's much loved and favourite woolly jumper in at 60 degrees and it emerged one foot long, three foot wide and as rough as a hessian sack, he was apoplectic with rage;

"It was my favourite jumper!," he shouted as he stormed off to work. I confess to having the most awful giggles as he held the deformed article aloft, stretching it to fully emphasise my incompetent laundering skills. In another, yet more disastrous episode, my mother had been given a beautiful sheepskin rug, it was dark chocolate brown, thick and luxurious and had been on her lounge floor a little over a week. I couldn't resist it. Surely the dust over the last 7 days warranted giving it some attention by now?.

In at 40 degrees it went with a mugful of Persil bio... Totally ruined. A sad, misshapen, unbendable shadow of its self. Mum refused to speak to me for a week.

So now we come to the part of the book where I have to introduce Kit Seymour. He was the pianist in a blues band called The Producers. Myself, Rupert and Mum had gone to see Peter Green of Fleetwood Mac fame at a performance he was giving in Worthing. Peter was a sad spectacle; a bowed, shuffling figure in scruffy clothes and sandals who wouldn't have looked out of place in a residential home.

"Ello Wurvin," he mumbled, ineffectually strumming the at least recognisable chords of Albatross. They left the stage after half a dozen songs and on came The Producers, who were superb, the keyboard player instantly catching my eye. Rupert, Mum and I returned home and I Googled the band to find out where they were next performing: 'Blues on the Farm' in Birdham in six weeks time.

I crossed off the days in my diary with the wild delirium of a prisoner due for release. The day arrived and having persuaded Ellie, a friend of my mum, to accompany me, we arrived in Birdham. I was a woman on a mission. It had been forty two days since the Peter Green concert and having survived on the nutritional intake of a field vole, I had managed to lose two stone. This impossibly efficient weight loss was down to 500 calories per day and the unusual regime of running up and down stairs. We're not talking taking the laundry up and down a few times a day, this was 45 minute sessions of me hurtling up and down at top speed. The weight loss was impressive if rather dangerous and all ultimately intended for the successful seduction of Kit Seymour.

Once at the gig, I knocked back three wines in quick succession which rendered me incapable of speech and swayed over to the jolly looking chap on their merchandise stand,

"I'm compliti and usserly in love with your peenist,"

"Are you now," he replied, beaming, "I'll go and find him for you."

Find him he did and Kit appeared. I wilt inwardly at the thought of it now, at my shameless flirting like that of an ovulating nanny goat. I cooed and purred and fluttered my three sets of false eyelashes and pressed my now slightly reduced in size, stomach against his. Men seldom turn down such a blatant offer unless the woman in question is exceptionally unattractive. He asked me back to his flat in Bournemouth. In my confused, drunken state I was convinced Birdham and Bournemouth must be close to one another because they both began with a 'B' and were near the sea. Ellie returned alone to our B&B and I stumbled through the crowd to find a taxi. Half an hour later I was on my way to Bournemouth.

"How far is it?," I asked. "A long way love, about an hour and a half, can you afford it? It's ninety quid,"

"Oh dear." I must have looked and sounded very forlorn because he said a cheque would be fine. We arrived at what I hoped was Kit's flat,

"Which one is it love?,"

"I'm not sure." I replied.

The taxi driver was a kindly chap and waited to see that I was safely inside before leaving. If not he said he would take me home free of charge, incredibly generous of him. I must have seemed an out-of-sorts, desperate woman, 'a donkey on the edge,' to quote Shrek.

In I crept. Kit was lying on his bed with a lit cigarette dangling from his mouth, and upon seeing me, crooned,

"Love! Love has come to me at last." Even through my drunken haze I remember thinking what a twat he sounded.

The night was uneventful and we both fell asleep. I awoke with an appalling hangover, somehow managed to locate his willy, relieved him manually and trained back to Rupert's house that morning.

As I'm sure you will have gathered by now, I am an obsessive sort. When I wasn't boil washing Rupert's jumpers, I was making fruit cake for his packed lunches, clearing the shelves of dried fruit and mixed spice in Tesco, in order to produce ten cakes at a time. And so, true to form, I became obsessed with Kit. I was still house-sitting for the agency and at each property I would lure him there with offers of meals and Jack Daniels on tap. I didn't then and still don't particularly like alcohol, apart from mulled wine, but in an effort to appear as a kindred, suffering, musical soul, I would join him in his wallowings of drunken depression.

It was during a house-sitting job in Kensington that I became terribly constipated and so bought some Califig, a dark brown, viscous liquid of which two teaspoons at bedtime was the recommended dose. I didn't plan to gulp the entire bottle down because I was (sort of) sexually involved with Kit and runny poo and sex do not combine well. Though truth to tell, our 'coupling' didn't happen very often as he didn't really fancy me much at all, preferring tiny mewling blondes. When sex did occur it was always when he was extremely drunk and as I was conveniently situated in the same house, he made the most of the situation. That said, I couldn't be risking a loose bowel movement during this time, but I was becoming increasingly worried about the finite capacity of my large intestine. Everyday I was consuming enormous quantities, the starvation phase having ended, but the food stayed put, my stomach felt like a small armchair was wedged inside it. I read the bottle;

'Take two teaspoons at bedtime. DO NOT exceed the stated dose.'

Two teaspoons?, thought I, ridiculous, how can two miserly teaspoons shift a weeks worth of food?!.

So I took a mouthful, figuring that was about five teaspoonfuls, let it trickle down into my stomach, examined the bottle again with its cheery little picture of a leafy fig sunning itself on a tree and reasoned that there was little chance of this simple fruit producing explosive diarrhoea. I finished the entire bottle and lest the reader suspect I elaborate purely for effect, hand on heart, I drank the lot.

Several hours passed and a terrible iron-like grip took a hold of my abdomen. It felt like my digestive system was in a vice (I now have a deep respect for the fig tree). I pooed and pooed and pooed and vomited. Excessive consumption of syrup of figs causes the body to expel intestinal contents from both ends it would seem. By bed time I felt as light as thistledown, I'm sure the scales lied when they read 11.5 stone, I felt as floaty as a size 8, cleansed, extremely tender internally and with a rectum like a rocket's exhaust pipe.

Another house-sitting job came along, and Kit stayed with me for a while at a gorgeous 16th century cottage in Warwickshire. One evening, having fuelled himself up on Jack Daniels, he came swaying into the sitting room and hit his head with such force on a massive, low oak beam, that I was sure he was going to sink to the floor unconscious. Even in his numbed state, he was calling,

'Fuuuck, fuuuck," and clutching at his head. The pain must have been immense as he had an enormous purple forehead the following morning. It gave me the helpless giggles and still makes me laugh writing it down twenty years later; a precious, arty musician, consumed with his own woes, smacking his head on a big old beam, haha!

Mentally, I was the most dreadful mess during that period. The neurological pathways and electrical signals in my brain must surely have looked like a firework display.

I had offered one day, to pick Kit up from the music shop he worked in near Oxford Street as I was house sitting in Golders Green at the time. Driving through London, I didn't have a bloody clue where I was or where I was going.

"Do you know where the shop is then?," he'd asked,

"Yep yep, not a problem," quoth I, trying to appear super cool and streetwise.

After two hours had elapsed of driving round and round the endless rabbit warren of London streets, I careered up to a pedestrian crossing, panicking by now as to whether I would ever find the damn place, and stopping only just in time to prevent my flattening a mother, her pram and its occupant. She looked at me in wide eyed alarm, together with the bus driver in the lane next to me, who was mouthing and gesticulating furiously. I ended up in Somerset Square, somewhere in London, swerving wildly between lanes, utterly lost, pulled out in front of a white van whose driver mouthed something along the lines of "you stupid fucking cow!."

I thrust two, cowardly and ineffectual fingers up at him, protected as I was in my little car. He screeched to a halt, got out and was about to open my door, presumably to give me a good beating, London style. He was black as a pint of Guinness and as endearing as Godzilla. I smiled sweetly and gabbled, "sorry." He retreated.

Kit was gradually becoming bored of our bimonthly meets, he being of an impetuous, musical nature. I meanwhile, was absolutely infatuated.

I had driven to his flat one weekend, unannounced, and knocked on the door. He appeared, cheeks flushed, presumably from busying himself in the gymnastics of copulation, and zipping up his jeans hurriedly. The sounds of a giggling female came from within. I ran wailing from his flat, roaring and crying, a scene straight out of Eastenders. Down the stairs I returned, climbed into my old Fiesta and hit the motorway with an empty fuel tank and no money. He didn't follow me. I was not merely a sausage short, I was in possession of no sausages at all. I have no recollection of the journey home, only stopping at a motorway service station, explaining I had no money and had just been obliterated by a man with whom I would have sacrificed a kidney for and borne children. Quite an offer being as I couldn't and can't stand the whining little blighters. The cashier had me sign a form and I was given £10 worth of fuel. Kit's only contact with me after that evening, was a voicemail to check I wasn't squashed on the Eastbound carriageway.

So that was that, the musician phase was over, at least for him it was. I spiralled into a deep and terrible depression that at its worst, saw me sitting in a country house I was taking care of at the time, with a bottle of pills and vodka. I made the sensible decision not to top myself.

The Kit episode triggered in me for the first time, something that had been waiting to germinate: Abandonment Anxiety. Every man I subsequently became involved with, whenever they lost interest, would trigger in me the same condition on a crippling scale which would wipe out normal, daily activities for weeks and months at a time. I absolutely wanted to die and wished from the bottom of my heart that I had never been born. This continued for the next 20 years, until I made the concrete decision to dabble no more in the world of dating. It was the best decision I have ever made.

Having sped away from the scene of the unzipped jeans and giggling female, I spent the next seven years Googling Kit, and finally tracked him down to a flat in Bristol. I sped off to the address some 250 miles away and pressed the communal intercom in the lobby. A familiar voice said, "hello?." I panicked and drove home, wrote a letter and posted it. It was returned with 'unknown address' written on the envelope, a handwriting I recognised instantly.

And that was it, the receipt of the letter finally laid the ghost of him to rest. My eight year obsession had nothing of course to do with his qualities as a person. He was a jobbing musician, of no more clout than a court jester. 'Twas I that were mad.

CHAPTER NINE

"No-One Sucks Cock Like a Man."

Having discovered the thrill of binge eating at the age of twelve and never having learnt or wanted to learn, the art of self induced vomiting, I consequently became extremely fat, interspersed with the occasional six months of maniacal dieting, usually instigated by some bloke I'd met who I fancied. At such times I would once again reduce my food intake from that of a Hereford bullock to a rabbit. My backside and waist would shrink rapidly and for a few, blissful weeks, I looked gorgeously feminine, attracting many an admiring glance. During these intensely feminine periods I subjected myself to Botox, wore false eyelashes, false hair, false nails, a false tan, false tattooed brows and a false beauty spot. I was a human landslide, the slightest vibration or whiff of moisture and the whole bloody lot would start to shift. Going on dates at this time was an unnerving experience as there was always a very real possibility that any number of bits could fall off or work loose.

Here follows a brief account of a few weeks spent with Sean, an Irish Metropolitan Police officer with a strong Belfast accent, of rather short stature, clean, oddly arranged teeth and a tendency to use the word 'cunt,' a little too often when greeting his cat, Pepper. He adored Pepper and upon arriving home at the end of the day, would grin lovingly at the cat, scoop him up in his manly Metropolitan arms, cooing,

"Arr Pippurr yurr liddle cont."

We'd met online, a site called Uniform Dating, and after a number of insincere email exchanges, agreed to meet. The chosen venue was a very busy and very posh wine bar, heaving with people on a Friday night and with barely enough room to jostle through the crowd to position ourselves next to the bar. Now am I alone here or does anyone else suffer from the condition of profound deafness when in a pub/bar/nightclub?. Unless it's a really quiet place, I quite literally, cannot make out a single word anyone says to me, so I've perfected the art of nodding and smiling on these occasions. I managed to just about make out what he was saying by staring at his mouth and interpreting his lip movements; that he'd asked me what I'd been up to today. It was an odd reply, not something a police officer would have heard very often,

"I drove to Gorse Head to look for fairies."

"Eh?," he replied, leaning in towards me in the hope I'm sure, that he'd heard wrong.

"I said," raising the volume slightly and using exaggerated lip movements as if he were the profoundly deaf one,

"I've been to Gorse Head moor, where folklore has it, there's a fairy fair!."

"Ar ooh kee, and dud yee air, fained any, you know, fairies?,"

"No but it's said you can hear the tinkling of the ponies' harness bells and the elves and fairies laughing but when you turn to look in the direction of the revelling, it fades away."

"Oh well that's a buddar va buggar, another drenk?,"

I stood there nodding and smiling, having long given up understanding the incomprehensible sounds and shapes his mouth was making. But I was feeling rather beautiful and more importantly, confident, as this time I'd found some industrial strength eyelash glue. As I sipped my wine I began to feel just a little pissed, which didn't make sense as this was only my second drink, plus I'd eaten a whole pack of pork and pickle pies and two Wispa bars on the way to the pub for comfort and courage purposes; my Met Police officer appeared to be getting smaller as if I was looking at him down the wrong end of a telescope. There wasn't any time to think, 'shit, better call an ambulance,' and as he continued to shrink, finally reduced to a one inch thumbnail at the end of my hallucinatory telescope, I remembered nothing more and woke up on the floor with the entire wine bar peering down at me, in a flurry of concern and noise.

"Shall I call an ambulance?," a worried waitress asked.

My date replied, rather oddly I thought,

"Noo sheez fane."

And up he hauled me in a rather unchivalrous, 'I'm arresting you on the charge of..' manner, bundled me into my pick-up truck, sat beside me and asked disinterestedly, how I was feeling. Without waiting for a reply he promptly leaned across, attached his mouth to mine in Alien face-hugger fashion and poked a wet tongue down my throat. I recoiled instantly and croaked aloud,

"Did you spike my drink?,"

He vehemently denied doing any such thing and we went our separate ways. I realised the next day that it could well have been a cocktail of the antidepressants I was on at the time and the alcohol. I shall never know. But it was a good lesson in not to mix alcohol and medication, and to avoid at all costs, men that call their cats cunts, however lovingly.

Over the years I have somehow managed to date six policeman, and as an escort, I saw five. Quite how I have accrued this unusually high number I cannot fathom. One date was with a chap in the C.I.D who appeared very keen indeed during our first date, but was never to be heard from again. Another tiny little policeman called Stuart, who given his petite arms and legs and overall dimensions, was given the unoriginal name by me, of Stuart Little. He looked about twelve years old and sitting in the pub with him, I felt like his grandmother. He leaned back in his highchair, sorry, chair, and fixed my mouth and chin with a look of studious concentration.

"You need to shave, I never thought I'd say that to a woman."

He was right. I was struggling to find a procedure that could deal with my black upper lip and chin hair. No matter what I tried; tweezers, razor, cream remover, electric shock, wax; I would be sporting a goatee within seven days.

And then there was Simon who was not a policeman. He was given the name of 'boiled beef n carrots,' by my mother, reason being it was all he ever cooked for us. I saw him for about two months and I'd begun the relationship looking very attractive; I was sat up in Simon's bed one morning, while he'd gone off, presumably, to begin the preparations for boiled beef and carrots. There were fitted, mirrored wardrobes in his bedroom and I remember seeing my reflection and not recognising the shapely, Pre-Raphaelite, smooth-skinned vision of loveliness before me, with its waist-length, dark and wavy tresses falling about the slender middle. The tresses were two foot long extensions as once again I'd been unable to resist the thrill of travelling to London to visit the trendy hair salon. Entering with a wallet of hard-earned cash and sporting lesbian hair, I emerged four hours later looking like Sophia Loren with no money for groceries for a month. I think I must have wrenched my extensions out by the roots about five times in total, until even I could see it was a ridiculous carry on. So I tried individual clip-in hair extensions, a bloody marvellous invention and at £15 for a set on Amazon, they looked fantastic. I simply unclipped them when the need to impress had passed. The only disadvantage was when a man became so overwhelmed by my gorgeousness that he was desirous of running his fingers through my hair. This activity I tried to avoid whenever possible as I would be forced to explain the very unsexy, complicated arrangement of metalwork placed all over my scalp. The one main advantage of clip-ins over permanent glue-in extensions was the fact that the glue-ins, however glossy and flowing they were at the start, after a week of being slept in, would give the wearer the appearance of a fully paid up member of a coven of witches, such was the impregnable tangle of coarse, black and matted undergrowth, masquerading as hair. The only way I could deal with it at this stage was to cut it off.

Boiled Beef n Carrots was a simple man of irritating routines who refused to change his ancient washing-up brush and who used shampoo as shower gel 'because it removes more skin cells.' He drove a blue Nissan Micra and possessed feet that in a standing and walking position were set at 45 degrees to his legs, giving him a Charlie Chaplin appearance. It irritated me to the point I simply could not look at his feet. His choice of car irritated me almost as much; a silly little car for a silly little man. The thing is he looked quite attractive on the website. In reality however, by the sixth date, the compulsion to slap him was a powerful one.

Doubtless I am simply an impatient old harridan who doesn't like 'nice' people but after the sixth visit to his flat, casting derisory looks at his clown feet and the alphabetically arranged collection of Depeche Mode and Stranglers CD's, we parted company. As mentioned I'd begun the relationship with BB&C as a picture of feminine beguile and beauty, as velvety and fragrant as a nectarine and pretty as a flower fairy; in lace bottomed size 10 pink leggings, ballet pumps and a figure hugging, cream, waist-length jumper, with little satin bows around the scooped neckline. By the sixth date I was two stone heavier, wearing my favourite baggy old brown, hand-knitted jumper which reached down to my knees, courtesy of an old Herdwick ewe who'd died the previous summer and from whom I'd kept the fleece from her final shearing before she bleated her last. The rest of the look comprised of practical work trousers, stout work boots and my own reedy strands scragged back into a scrunchie.

"You're bigger than when I met you," he remarked one evening, four dates in. (b..b..b.baby you just ain't seen nothin' yet, I inwardly chortled)

I was thrilled to bits one evening when Boiled Beef suggested a Chinese takeaway. Begrudgingly I placed an order for a woman with a normal appetite as God forbid he should witness my true capabilities, and sat down to eat in a delicate, semi-interested fashion.

At 5am I awoke with a frenzied desire to get to the leftover cold takeaway in the fridge. Off I stole, and stood in front of the open fridge door in rapturous delight, cheeks bulging with stale prawn crackers and congealed sweet n sour pork balls.

Fuck me if he didn't appear at the fridge, "are you still peckish?," he politely enquired.

BB&C had a big tub of peanuts and raisins in his sitting room, the size tub which the old-fashioned sweet shops used to create assorted displays with. It was three quarters full, about 2kg I'm guessing. Every time Boiled Beef went to the loo, I would be off the sofa like one of those child's toys you pressed down, that sprung up after a few seconds at high velocity. After I'd leapt to the tub and wolfed down as many peanuts and raisins as time would allow between him weeing and flushing, I would vault back to the sofa and assume my former feminine pose. Eventually he remarked on the inexplicably low level of his favourite snack. Poor Boiled Beef, he deserved a nice girl.

I also met an Iranian man online and very dark and attractive he was too. Sadly it transpired he preferred the look and feel of a penis in preference to a set of breasts and he smoked opium. At the beginning of our relationship my usual obsessive dieting kicked in and I would plan my outfits down to the last hair clip in order to win him over. He lived in Islington, and being now a seasoned traveller around London, I would head off every weekend to see him.

He had a preoccupation with bottoms, specifically the orifice of the bottom and would constantly press me to agree to his putting his willy in mine. Eventually after a month of refusing, I gave in. It was a heinous act, small wonder it is forbidden in the Bible. I am not exaggerating when I say that I couldn't sit down for two weeks having developed unbearably painful, sultana sized piles. How the hell gay men carry on I've no idea.

Anyway the Iranian became gradually less enthusiastic about my weekend visits and after a three week interval of not seeing one another, I arrived in London, expecting him to be at least a little desirous of my charms. Instead, he grasped my shoulders, beamed and gave me a huge kiss, of the granny variety, not the boyfriend variety. He then gave each of my breasts a single, fun-filled squeeze, and imitated a 'honk' sound, such as one might find on a veteran automobile. I found this to be strange behaviour for a heterosexual man and so when his head was on the pillow that night, mouth open and snoring, I decided to read his text messages. Turned out the little tinker had been indulging in all manner of penis on penis activity with an impressively long list of men.

The next morning he awoke producing his regular symphony of flatulence. I meanwhile stood ready and waiting by the bed, his phone in my hand;

"And what the hell is this?!," I spat. He sat on the edge of the bed, still groggy from sleep, head in hands, and sounding most piteous in his small Iranian voice;

"I am bisexual and I am a liar. Ok? I'm sorry."

Poor chap, I felt sorry for him, life must have been very confusing. So I put the kettle on and after a brief chat we agreed to stay mates. He's now living with a guy and we still meet up for a chat sometimes. During one of our chats, sat in a fish and chip shop in London, I asked how his relationship was going,

"Well, I really love the look of a woman," he replied, using his hands to draw a shapely, imaginary woman in the air.

"I love their backsides, their waists, women are beautiful."

I sat, eyebrows raised, waiting for the punchline. He looked at me very solemnly, leaning forward in his chair..

"But no-one sucks cock as good as a man."

I fairly choked on my pea fritter.

Poor old Rupert, I'd ended our six year long relationship a few months after meeting the jobbing jester and broken Rupe's heart. The last I heard he was married and living on a farm in Suffolk.

The next career move was a farm in Gloucestershire, where I had the job of dairymaid. Doesn't that sound rustic and lovely? It was not, it was sixteen hour days, everyday, spent alone in a tiled room, full of strange looking stainless steel equipment, attempting to produce skimmed, semi and full-fat milk, cream and butter. The herd of 140 Friesians were milked by the herdsman, and I was responsible for doing things to it once it began flowing through the pipes and into the vat in the dairy. Skimmed milk, you'd think, was a simple enough thing to produce: the raw milk was pasteurised and put through a spinning thing that spun all the fat out. Unfortunately the farm sold all their milk and milk products directly to local customers and within days there were complaints flooding in that the skimmed milk had a thick layer of cream on top.

Making semi skimmed milk involved skimming the full fat milk, then putting exactly half the original volume back in as whole milk, thereby creating semi skimmed milk. It was all very confusing and very approximate and would not have impressed todays milk buyers at Tesco. The only bit I didn't cock up was bottling the full fat milk as the cows had done most of the work already.

Cream production involved spinning the cream that resulted from the skimming process and agitating it until it thickened, the thickness determined by having it run over your finger, high tech stuff. If it didn't drip off, it was double. If it did, it was single. Inevitably, calls began to come in regarding the unpredictable nature of the farm's cream; cream so thick it was bending spoons, and cream so thin it disappeared like water when poured over corn flakes.

After one week, the farmer threw open my cottage door and announced,

"You may as well clear off, you're no good ere."

Too bloody right I thought, much relieved as I packed my little Fiesta up to the gunnels once more. Within a fortnight I was on a plane to Aberdeen to be met by a huge farmer with a black beard who was in the process of setting up a B&B in Scotland on his newly purchased beef and arable farm. I was to be interviewed for the post of housekeeper and farm assistant, stay the night and return home the next day. All went well and that night there was a barn dance as fancy dress, to be held on a nearby farm. Blackbeard invited me along and a kindly neighbour's wife provided me with a wench's outfit. For someone who doesn't really enjoy alcohol, I drank an awful lot that night, was hauled upright from a crouching, vomiting position over a muck heap by Blackbeard and helped home. I have a hazy memory of him removing my mop cap in the most chivalrous manner and putting me to bed. I was rough as a rough thing the next day, and in between dashes to the loo to be sick, was offered the job. I declined the offer, it was so bloody cold up there, not my cup of tea. And so, once again on the farm labourers scrap heap, I continued to apply for jobs. And the more remote and bleak the farm the better...

The 550 acre farm in Argyllshire, Penrhyl Crag Farm, could not have been any bleaker, and so were its owners, Margaret and Donald McAlistair. Donald was small, wiry and red-nosed thanks to decades of knocking back the best Scottish whiskey and could easily outrun a Scottish Blackface, an incredible feat to witness. (Scottish Blackface, affectionately referred to as 'bloody Blackies' are the indigenous breed of turbo-powered sheep that dot the upland farms of Northern England and most of Scotland).

Margaret, Donald's wife, was petite, pretty and very brusque. There were virtually no trees on the farm, just hundreds of unforgiving windswept acres of tussocky cropped grass, eaten low by Blackfaces. One freezing cold March afternoon I was instructed to 'geet ah wee an cowp ram in hundred acre, heez ah poo-urly foot.' Translated this meant I was to catch and turn the ram in the field known as Hundred Acre. Problem number one: catching a 100kg ram. Problem number two: catching a 100kg ram in a hundred acre field with no sheep dog or quad bike. If the farmer had asked me to build a space capsule from tractor parts, set off for the moon and bring him back a rock sample by lunchtime, it would have been as achievable.

I had gone to Penrhyl Crag for four weeks during April to help out with the lambing of 1000 Blackface ewes and the milking of 500 dairy goats. There are approximately 60 breeds of sheep in the UK, including commercial crosses such as the 'mule,' a milky, tidy looking ewe with good mothering instincts, the result of crossing a Blue-faced Leicester ram with a Swaledale ewe. They are in no way related to the donkey. The hill breeds such as

Herdwick, Swaledale, Rough Fell, Kerry Hill, Derbyshire Gritstone, Scottish Blackface and to an even greater extent, the primitive breeds such as Soay and Hebridean, are noticeably wilder than their chunkier, more placid lowland breeds such as Poll Dorsets and Southdowns. No prizes which type of sheep I keep nowadays in Cornwall.

The rocket-fuelled Blackface ram steaming around Hundred Acre field had no intention of being caught, and judging by the mph he was notching up, his feet couldn't have been that bloody poorly either. I stood at the gate and watched the distant blob of wool, now stationary in the distance. An admission of defeat would have resulted in a sound Scottish bollocking so I sought out the help of the surly vet student who was at the farm for a month to gain lambing experience. He was a tall, heavily built, rugby playing 22 year old, perfect. We found the keys to the quad bike, I hopped on behind him and we set off, grim of countenance and gripping our sheep crooks. Ten minutes later a 100kg Blackface ram was spread eagled on the grass with my heroic vet student sprawled across him.

To the reader who has never attempted to restrain a sheep, which I'm kind of guessing is the majority, it is difficult to describe the inordinate strength and technique required. Sheep, that is to say, those above 50kg, are immensely powerful and most average mortals cannot hope to stop a sheep from propelling itself forwards by instinctively but mistakenly placing a hand in front of the neck. The trick is to place a hand beneath the jaw. Only a light touch is needed as by tilting the head upwards, the sheep is no longer able to propel itself from first to fifth gear. The jaw therefore is the throttle.

Watching the young chap's prowess at catching speeding sheep, I realised with dismay that this was a prerequisite of shepherding, particularly on the exposed uplands of moor and fell. In stark contrast my mollycoddled and tame flock are currently crashed out on deep straw, cudding away and gazing smugly out at the foul weather. Quite often, I'll take a flask of tea and a packet of Ginger Nuts on a wet afternoon, and sit amongst them, enjoying the peaceful sound of munching, cudding sheep.

The method the vet student used to catch any single sheep was as follows...mount quad bike and imitating a border collie by weaving left and right, direct the sheep towards the corner of the field. The key to success at this stage is the ability to anticipate the next move of the animal, something I'm actually pretty good at now. Incidentally we are not talking neat little field corners of 90 degrees but wide sweeping 'corners,' big enough to turn a twin axle lorry in. The sheep, sensing imminent capture, will turn away from the approaching field corner and hurtle away from the shepherd, it will almost certainly then shoot left, right, and stand motionless for twenty seconds before motoring off into the distance once more. A sheep in good fettle can easily power across a field at 25mph if he or she feels so inclined, therefore the quad driver has to have some pretty nifty moves up his sleeves to outrun her. Catching ewes was essential at this farm because they ran an outdoor lambing system, and many ewes needed help giving birth. Countless times we needed to catch ewes that just had a head hanging out of the vulva, or sometimes, just a tail. Swift intervention was then needed if one was to save both lamb and potentially the ewe, depending on how long she had been in labour. The vet student would catch her eventually of course as I watched on in awe and wonder, mouthing 'How the hell?..'

I don't know what it was about the sight of him during this activity, driving frantically and erratically in response to the sheep's movements, ear flaps on his deer-stalker hat flying up and down, a look of grim determination on his chubby red face, frozen into a humourless scowl by the bitter Scottish wind, but I was rendered helpless with giggles. Not much made me giggle in life but by Christ this did. I would begin the task straight faced and earnest, at the ready with lambing lubricant and ropes and watching on in deep concentration. Then nearing the point of capture, helpless hysterics would begin as he drove in for the final swoop, catapulting himself from the quad bike which continued on without its rider, and grabbing hold of a woolly body part, both shepherd and sheep still airborne, down she would come with him on top. 'Ged over 'ere!!,' he would yell.

'"Go and catch the ram", he said.'

I found outdoor lambing, as opposed to indoor, upsetting because of the large numbers of lambs that died, needlessly to my mind. A final check of the flock at sundown and then again at 7am, meant many lambs were lost during the night. The arguments against lambing indoors are the extra costs incurred, eg: straw for bedding, of which an awful lot is necessary to keep the ewes clean and comfortable, hay for feeding, lighting and of course, paying someone to be on lambing duty each night. My simple brain could never fathom why anyone would want to lamb lowland flocks outdoors; saving the lives of two lambs during the night means you've already covered your costs. Hill farms however lamb outside because the sheep breeds are tougher, with stronger maternal instincts and produce more singles than twins, so overall the survival rates are better than for lowland flocks lambing outside. Even so, the death pit that was dug for lambing casualties at Penrhyl was pretty full by the time a month was up.

Sod that, give me a cosy, brightly lit barn, and contented ewes in deep straw.

Donald and Margaret had two young daughters; Chloe, aged about two, who screamed and wailed constantly and flung her food with surprising accuracy at the ceiling during mealtimes, where it remained, cemented to the plaster. I couldn't bear the noise levels at these family meals, craving my thirty minutes of peace and respite from lambing. So one day I took myself and my midday meal to the living room. This didn't go down well with Margaret. "Wat jer meen tekin yiz vittles in tuther room?!." From then on the atmosphere was a bit strained, which complemented the freezing weather perfectly. Chloe's sister, Claire, was a wonderful little girl. Aged just five, she devoted her days to me and strived to graft as hard as an adult, lambing ewes and shifting piles of fencing posts. When I left after a month, she was crying her little heart out. I was much moved, lovely kid. Chloe would pick up everything her little ears heard, which on a farm can be very colourful. We were all sat around the breakfast table early one morning and Donald in mischievous mood, knowing full well the response he would get, said,

"Wat arr wee dooin teedee thun Chloe?," her face lit up and she beamed at her Dad,

"We're gonnee hammer thi Blackies!." Translated this meant they were to gather the 800 Scottish Blackface ewes off the fell and administer various medications. Much giggling from everyone.

Margaret had her sister to stay one weekend and they and the two girls had all gone to feed Michael the horned, bad-tempered, testosterone fuelled Blackface ram. It was well known that

Michael entertained himself on a daily basis by thundering aggressively towards anyone that entered his field, his goal to shatter kneecaps. As the girls entered the field with their bucket of sheep feed, their mothers leaning unconcernedly over the gate, Michael turned to face his enemies, huge horns lowered and prepared to charge. Chloe's cheery little voice rang out, confident and bright as a bell,

"Fuck off Michael!!."

A deft emptying of feed into the trough and the girls had exited the field just as Michael launched himself across the short distance to the trough at an impressive speed.

At the side of the lambing field, we had a large enclosed yard with a row of lambing pens for those ewes and lambs who for endless reasons, needed some extra TLC. A tin-walled and tin-roofed shack was where poorly lambs were tended to. A heat lamp was suspended over a deep, straw filled box and any lamb born prematurely, suffering from hypothermia, hunger, or without a mother due to her having died or her rejection of the lamb, was placed in the box and ministered to accordingly. In an ideal sheep world, all ewes should rear twin lambs. In the case of a lamb being fit and well but having no mother to suckle from, either for the aforementioned reasons or a lack of mothers milk, it is necessary therefore to try and find a foster mother for the lamb. This is always preferable to bottle rearing because ewe milk replacement powder is as dear as cocaine. Mother Nature however is no fool and simply plonking a bewildered lamb under the milky udder of an unrelated ewe, almost always results in one very angry sheep. She is well aware that this interloper is not her offspring and will aggressively put a stop to its attempts at suckling by ramming it with her head, easily breaking its ribs and potentially killing it. This is not stupidity, the ewe is instinctively reserving her milk for her own lambs. But she is not so intelligent that she can be persuaded to rear an unrelated lamb due to the price of milk powder. Therefore a contraption called an 'adopter crate' is used. This holds the ewe's head so that she cannot turn to hurt the lamb. However the ewe can still get up and lie down in comfort and feed. After a few days the ewe is released and in about 60% of adoption cases, she will, as if by magic, have accepted the lamb as her own. A more successful method of fostering a lamb onto a ewe, is 'wet fostering,' whereby as soon as the ewe gives birth to a single lamb, you need to grab an orphan ASAP and rub it in the birth juices before the mother has turned to realise the deception. If successful, this then results in the ideal ewe and two lambs. A slightly more squeamish method is also necessary in certain situations; a ewe that has lost her lamb/s, can be fooled into thinking that it has risen from the dead by skinning it and placing the new overcoat on an orphan. Sometimes this works, sometimes not.

    The work was so tough and the hours so long that there was no room for squeamishness or sentimentality. I would take a very sharp knife, having sharpened it on one of the many stone walls, and slit the skin in a complete circle around the neck, around the knee joints and hocks, with a final slit across the inner thighs. It then remained to simply pull the entire skin off over the head and place it on the orphan lamb, who by now was looking pretty pissed off by the whole affair and would totter off, complete with his two tails, towards his adopted Mum in the hopes that he could fool her. As one can imagine, skinning can be a bit messy especially if the knife isn't sharp enough or the skin particularly tough. Margaret's pregnant sister, Liz, decided to take a wander one crisp, sunny April morning, which unfortunately took her through the lambing pen enclosure. I stood outside the intensive care shack, freshly skinned lamb in one hand, bidding her a good morning and strode across the yard to dispose of it in the death hole. Suffering from morning sickness as she was, she threw up on the spot and returned to the farmhouse, spluttering and retching. In retrospect, she should not have been around pregnant sheep at all. Donald meanwhile had managed to skin a stillborn 45kg suckler calf, no easy task. Using baler twine, he had tied the grim overcoat onto a three day old calf whose mother had died. The foster cow readily accepted the new calf, amazing really as it looked unlike any calf ever born, with two tails, four ears and stunk something terrible.

I carried out all the tractor driving on the farm and loved it as it was a break from the endless manual work. The vet student, chunky and capable as he was, was nervous at the wheel of a big John Deere, so I took over the job of carting big round bales on spikes and feeding the cattle. I became pretty nifty after a month of this, spiking two huge, round bales on the front loader and weaving my way through throngs of bellowing, hungry cattle, I would drop one bale into a ring feeder, jump off tractor, climb into feeder through deep mud, cut strings and remove netting. Back on tractor and drop second bale in other ring feeder. Speed was essential. Longer than a few seconds in one place and you stood a real risk of being suctioned to the spot in your wellies by the mud and crushed by cattle. Even Margaret had to admit "aye yurr nay bad at oll weet tractuz." I wasn't however prepared for the sheer strength of the winds so far North. On my third day at the farm, I drove into the field to feed the cattle, opened the tractor door and had it wrenched from my grasp by a powerful gust. It swung back violently against its hinges and smashed all the glass into hundreds of pieces on the ground. Donald was surprisingly ok about it "aye thi students allus brek thi winduz." Two days later I smashed the other door and a week after that the rear window. Appalled at my incompetence I went cap in hand each time to Donald, expecting him to snap but he maintained total calm over his now fully ventilated tractor. By the end of lambing, the windscreen was the only intact glass.

My month at Penrhyl Crag eventually came to an end and after bidding a farewell to the family, I was soon crashed out on the train back to West Sussex and back to the shambolic old caravan I had been staying in prior to my elopement to Scotland.

'A handsome Swaledale ram'

CHAPTER TEN

The Friendly Cow All Red and White

> The friendly cow all red and white,
> I love with all my heart.
> She gives me cream with all her might,
> To eat with apple tart.
>
> — Robert Louis Stevenson

The caravan in West Sussex was to be my living quarters for the next month. Situated on a large sheep and cattle farm, I was to be the night-lamber with sole responsibility for 500 heavily pregnant ewes. The farmer, bursting with generosity had agreed to my use of the caravan provided I 'pay my way.'

Pay my way! Jesus, for what exactly?. There was more comfort to be found sleeping under a blackthorn hedge. The door, whilst held shut with baler twine, still revealed a two inch gap through which the chilly April wind blew. Rain dripped through the rotting roof, my toilet was the muck heap and I washed and cleaned my teeth in the water trough in the sheep shed. Obligingly I paid my way by helping out in the farmer's stable-yard every Saturday morning. As you may have gathered by now, horses are not my strong point, they bloody terrify me. He bred some breed of horse I'd never heard of, a genetic mutation between Sir Lancelot's massive medieval war horse and a cheetah. These beasts were colossal, glossy black and solid muscle. I wept as I looked at the 18 hands of pulsating power looking back at me from the field.

"Get Bella in from field and put her in her stable," he muttered, disappearing into the farmhouse for morning coffee.

She looked evil and as black as the devil's cooking pot. I was crapping myself. The distance between the horse and her stable was only about 40 foot but it looked like a mile. I opened the stable door in preparation, approached the horse and managed to put the halter on with its attached rope. Immediately she began to dance around. There was no bloody way I was doing the tango with 600kg of horse. I knocked on the farmers door and he stumped off, all 6'5" of him to the field, tutting at my incompetence as Bella trotted meekly behind him to her stable.

And so to the job of sheep for the next month or so, it was an usually late lambing, late April/early May but having stocked up my caravan with a huge supply of carbohydrates and tea, I attempted to prepare myself for the 13 hour stints in the lambing shed. My hours were 6pm to 7am and it was non stop, though that was to my great advantage as the weather was so bloody cold that year. A typical night spent lambing involved delivering lambs, fostering on lambs, moving ewes and lambs between pens, dipping navels in iodine, stomach tubing poorly lambs, tailing, castrating, bottle feeding, mucking out and disinfecting lambing pens, strawing up, haying up, filling endless water buckets, foot-trimming, ear-tagging, putting in and removing prolapse retainers, drenching for twin-lamb disease, milk fever, mastitis and watery mouth, mixing up powdered milk and spray marking individual families before they were turned out to the field in the morning, once I and the shepherd were happy that the ewe and lambs were well bonded and getting sufficient milk.

On a good night, when all was running smoothly, the work was very satisfying. One particular shift produced 38 lambs which would have been fine except the head shepherd, James, had been a bit relaxed about the number of individual pens he'd constructed in preparation for the month ahead. It was pandemonium as every time I turned around another ewe was lambing, so I searched out pallets and spare gates which were lying around the farm and cobbled them together with baler twine. All this in the dark of night and a very poorly lit lambing shed. I was mighty glad to see James at 7am, and crawled back to my caravan, peeled off the stinking plastic overalls and sank into a blissful sleep. Fortunately he had offered the use of his washing machine, tumble drier and bathroom whenever I needed them. It was wonderful to wake up in the late afternoon and to immerse myself in a deep, hot and fragrant bubble bath, put on fresh clothes, enjoy a full cooked breakfast and head back to the expectant girls for the night.

One freezing morning at about 4am, a ewe had a full uterine prolapse, something I'd not dealt with before, so reluctantly I had to call James and rouse him from sleep. He was marvellous and on the scene within ten minutes, suture and needle in hand, first cleansing the engorged organ then carefully placing it back inside the ewe whilst I held the vulva together. He stitched her together, gave antibiotics and painkiller and amazingly she made a full recovery. I did question my chosen career during that little episode, knelt in the straw with bloodied arms in the pitch black of a bitter April night.

Any rest time between ewes I spent in the caravan, drinking tea and eating Hobnobs, rustling through the printed pages of a list of farmers and country-minded people, all looking for a suitable mate. Internet dating not being available back then, I had responded to an advert in the Farmers Weekly which read, "Just Woodland Friends." I rang the number and spoke to a friendly Mrs Tiggywinkle type character, who for £25, sent me a long list of boiler-suit and tattersall shirt clad bumpkins:

'David, 41, Leicestershire, tenant farmer...'

I drew a black biro through David, I needed permanent bricks and mortar not a rented farm.

'Horace, 27, attractive, 6'3", enjoys hunting, pubs, looking after his 200 cow Friesian herd and (yes you guessed it) cosy nights in by the fire with a bottle of wine and a film.'

Too young. I persevered.

'David, 36, manages family-owned (looking good so far) dairy farm in Haverfordwest, (Christ that's miles away) dark hair, attractive. Looking to meet a slim, funny, (I can do the second bit, the first could be a challenge) country-minded lady for good times.'

Yep, definitely worth a try. I left a voice message on his mobile and that evening whilst grabbing a ten minute break from lambing, the phone rang and a dark, heavily accented Welsh voice said,

"Hellaw, is that Cathy?,"

"Yes hello there!," I pipped, hoping the dog tiredness didn't come across in my voice. The conversation flowed easily and we both fell in love with each others voices, how bloody ridiculous aye?. Weeks past with hours and hours spent on the phone to one another and eventually a date was set for us to meet. The expectant ewes were now down to below ten in number. I was therefore no longer required and gratefully banked my cheque.

We met at a pub local to me, in Little Bignor in West Sussex, fair play to the bloke, that's a long drive from West Wales. I arrived early and sat hunched down behind the steering wheel praying he looked more like the handsome Welsh frontman, Kelly Jones from the Stereophonics than Aled Jones.

A short balding man emerged from a 4x4 and walked into the pub. Oh Christ lets just hope he's got charisma...

.....There was no chemistry whatsoever but being as I'd paid Vodafone a small fortune, I figured he was worth a trip to Pembrokeshire. A day was arranged.

I drove for what seemed like weeks to the edge of the Atlantic and spent five long days working on his farm. What the hell, I decided to make lemonade from lemons and ate like a goddamn horse whilst there. No sex was forthcoming, his willy, though large, didn't fancy me and I didn't fancy it. I stayed in the farm's guest cottage and joined the family for meals, which suited me fine.

What I'm about to relate is such a cliché it sounds completely made up, but it happened. Whilst I was there David was going to the hunt ball, something he did every year. He invited me along, how very decent of him. It was a black bow tie and nice dress do and I have to confess I did look pretty good; a fitted, plum coloured velvet dress, lots of glittery jewellery and a pair of incredibly feminine, sparkly red, strappy shoes which I have absolutely no idea how I forced my size 8 platters into. I emerged from the cottage looking and smelling good enough to eat. He seemed well pleased with the vision in front of him. As I stood in the yard, a car came down the drive and a blonde, twenty something girl got out. The sneaky little Welsh fucker had double booked! He'd asked her weeks before and had forgotten, so he told me. An awkward moment followed and she drove away, feeling as much of a prize dick as I did no doubt. The evening was not looking good so far. Once at the hunt ball I decided to numb the situation by getting drunk as quickly as possible. Here I was, stuck on a dairy farm in Wales with a slippery little weasel who considered himself the Tom Jones of the Friesian world. He leant across to me darkly as he drove us to the ball in his Landrover; "I aff to be vairry care fill what I say to women in nate clubs you knaw, you see I'm a millionairrr on peepah." Wanker.

I was in excruciating agony in the strappy heels and was padding about barefoot within ten minutes of our arrival at the ball. He spent the evening whirling about the dance floor with anyone that would have him and I sat myself at a table, completely pissed by now, bloated with hog roast, and attempted amiable banter with his friends, trying my hardest to at least give the impression of having a wonderful evening with my new two timing, millionaire-on-paper, twat of a Welsh dairy farmer boyfriend, even though he smelt permanently of silage before and after a bath and hadn't managed an erection for the three days I'd been there.

A woman I suppose of about 25 years of age and approximately a size 14 was sat opposite me. I knocked back another mouthful of red wine and announced cheerily, slurring badly and genuinely convinced my announcement was of a complimentary nature,

"You're such an attractive lady, you'd be so beautiful if you lost two stone."

Yep, I really said this, what the fuck was I thinking?! I have no recollection of the rest of the evening but when I appeared at the farmhouse table for breakfast the next morning, his mother bustled furiously into the kitchen,

"Go on, get out, we don't want your sort here!," as she flicked me out of the room with her tea towel. My well-meaning comment had apparently upset the girl and most of the agricultural community of Pembrokeshire in less than twelve hours. The peasants had revolted and I was pitchforked out of the county.

I stayed with my aunty Judy, in Narbeth for the duration of the stay. In need of cash by now I applied for a job at the local creamery. This didn't involve old butter churns, Jersey cows and frilly caps. It was an enormous hanger filled with vast steel vats and miles of pipework and the rhythmic clanking and whooshing of the forming of thousands of packs of butter. I stayed there for one day. I was in my mid thirties at the time of the short lived butter career and the life enhancing affect of a nice normal relationship had so far eluded me. During this time I'd slimmed down a fair bit, had stopped pulling my lashes and brows out and was altogether prettier. The affect of lashes, especially when clever makeup skills are applied is transforming. Mr 'Millionaire-on-paper' had said to me one evening whilst we sat in his car,

"You gnaw, aim shooer you get prrettier evree dee."

He was quite right too as every time I saw him, my lashes had grown a little longer. It was always a tense and terrifying time both as a child and as an adult when I had managed to grow my facial hair. Terrifying because I held in my hands the pretty/ugly dial and within a few short frantic minutes could render myself as bald as a Christmas turkey.

After a couple of weeks, Judy had a call from a friend, Jemima Entwistle, who needed help with her family's newly renovated country house in Scotland and it's attached 150 acres. Jemima's husband, Henry, was an investment banker and together with their three children, would spend the week in London then fly to Scotland every Friday evening to frolic in the countryside for the weekend. This all sounded irritatingly familiar. Probably an ex dairy farm whose previous occupants, like so many dairy farms up and down the country, could no longer make a living from the monthly milk cheque. The farms would then become rich pickings for the wealthy who fancied a big slice of the English pastoral idyll.

I arrived at the huge farmhouse on a Saturday morning and was greeted by a good looking man in his mid thirties who, it transpired, had already had the old milking parlour, dairy and cubicle shed where the cows used to sleep, gutted and converted into a play area, bar and barbecue set up, plus of course a newly installed sand-school for the numerous horses which grazed the lush pasture. Henry, having had absolutely no dealings with or knowledge of horses in his hitherto urban existence, was stocking up his patch of England as he felt all English gentlemen should; with anything and everything connected with equine, from bubblegum pink barrows to brand new saddles and bridles.

The fields had been fertilised heavily for generations in order to provide a thick, calorific sward, perfect for a herd of craggy old Friesians pumping out 20 litres of milk a day. But a horses digestive system is not built for a diet of sugar and protein rich ryegrass, it renders them lame and obese. So to keep the beasts trim and prevent them from hobbling, hundreds of metres of broad, white, electrified tape divided up the acres of grassland, colourful wheelbarrows and buckets dotted the fields, and the horses, mysteriously stripped of their natural shaggy coats, wore a complicated layering system of rugs. The whole thing confounded me, what the hell was happening to our once productive farms?.

I set to with steely determination in my new job, scrubbing the house, sweeping yards, cleaning tack and mucking out the horses. I'd been there about a month when Henry said to me one morning as we stood in the stable yard,

"Could you have this horse groomed and tacked up ready for me every Friday please."

I can only assume my expression must have read "fuck off matey, tack her up yourself," because almost immediately he continued with,

"It's ok I'll do it."

Can anybody enlighten me as to why these newcomers to the countryside fill their land with horses? Why not a herd of glossy, black Angus cattle or Swaledale sheep? I have nothing against horses, they are magnificent animals, indeed they have fought in our wars and sacrificed their lives in doing so. They have worked the land and hauled all manner of goods about the country for hundreds of years. But we don't eat horses and human numbers are increasing. How is the replacement of beef, dairy and sheep farms with horses sensible? Doubtless Mr Investment Banker expected milk in his coffee every morning. Consider then, his reaction when the farmer on the adjacent property decided to convert from arable and pigs to a 300 cow milking unit. He was outraged and managed to put a stop to the entire project. I left soon after.

Talk about from frying pan to fire; I'd seen a job advertised in an agricultural magazine which involved looking after animals including sheep and pigs in Hampshire. Having found that generally speaking, people who keep livestock are a sensible and grounded lot, with a natural empathy for the trials and tribulations of agriculture, I was disappointed to discover upon arrival that my new employer was a hedge fund analyst (not hedges with leaves, hedges with money) who had just bought a pet lamb for his three year old daughter, without the faintest idea of how to look after a very small sheep. The 'pig' bit of the advert referred to something he'd always liked the idea of, pigs. I set off for the local agri supplies store and purchased lamb feeding bottles, milk powder, lamb cereal pellets, hay and straw, plus a few syringes and needles for the inevitable problems.

As before, the six bedroom Georgian farmhouse was a weekend home to which he returned to every Friday afternoon with his daughter, Daisy and wife Arabella. Arabella was terrified of the countryside. The trees confounded her and she was mortally afraid of being stabbed to death in the dark on the six metre journey between the Volvo X5 and the huge front door. She would walk sorrowfully around the three acres of gardens, head bowed in abject misery, looking woefully down at the mysterious asparagus patch, her mohair Burberry longline cardigan pulled tightly around her, "how do you cook these?," she had said to herself in quiet despair.

I was mixing milk for the lamb early one morning as hastily as I could to put a stop to its bleating demands for breakfast. Meanwhile Mr Hedge Fund Analyst, bleary eyed, leaned out of his bedroom window,

"Could you stop the lamb making a noise please, I am trying to have a lie in."

I couldn't think of a suitable reply to that one.

The local farmer, Simon, who lived a mile from this property, farmed potatoes and sugar beet and also had a mobile phone mast on his farm, a structure which had been there for several years and earned him some much needed extra income. They were a lovely family and I would regularly spend a couple of hours sat in their kitchen, drinking tea made on the smokey old Rayburn and wolfing down homemade cakes made by Alice, Simon's wife. He told me that Mr Hedge Fund had begun proceedings to have the mast removed as 'it offended him.' Similarly, Simon held, for five Saturdays per year, motorised go-kart sessions in one of his fields for the local children. Mr Hedge Fund, after many months emailing the various authorities, put a stop to it. Money talks, I witnessed this first hand one morning; Mr HF walked into the field where the go-karting was taking place and announced to the farmer,

"I come down here for peace and quiet. I'm a millionaire and I can put a stop to it."

Understandably it didn't take long for the surrounding residents to develop a strong dislike to the new incomers. This is very often the case with city weekenders. They alienate themselves, install the standard, "no admittance to peasants," electric wooden gates and live an entirely enclosed existence whilst residing sporadically in the countryside. The type of people who have succeeded enough in business to be able to buy up farms and farmland did not get where they are by being nice. They got there by being forceful and resourceful and generally, well, used to throwing their weight around and getting what they want. So locals really don't stand a chance.

It is a sad fact that a large proportion of people living in rural Britain today are not of a rural background, disposition or attitude. They fill their Waitrose trollies with butter, milk, cheese, wine, steak and eggs. And yet I can guarantee were a dairy/beef/egg production farm to be set up in the vicinity of their immaculate residences, they would be outraged and put a stop to it, one of the main objections being the smell and animal/tractor noises. They seemingly want to live in a green, unchanging capsule, a picture postcard world where they can ride their horses and entertain their children and guests. But when their perfect world collides with real farming and a glimpse of where and how the contents of their fridges actually originate, they simply can't handle it.

My little patch of England here in Cornwall has not escaped the invasion of the townies either; there is a dairy farm a couple of miles from here whose weekend-only residents complained bitterly about the sound of a traditional old cowbell around one of the Jersey cow's necks. The bell was eventually removed by the farmer, it having been ding donging happily away for decades. Another resident who had recently moved down from London, strictly forbad the mucking out of animals at weekends, the smell of manure being deeply offensive to his delicate nostrils. The dairy farm in question had been in the same family for 200 years. My personal opinion is that if farmers were paid a decent price for their produce, ie; double the current rate, the countryside would be producing more feed and less golf courses, horses and land for development. Food is precious, too freely available and too cheap, far too cheap. And as a direct consequence of cheap food, we buy too much, eat too much and throw too much away complete with all the endless packaging. I am not saying that everyone who lives in the countryside should be into farming, but what I am saying is that it is fundamentally wrong to buy yourself a piece of country life and then proceed to jack boot it around, objecting to and putting a stop to, everyday farming practices. After all, I wouldn't move to Kensington and complain to the local authorities about the traffic noise. If you don't like the sound of mooing/bleating/crowing and animal smells then may I suggest a desirable residence in Surbiton-upon-Thames or Wimbledon Village with expansive gardens and hedges high enough to give the occupant the impression of living in the sticks.

Anyway, I made some feeble excuse to Mrs Hedge Fund about not fitting in and made for the exit as quick as I could, having arranged to spend a months work on a sheep farm in Cornwall. This left a gap of three weeks during which time I needed to earn money so I reluctantly took on a two week temporary housekeeping job via an agency in London. How the hell I wangled it to be accepted onto their books I will never know. I had sat nonchalantly in the immaculate waiting room next to a warm radiator and a plastic cheese plant, along with two other hopeful maidservants who I'm sure were a lot keener than me at the prospect of scrubbing pots and pans for the wealthy. A offensive odour of goat wafted up from my fleece coat as I sat, hand poised with biro held aloft, over the questions that read:

'Please tick your experience levels of the following: silver service, waiting at table, uniformed butler services, preparation of dinner parties for over 25 people.'

I lied fluently and ticked any and every box. Christ it was only two weeks for gods sake, I could wing it. The beige clad, Chanel perfume wearing lady at the office reception had handed me a printout of jobs that had become available. One position was as housekeeper to a Duchess, to whom all staff were contractually obliged to curtsey to every morning (over my dead body). Another grand house situated in Wiltshire forbad the presence of squeezy sauce bottles owing to the 'rude' sounds they produced. I didn't make that one up, promise. They all sounded appalling but I eventually agreed to do a two week housekeeping job for a wealthy, middle aged couple with four sons in Surrey. It will come as a surprise to most readers to hear that I am actually a very thorough cleaner, that is when I am absolutely forced to do it. My own home was cleaned for the first time in six months last week. I had to borrow the gardener's rake to deal with the straw and dog hair before I could vacuum. However in my new job I cleared and cleaned kitchen cabinets and sorted through spice and condiment cupboards whose sell by dates were in shillings and pence. I powered through the contents of enormous containers of kids toys, all plastic, all crap, all unnecessary, all unused. Filling loads of black bin bags with this detritus, I made many undercover trips to the tip, furtively chucking bulging bags of mass produced Taiwanese bollocks into the back of my truck. Subsequently an altogether leaner, tidier house was revealed. I was extremely pleased with the results and the wife was impressed, not to mention in awe of how I had managed to minimalise the kids' rooms. The secret of course was that half the stuff was now in landfill.

One morning, whilst cleaning the five year old's bedroom, I dusted a DVD on his computer desk entitled 'Wet Red Gash.' Being pretty certain this wasn't a training video for paramedics, I thought I'd better let the mother know that her little boy was maturing at an above average rate. She didn't seem fussed at all. Turned out the elder teenage brothers would watch any old thing on anyone's computer, including hard porn.

After a particularly long day of cleaning and then clearing up after a large dinner party for them, I nipped across to my granny annexe for a wee and a quick cuppa. On my return she demanded to know where I'd been and what was I thinking of, 'abandoning her in the midst of all this mess.' I buttoned my lip, waited till she left the room and let her three smelly old retrievers lick and teeth scrape until perfectly clean, three huge roasting tins which I had cooked the party's roast lamb and chicken in. Good as knew and sparkling 'clean,' I replaced them unwashed in the cupboard.

At this time I was dating a psychopath who scared the bejesus out of me, the aforementioned Ryan. He had no money, no driving licence, no prospects and no control over his anger. I dumped him after six weeks. One evening as we sat in the sitting room of my annexe he announced,

"I need ice cream, they've got everything, they'll have ice cream. Go and ask them for ice-cream."

"What?! It's 9pm, I can't just knock on their door and ask for ice cream!."

True to form he lost his temper immediately and stomped off out into the dark, his intention being to walk to the pub and exchange his watch in return for ice cream. Enough said, the man was insane. I was well rid.

When the two weeks were up I packed up my little car and trundled off to Cornwall to get stuck into sheep work. The farm was near Truro and was absolutely stunning, a tenanted National Trust property, farmed by a young couple and their thirty something son. I was to be helping out with the general MOT'ing of 800 Poll Dorsets, a lovely calm breed of sheep, very different to the mad Scottish Blackfaces. Poll Dorsets are exceptional in that they are able to conceive much earlier in the season and therefore lamb from November onwards. One of my jobs before it became dark in the afternoons, was to drive around the fields and check for 'cast' ewes. Not as in sheep chosen for their acting abilities, but 'cast' meaning stuck on their backs. It's easy to up-end them and they generally give themselves a thorough shake and toddle off, a little embarrassed to having been stuck in such a ludicrous position for several hours. On a more serious note, if not discovered and uprighted, a cast sheep will eventually die of heart failure due the unnatural position of its internal organs, or it will have its eyes eaten by corvids and its belly torn out by foxes whilst still alive. The role of the shepherd is, as you can see, a vital one and not as simple an occupation as the uninitiated might believe. On this particular Cornish farm, a number of shearlings (young sheep) had inexplicably given birth back in December. It turned out that the previous shepherd had been incorrectly castrating lambs during the two years she was there and subsequently many of the male lambs were fully functioning and had been merrily shagging their own mothers and sisters and any other fertile female sheep in the vicinity. The castrating of a lamb/calf or goat kid is carried out using a small, specially designed rubber ring and a metal applicator called an 'elastrator.' This must be done by law within seven days of the animal's birth, no later. I always wait until the lamb has been drinking successfully for at least 24 hours and that the navel (umbilical cord) has dried and begun to shrivel, which happens about 48 hours after birth. By this time the lamb has a strong bond with its mother and a full belly of milk. I administer a small injection of painkiller before placing a rubber ring over the scrotum, ensuring both testicles are sat completely within the sack. The ring is released and within about six weeks the scrotum has dropped off due to an absence of blood supply. If the ring is released before ensuring that both testicles are contained within it, then the lamb is potentially fertile once it reaches approximately three months of age. It is also important to ensure neither teat is trapped within the rubber ring. Occasionally a lamb will have a testicle that will not drop down into the scrotal sack. Such lambs are called rigs and I spray them with a coloured mark so I can spot them in the future and repeat my efforts at castrating, with veterinary intervention. There is a sheepy contraceptive device for ewes which involves the ewe wearing a leather flap covering her lady parts. Personally I would never trust this method, a randy ram will always find a way.

On a very different note, would you like to hear the story of Timothy Tired? Twas yet another delightful little fling as you shall read.. I met TT on a dating site called Dating Direct after I'd returned from Cornwall. He worked for the National Trust as a wildlife warden. I suppose I quite fancied him though he had a horribly dangly foreskin, and once, having spent the day together and myself suggesting I cook us an evening meal, he announced, "I think you'd better go home, Timothy tired," and so his name was born, although "knobhead" would have sufficed. We went for a walk together one morning on the South Downs in West Sussex and as we trod the steep chalky path, he turned to me and said,

"I chose a steep route to help you with your weight loss," I sure do pick 'em. He certainly was a slightly odd character. I was sat reading a book alone one evening and a piece of paper fell out, obviously intended to be found and read by me. I can't recall exactly the words he'd written but it was something along the lines of; 'and just like a planet's moon, so the smaller you become, the more I will be drawn to you.' This was a direct reference to the fact I was dieting at the time. The words 'fucking' and 'wanker' popped into my head as I read this loving missal.

After about three months our dalliance began to fizzle out although I'm pretty sure their hadn't been a lot of fizzling anyway, and as per bloody usual, the madness at the panic of his possibly leaving me set in. Only this time it was madness with a £300 price tag. It is unbelievable now to think I carried this through, but in complete desperation to keep his affection for me intact, I bought him a chainsaw, a £300 bloody chainsaw! (He'd mentioned to me some weeks previously that he needed a new saw). The affect was not what I had hoped for. He was furious and and left me several roaring voicemails, insisting I return it to the shop immediately. I was disappointed at his livid rantings and perplexed as to why a shiny new orange chainsaw couldn't buy me love. So that was that. We parted, Toby Tired of the dangly foreskin with a top quality piece of woodland maintenance kit and my moronic self, £300 worse off.

CHAPTER ELEVEN

She Is Not Any Common Earth

> *She is not any common Earth,*
> *Water or wood or air,*
> *But Merlin's Isle of England*
> *Where you and I shall fare.*

Having lost my heart to the beetle counter, I was not in the sunniest of moods and so decided to spend some time in Scotland. Tanera Mor was my destination and after a plane flight, bus, taxi and short boat ride, I finally arrived. A blissful week was spent in a small bothy heated by an open fire. I made Clootie dumplings the size of footballs and generally wafted about the heather with the wind in my hair, loving every minute of the isolation and bleakness. My only human encounter was with a lonesome fisherman, Stuart, who had paddled me across in his little boat from the mainland upon my arrival with my supplies for the week.

Stuart was convinced I was the Highlands and Islands answer to Julia Roberts and made it his mission to 'cover' me, in the agricultural sense, at least once during my stay. Stuart wasn't in the least attractive, was far too young for me, smelt of salmon and 'wooed' me by rowing us across to look at the salmon cages where I watched the poor little blighters trapped in the underwater equivalent of sow crates. However I was raw after the chainsaw experience and any male attention helped to neutralise the battles going on in my head. In the absence of a nice restaurant and menu to choose from, he gave me a colour chart illustrating the many shades of pink your intensively farmed salmon could be, according to the density of colourant added to their feed.

Ok, so what are the chances of being on Tanera Mor, an island consisting of only seven dwellings, and myself equipped only with a toothbrush, flannel, change of underwear and £30, only to be rogered by a fisherman with the smallest willy in Scotland, who had just one condom which he managed to burst. It could only happen to me. His willy was absolutely with no exaggeration, the smallest I had ever seen or felt. It sat inside its rubber casing like a lonely cocktail sausage inside a carrier bag. Stuart must surely have been conscious of its Lilliputian dimensions and endeavoured to make up for it with the most ferociously energetic thrashing around on top of me. It was all most disappointing and I longed to return to the sanctity of my little bothy. I could feel no sensation of a willy at all in the vicinity of my vagina so how the hell he managed to burst a hole in the condom I have no idea. As it was we had to somehow find transport to the mainland doctor to obtain a morning after pill. But still, at least I wasn't in calf to a salmon fisherman and the week away had been wonderful. Whilst on Tanera, I had a look through the Farmers Guardian and saw a vacancy for a general farm hand in Yorkshire, Gallows Farm on Silsden moor. This of course is the year of the dastardly deeds, covered in the second part of this book.

By early 2006 I had decided that never would I again resort to escorting and moved to a farm in Derbyshire, Clartie Farm, to make a fresh start of things. Owned by Penny and Kurt O'Connor who initially only wanted help for a year, I ended up staying for ten years, a record I still hold to this day. They were a lovely young couple with a new baby and had bought a 25 acre smallholding with the intention of investing in some animals and opening up to the public. It was a fantastic experience and I accrued an awful lot of knowledge about an endless variety of animals, right through from tortoises to Shire horses. I'm also certain I unwittingly produced a lot of vegetarians through entertaining our urban visitors; when you've been born and brought up in Croydon and your only experience of sheep is a delicious, sizzling offering of roast lamb, rosemary and garlic, to then see it bouncing around enjoying a bottle of milk and a scratch, is too big a void to expect a town dweller to bridge. On the many farms I had worked on however, the farmers and their children who had all grown up with the yearly cycle of shepherding, involving dead lambs, live lambs, placenta and bad tempered rams, all ate meat and had a deep seated understanding and ability to give an animal a good life, a swift and painless end and enjoy and appreciate a well earned Sunday roast. I have nothing against vegetarianism, indeed I cannot bring myself to eat lamb during lambing! However the real concern for me is not just the disconnect between the majority of the population and the origins of their food, it is the apathy and indifference to the countryside and the wildlife it contains and its shocking decline.

    I feed wild birds all year, as advised by any bird expert. People tend to stop offering feed in April which is when the birds need it more than ever as they are rearing their young. I have eight bird feeders in my garden all offering different feeds; suet balls, niger seed, mixed seed and peanuts. Six years ago I was spraying acres of nettles and thistles with herbicide and feeling very smug about it too. Sat one evening listening to Radio 4, the guest speaker spoke of the massive decline in once common farmland and woodland birds, the main reason being we have reduced their food plants and therefore insects and breeding habitats, by draining the land and using pesticides, herbicides and fertilisers. I stood and watched swallows swooping across the fields the next morning, their spectacularly skilled aerobatics mesmerising, scooping up beakfuls of insects as they went, insects and butterflies whose larvae depended on nettles, thistles and ragwort to grow and survive. I threw away the knapsack sprayer and disposed of the chemicals that very day. Overly invasive nettles were strimmed only when and where needed.

'My favourite Highland cow, Flora'

My ten years at Clartie Farm were wonderful. I lived in one of the old pig sties that had been converted into simple accommodation, and I do mean simple. I would lie in bed listening to the snuffling and grunting of the sow and her litter who lived in the unconverted sty next to mine. My piggery was tiny, a stone wall had been built through the middle to provide two piggy sized rooms. One half was a sitting room and kitchen and the other half a bathroom and bedroom. There was no plasterwork, just the original stonework, a slate roof and two deep set windows through which I would watch the birds feed from the numerous feeders stationed about the farm yard. A wood burning stove kept the sty as warm as toast.

The farm gradually attracted more visitors year on year as our collection of animals grew. We prided ourselves on having absolutely no plastic play equipment, none. One morning I was bedding up the barn and a little boy of about three, was calmly and quietly stood in a pen of six month old lambs who were about the same height as him! He was completely entranced at these woolly, gentle animals, something he'd only ever seen in books I would imagine. His face wore a serene smile as he worked his hands through the mass of warm fleece, it was a very tender moment. Not every child was as wondrous as that little boy; one very busy, hot summers day at 4pm, the scheduled time for bottle feeding, a group of twenty adults and their attached children descended on me. Unfortunately I only had one bottle of milk and one lamb with which to entertain the mob. I made a damn fine job of it and succeeded in having every child (almost) have a turn at holding the bottle before the milk ran out, not bad going as strong, older lambs empty a bottle within minutes. More adults and kids arrived and a desperate clamouring began as parents attempted to jostle their beloveds to the front. I sensed this was going to end badly. The humidity and my temper were evenly matched that day. Alas the milk ran out at the final child, whose particularly pushy father, having fought his way through the throng was determined his son should feed a lamb,

"Go on go on, quick quick! Hold the bottle!."

Much face crumpling ensued…

"Dadeee," he wailed, "I wanted to feed the lamb,"

Now I had just spent 120 seconds engaged in intense activity, smiling and tending to the needs of 50 or more agitated members of the public, in 25 degrees centigrade, armed with a bottle and one small sheep. I was beginning to hallucinate, visions of ice cold cider and an easy chair under my favourite oak tree, filled my head.

"But I weeelee wanted to feed the lamb Daddy," he howled, until the urge to stuff the bottle teat into his wailing gob was overpowering.

"Is there no more milk?," the father asked, as I looked at him blankly, with a very obviously empty bottle in my hand.

Now look folks, I'm not proud of my reaction here ok, but sometimes the pressure builds up and has to find a way out or it's a mental institution on the cards by the time you're 40 years old. I blurted at the child,

"Well it was a bit stupid to get here so late wasn't it? You should have got here earlier!."

The father looked at me in astonishment.

"Are you saying my son's stupid?"…

A slight pause followed as I weighed up the consequences of choosing one of two possible replies. Unfortunately for the father, I had had enough by now and replied with an emphatic,

"Yes."

He grabbed his son and stormed off to the shop to find, I would think, the manager. I awaited the inevitable call over the two way radio;

"Hello Cathy, could you come up to the shop please..."

"I've just had an irate father here complaining you called his son stupid and I have had to refund his admission fee. Did you actually say this to him?."

I looked at Penny rather sheepishly and admitted that yes I had indeed called him stupid and regretted my actions. She seemed happy with my apology and nothing more was said of the incident.

One day we had a group of blind adults visit the farm which I always found very moving. Sirius, our magnificent 19.1hh Shire horse was led into the stable yard and the group were able to stroke him if they chose to. One softly spoken lady in her forties nervously asked me to help her. Taking both her hands I placed them on the horse's massive shoulders, much much taller than her own. She stood there a long while, feeling the warm beast under her hands. Sirius was the gentlest of horses imaginable. He would lift his huge feet and hold them there in order for me to pick out the mud, I had no need to support the weight of them. He was the perfect gentleman. One day he accidentally trod on me as I lead him out to the fields for the night, it felt like he was standing on my foot for several minutes, though it would only have been seconds. I smothered my foot with arnica cream once home and within hours an enormous and highly impressive black and purple bruise developed.

If any animal were to show signs of aggression towards people, we couldn't keep it as a matter of safety. A case in point was Inky, a Greyface Dartmoor ram lamb. I'd reared him as a tiny little orphan and as the weeks and months rolled by, he became bolder and bolder, gently pushing against me as I stood to feed him his breakfast. After three months Inky was a solid six stone barrel of sheepy manliness and was growing rapidly by the day. By the time he was a year old he weighed twelve stone and spent his days grazing peacefully amongst his harem of Dartmoor ewes, until that is, anyone dared to enter his field, whereupon he would dip his massive head and shoulders, sprint from 0 to 20mph in seconds and have you flat out on the ground. If not stopped he would then continue the attack by breaking as many of your bones as possible. My tried and tested trick was to throw their breakfast into a trough over the fence, then leg it through the gate, fill up the hay rack and hot foot it out of there before he'd finished his breakfast.

When Inky was about eight months old and before I was completely aware of his bruiser capabilities at the time, I entered his pen one cold winter morning to replace his wall-mounted mineral block, the only tool needed being a hammer. I was squatting on the straw (amazing, just amazing, to think that once upon a time I could actually 'squat') and tapping the small pins back in to secure the new mineral block, when I received what felt like a blow over the head with a block of wood. Dazed, I looked up from my pronate position on the straw to see Inky's enormous woolly head looming down on me, wearing a furious expression that said "joo wanna a bit more where that came from?!," as he prepared himself bodily for another run-up.

If I'd been a small child, I reckon he'd have killed me. As it was, I grabbed my hammer and bopped him on the head, feeling a little guilty doing so, despite my predicament. He came at me again. I bopped him on the head, harder this time. Still he came, another harder bop. He came at me a final time and I sprang over the gate just as his solid head made contact with the wood of the gate. Rams have evolved to have immensely hard heads in order to defend their breeding rights, but being sentimentally attached to Inky despite his killer instincts, I didn't mention the incident to Penny. Two weeks later she announced she'd booked him in at the abattoir as he'd just knocked her clean over one morning. Poor Inky.

Kurt, Penny's husband, was a practical, no-nonsense ex dairy and sheep farmer, and though fantastic with the animals, his PR skills were not quite so well developed. He had been running a small PYO asparagus enterprise at Clartie farm for about three years. One day a shiny white sports car purred into the farmyard and a middle-aged woman in heels got out and tottered off to pick asparagus. I think she was expecting a tidier set-up, more akin to the fruit and veg aisle at Waitrose but with a nice countryside view. She appeared an hour later, flustered and limping with not much asparagus...

"There are nettles everywhere! It's totally unacceptable. How am I supposed to pick asparagus and not get stung?!,"

She had a good point but hadn't reckoned on Kurt's volatile nature...

"Nettles?!," he roared, "of course there's bloody nettles!."

She was outraged, returned to her car and spun away on the gravel, yelling "rude bastard" out of the window. Kurt in his customary, 'the customer is always right' attitude, sent a parting shot of,

"Fuck off, go on, just fuck off!."

Farm visitors looked on, marvelling at this rustic scene unfolding before them.

One morning, our cook arrived as usual for work, wearing his regular, 'another day in the poorhouse expression,' and mumbled,

"Saw Robbie Williams when I was pickin' up bread this morning."

"Robbie bloody Williams?!," we all chorused, "are you sure?!,"

"Yep," was the reply as he turned his fryers on for the day's cholesterol soaked offerings. Turned out it had indeed been Robbie Williams.

I was feeding the cattle one morning in the barn and who should I spot wandering about, but one Gary Newman who appeared to be being 'walked' along by a heavily made up, black-haired woman, clinging to him as one might to a rubber ring whilst stranded at sea. Gary, managing to free himself a little from her tentacle-like grip, said,

"Have you got any goats for sale?," delivered with such typical coolness that I half expected him to follow it up with, "here in my car, I can only receive…"

His companion managed to force an expression through the paralysis of botox exclaiming,

"A goat! What joo wanna goat for?!."

I left them to it.

After ten years, I decided a new challenge was in order, after all, ten years was a record for me and I had absolutely loved my time there. Sadly, the subsequent challenge of taking milk samples from a herd of Friesians proved to be too much for my rather slow on the uptake 'cow chewing the cud' mental abilities. After a days work of sampling I was left feeling the same after learning our brilliant female vet was also an accomplished double bassist in a London symphony orchestra. Just shoot me now.

Taking milk samples from each cow involved moving with dexterity around the herdsman in the 'pit,' who was busy milking the cows, with their multitudinous pipes and tubes attached. The precious trays of individual, tiny milk-sample pots sat on the bulk tank in the dairy at the top of the steep pit steps. The 'milking pit' was a sunken 25 foot x 10 foot area, lined either side with milking clusters. Being sunken, the cows' udders were then at a working height which allowed the milker to go about his business without having to sit and crouch as he would have done in ye olden days.

As each group of cows entered the parlour, the herdsman would wash and dry the teats before attaching the milking unit or 'cluster.' Once milk began flowing into the jar, I would syphon off 50mls into my little pot, snap the lid on and return it to its tray. Every pot was pre labelled with the 'freeze brand' number of each cow so it was vital that the correct sample was placed in the correct pot. This all sounds relatively simple. Unfortunately I too am simple, probably the forceps used at birth. By the time I had legged it up the parlour steps and into the dairy, placed pot in tray and returned to parlour to sample the next cow, it would take me a couple of minutes to work out where I'd left off. The cows were all black and white and the freeze brand numbers on each of their thighs had very often faded or if her backside was more white than black, the freeze brand was on a black bit of the cow, out of my view. Freeze branding is, as mentioned previously, stamping a number on each cow in large, legible numbers, but branding is only possible on the black parts of a Friesian. In these cases I had to ask the herdsman which number she was and after five minutes of me peering at her backside be it black or white, he'd be letting that group of eight cows out and ushering the next lot in.

It was all far too frantic at 5am in the morning and by the time 8am had arrived and I had peeled my waterproof leggings and apron off, I was knackered and reeked of milk, urine and dung. It wasn't for me.

And so to my final job before I settled down in Cornwall, where I reside now. An 800 acre estate in Devon owned by Lord and Lady Stanhope-Milton, my job there was as general farm worker. Lady S.M was in her 70's, jolly nice and always provided an enormous container of biscuits and a bubbling tea urn, all day in the barn. She was by now, happy to be addressed as 'Lady S.M.' Once, I had made the grave error of using her christian name, Margaret, as she threw hay bales to the baaing ewes one morning. She shot me a royally disapproving look that instinctively had me reaching for my cap with which to doff. She would get thoroughly involved with all farm activities; lambing, machinery work and even changing the oil on the big old Ford tractor we used to muck the barns out with; she stood, with thick, black oil smeared across her face and overalls, at the back of the beast, having wrestled off the oil cap and positioned the container under the sump.

Lambing having long been over back in January, and before my arrival, the big empty sheep barn needed mucking out and she would allow no one except herself to carry out the mechanised part of this job. She flew around the barn with the huge fork attachment on the front of the tractor, niftily getting into awkward corners and scooping up enormous piles of dung and straw which she dumped into the waiting trailer. I meanwhile, hobbled around after her with a hand fork removing dung from against the sides of the barn which the tractor couldn't reach. She would 'honk honk' from the cab to alert me to any muck she presumed I had not spotted. The honking continued throughout the two hour operation until I'd have cheerfully impaled the old woman.

Having scuttled about hither and thither with my fork, meekly excepting my extreme subservience as it was temporary, I would look wearily across at the young farm lad, Steve, who had also been appointed as a cap doffer. He was one of those cheeky, good humoured lads who you can't help but like. As she chugged off up the barn on the final run, honk honking as she went, he wandered up behind the tractor, loaded an imaginary shot gun and peppered her like a rabbit.

The flock of Poll Dorsets she kept were a plodding, calm breed of sheep who she lambed in December. This breed has been bred to be one of very few that are able to conceive as early as June, five months being the length of a ewe's gestation. The benefit to the farmer of lambing mid winter, is that the lambs are finished and ready for slaughter by April/May, thus earning the farmer a premium as spring lamb is appealing for the consumer. Personally I don't agree with it, it goes against nature. Naturally sheep will lamb in the spring when there is plentiful grass and kinder weather. 'Spring lamb' is a misleading phrase for the uninitiated. Lambs are spring born, correct, but they are not ready to eat in the spring, unless that is you have a liking for an extremely small leg of lamb for your Sunday roast.

It was a beautiful farm with an enormous Victorian walled garden, wherein was grown all manner of fruit and vegetables. One of my jobs was propping a ladder against a very old mulberry tree and picking the fruit. If you've never tried a mulberry, do. They are quite delicious and unlike any other berry.

When I first began working there Lady S.M had no working sheepdog, just an insane but loveable collie called Frib, who bit everyone she saw except me. Occasionally she was to be found amongst the flock, having escaped, attempting to move the sheep to the next county. We loved each other, Frib and I. Consequently moving and gathering sheep involved poor Steve and myself running around the hundreds of acres with much arm flailing and 'woop wooping.' Lady S.M meanwhile would be zig zagging across the fields in her Landrover, 'parp parping' on the horn. At the end of one particularly long and exhausting sheep moving exercise, she relented, seeing Steve and I collapsed on the grass. A few calls were made and Moss, a fully trained working collie was delivered the next day. Costing £1000, at ten years old Moss was worth his weight in gold. It didn't matter what instructions you gave him, he ignored them all and just got on with the job, instinctively knowing what was required of him.

'Frib and Moss'

My four years in Devon came to end and I was loaded up with fresh lamb, veggies and fruit. I made my way, pick-up bulging at the seams, to my new tenanted smallholding in Cornwall, which is where I write from now. It has been a jolly good laugh recounting all these tales and I hope they've provided a little pleasure to at least some of you. The rest of you miserable gits can just sod right off. Cathy x

Epitaph

Care no more to bow and weep

All Earthly toils thou knew must sleep.

Fear no more wild winter's rage

To thee all nights lie as the days.

Rhyme and song in thee have rest,

Thy task be done, thy courtyard swept.

No minstrel's sad humming

Nor sorcerer's vile cunning.

As mighty elms to dust must come,

Thy hands be still for thou art done.

— Samantha May 1997

COCKADOODLEDOO

Part Two
A Ghastly Business

January 15th 2005

Oh holy fuck, today is my first escort booking. I feel as calm and professional as a gas boiler engineer having successfully lied his way into the post of Chancellor of the Exchequer. I am fucked, this is truly dreadful. I am a dreadful person! no no it's fine. You're just fine. Everyone has to make their way in this world. You never found your farmer so needs must. Be calm and wear a condom. This time tomorrow you'll be gloating over the money.

….Hmm, well, it wasn't so bad. He seemed to sense I didn't have a clue what I was doing and after a lengthy chat on the acting ability of Keira Knightley in Pride and Prejudice and any other topical subject I could dredge up in order to postpone the dreaded deed, we microwaved some hot dogs, brewed a pot of tea and for the last ten minutes I tugged away determinedly at his manhood like a blackbird on the lawn with a worm. Not too bad at all for a first attempt. I drove home in a fog of mild disbelief, feeling like I'd witnessed a murder scene, shocked and disgusted at myself, but the lure of £20 notes led me onward.

January 23rd 2005

I'd only charged £30 for my first half hour outcall which he told me was ludicrously cheap. To him maybe, but compared to two hours of dry-stone walling at 2000 feet, out on the Yorkshire moors, it seemed like a kings ransom. Driving along in my pick-up truck on the way to a second booking and now officially a prostitute, (oh my GOD! I'm going to hell in a handcart) mobile in one hand, pizza in the other and no seat belt on, I was passed tonight by an unmarked *police car from which the three unimpressed looking, uniformed officers all waggled their fingers. I stunned them with a dazzling smile and wolfed down my pizza.*

Having driven for what seemed like bloody miles in torrential rain and darkness, I ended up on a large, dubious looking council estate where I expected to be hauled from the security of my truck and stabbed to death with heroine needles. It was extremely depressing. Endless rows of hutches, or flats as they're commonly known, all containing life's wretches, and all eating microwave curry and watching Jeremy Kyle. I was scared, very scared, having only ever known life on a farm, and though farm life is tough, it is simple, relatively safe, and far from the clutches of life's Fagins, mostly. I parked the pick-up and found flat number 32. He appeared at the door at my knock and after I'd introduced myself he said he had family at home so could we use his car? His car? So we sat in his Mini and he gave me £50 and two wooden clothes pegs, after which I placed a condom on his willy and engaged in some very amateurish sucking. He meanwhile had put the pegs on his nipples and proceeded to pop his weasel very quickly. I hurried back to my truck. The oddest thing was a large, tortoiseshell cat had sat motionless on the bonnet throughout the entire performance, staring unblinkingly at me. I returned at long last to my blissful gypsy caravan and crashed out in bed with Fly and Nellie, two of several collies here at Gallows, they all take it in turns to sleep in the caravan. The moors suit me, they brood and I brood together. There is a huge pull to this wild landscape, no surprise that Wuthering Heights is my favourite book, I would love to have met Emily Bronte. The way I was driving tonight, I nearly did.

'Nellie and Fly'

January 27th 2005

My caravan or hut as I call it, is small but perfectly formed with a tiny single bed that sits widthways across at the end and which is raised up high so that the window sill is on a level with the duvet itself, very handy for lambing as I can lean out whilst still in bed and with a good torch, check all is well with the pregnant ewes. I blitzed the hut today and beautified it, having made the decision to see clients, wherever possible, in my home surroundings instead of driving out to ghastly urban areas that filled me with dread. Living in such a small area and working with animals who frequently end up in the hut if they are poorly, can quickly turn my home into a scene of carnage, so I have a very quick and efficient system for transforming exceedingly hairy dog hut into rose-petalled boudoir with which to entice the breast-starved men of Yorkshire; a quick spritz of vanilla room-spray, remove dog to dairy, cover hairy bed and floor with throws and I'm good to go.

'A pretty little hut sometimes'

I saw a chap the other day who was your typical Londoner, a long way from home. He sounded very keen on the phone but as he steered his BMW X5 through the slurry of the collecting yard he emerged from his car looking less than impressed. "Still!," I said cheerily, "I don't suppose you see much mud in London!." "Well, yes a little but not on this scale."

January 31st 2005

Ok so it's been a crappy day. I am in a terrible mood. Today was the designated delivery day for my 150 bales of oat straw. Having had the Devil's own job of extracting text replies from the useless pile of horse shite farmer that I'd ordered them from, I eventually managed to pin him down to a day that he could get here. 'He' didn't arrive with the straw but three acne and pustule covered youths did, presumably selected at random from his team of misfits and oompa-loompas. I watched with a growing sense of foreboding, the tractor with attached straw-laden trailer slowly making its way up the steep hill before it began to wheel spin, lose traction and slide thirty foot to the right, finally coming to a standstill halfway up the hill. The driver grappled with various gear sticks and throttles and succeeded in carving a network of two foot muddied deep ruts into the ground.

"Course thissle cost ya a loaduv extra money cos we've got stuck and it's cost toime," muttered a youth. Me, having spotted the nearly bald tyres as the tractor approached, pointed out that, "had the bloody thing had some tread this wouldn't have happened!." This comment was not warmly received, particularly as it had been pointed out by a female and worse still, because they knew I was right. After much chin rubbing and grunting they decided to return to their farm some fifteen miles away and return with a 'better tractor.'

Upon their reappearance an hour later, another tractor, complete with new tyres, hauled both stuck tractor and trailer with ease up the hill.

"There you go lads, what did I tell you," and all the while cursing their brutish stupidity. This remark was ignored. The more unpleasant of the three threw a 'wadda YOU know fat old lady,' look, in my direction and spat,

"Where's it goin?,"

"In the barn," I replied (where else you bloody simpleton).

The straw was appalling. If the man had made teabags, mine were the floor sweepings. I'd been ripped off in the fullest sense of the word. £3 per bale and they were less than half the weight they should have been. Most of them fell apart when they were picked up and the ones that didn't, weighed about 35kg each and were rotten as a pear because they'd been baled wet.

"Were these baled by a blind person with a knife and fork?," I asked one of them forlornly, hoping in my feeble female way that adding a little jaded humour would lighten the gloomy atmosphere. The nicer of the three said,

"Yeah you might wannoo av words wiv im 'bout this ere straw."

Words! Thought I, bollocks to words! I'm thinking bread knife in every tyre on every vehicle on his shitty little rented farm. They all sloped off with their collection of tractors, trailers and pickups and left me to clear up the devastation. The same day, the same bloody day!, I forgot to take payment upfront from a guy before I did the foul deed and he drove off having had a free handjob. I lost £70. There are winning lottery card holders who didn't check their numbers in time, happier than I was that day. I was beyond angry. I was exceedingly depressed and went to bed at 6pm after a supper of three Wispa bars.

The next day the 'stack,' if you could call it that, had collapsed and I spent the day barrowing loose straw into a huge heap. I left the farmer a 'firm' voicemail and sent a 'firm' text but never heard from him again. May his corn be infested with blight and ergot.

February 3rd 2005

Another delightful collection of texts arrived today whilst I was in the midst of footbathing the ewes. Sheep don't like going through footbaths and it takes much persuasion and rugby tackling. This I'm sure influenced the content of my replies. Sit back with a cuppa and be wide eyed at the ingenuity of the male of the species. Is it any wonder my uterus recoils in horror at the thought of copulation...

"Are you interested in filming video clips or a live web cam of a young guy sucking your toes and swallowing your urine, you don't have to show your face, £300 an hour,"

"I don't care if it's £10k an hour with a years supply of icecream, it's a no from me."

What amazes me is that there are people out there, walking amongst us, who suck toes and drink wee. And here's another classic, bless him. A few English evening classes are in order I think.

"Hi possible, antes hora tomarnos 17.00h. Hoy to much. Bye am Daniel."

"Sorry but the language barrier is going to be a problem. Bye am Delilah."

I had a candle-making session today that produced a big pillar candle the colour of a decaying corpse, with purple and black blotches like a Black Death victim. My fault entirely as I do tend to get a bit carried away with mixing different dyes. I shall enjoy it once it's lit as I can't see anyone wanting it at their dinner table somehow.

Saw a pilot today, god they're an arrogant bunch. He was French Moroccan, about 5'4" and chubby with the milk-coloured skin of a Middle Eastern and the seductive (apparently) accent of the French. He had dark, floppy boy-band hair that he took great sensual pleasure in constantly sweeping away from his face. I don't much like fingers through the hair thing. Hair can be dirty and hair comes out, probably over my lovely white bedding. But he was quite a nice chap and was cheerfully boasting of his love for his wife and children and the love for his stunning Moroccan cabin crew long-term girlfriend. One in every port methinks.

"Hey, I'm looking for a slave for 3 days a week, you will receive cash for three days upfront, £1000."

"Try the job centre."

An assortment of delightful texts:

(Me) "Hi, sorry I missed your call earlier,"

(Him) "I'd call you back but I'm in the middle of doing something,"

(My guess is he isn't baking a cake)

"Mind if I ring you whilst I'm doing something?,"

"Yes I bloody well do mind, you ruinous individual."

"Hi Delilah will you massage a 36 year old with a tiny cock?,"

I couldn't think of a witty reply to this one.

"Hi do you offer oral, anal, cim and deep-throat?,"

"No. Tell me, how would you fancy a penis rammed up your backside, down your throat and its contents spurted down your gullet?!. Precisely. So why would I?."

And listen to this one, is it any wonder I prefer the company of sheep and collies:

"Hi, I'm working near you today, are you available?,"

"Hi yes I am."

"Can I rim you? I like a smelly bum, sorry if that's odd."

"Damn right it's odd, no I can't help you. Try a homeless person, you'd smell her bum at fifty paces."

"Oh that's a shame. I just like a big lady with a shitty bum hole for me to lick clean, thanks anyway."

"Morning Delilah, saw your ad, you look very juicy, I'd like to suck on you, when are you available?,"

"I'm not a bloody nectarine."

"Just read your profile, do you fuck mixed race UK born and bread?,"

*"The correct spelling is **bred**."*

February 5th 2005

My right leg hurts so much that the thought of shagging is as enticing as a ten mile run across a Cumbrian peat bog; I was walking my flock using a bucket of food as the lure, the whole thing was going like a dream when out of nowhere a one year old ram lamb head butted me on the side of my left calf. Jesus the pain, I thought he'd broken it. Anyway, ever the devoted shepherd, I vaccinated and foot-trimmed everything, having taken a handful of painkillers. Good job done but I can hardly walk.

How bloody dare people complain about the price of lamb. It should be £100 a kg.

February 10th 2005

My profile now states that I do not offer kissing. I mean really?! Kissing? Here's the thing ok..kissing a stranger is worse, much worse than having them invade your lady parts. Whilst going along with it I managed to endure kissing by imitating, very poorly no doubt, the scene in Shrek 1, where Lord Fahrquart cranes his head up to princess Fiona, braying 'kiss mi.' Anyway it generally made clients laugh which distracted them from their real focus. Being kissed by a paying stranger is like oral rape and I simply can't abide having teeth and saliva of an known hygiene rating anywhere near my mouth, so it's off the menu for good, along with their mouthparts in the vicinity of my front bottom. Highly risky disease-wise and akin to licking the bottom of a wheelie bin every week in terms of safety. I knew a man who contracted gonorrhoea through having an infected escort suck his unprotected willy.

Saw a man last night who told me he worked in the city as a banker. This was greeted by a polite expression of acknowledgment and puzzlement by me, as I have no idea what this actually means. I'm fairly certain it's not the same banking as the bored cashiers asking, 'if you'd like to enter your pin and press enter please,' all day long. He got out of his shiny new car, wearing a slightly shifty expression that I hoped wasn't the same expression worn by serial killers of prostitutes, (which reminds me, I must organise a will) opened his boot and produced a brace of pheasants that he'd shot that morning. At his request, I produced a kitchen knife and he deftly carved off the succulent bits, tossed the carcasses in the hedge and handed me the breasts. I thanked him profusely and said I would enjoy them with a pepper sauce. I ended up giving them to the dogs, it just felt a bit weird. He said after our 30 minutes of paid grappling that, 'visiting me was the oddest experience he'd ever had and that escort-wise I was terrible value for money, but character-wise I was terrific value for money.' I decided to take that as a compliment. He took a bit of a shine to me and sent me random texts that evening suggesting a drink together one day. This happens occasionally. They then think about it for 24 hours until it dawns on them:

'Oh my god she's a whore, my family would disown me and I'd be fired.'

They're right of course. I shall die a spinster but a contented one.

Text this morning:

"What shoe size are you mistress? I would like to buy you some sandals if that's ok?,"

"Size 7, do you mean sandals as in Jesus of Nazareth sandals?,"

(Long pause from man)

"Ah, I gather from your disappointed silence that you were hoping for a size 4?,"

"Yes, what size are you?,"

"I have just told you, 7."

"Shall I buy you some sandals in a size 7?,"

"Well a size 4 would be rather pointless wouldn't it? I take it your texts are with a view to making a booking?,"

"Not an escort booking, I'll just bring the shoes and maybe stay for fifteen minutes just to lick your feet and drink your piss, how much will that cost?,"

"WTF?! Go and find a weak bladdered woman who's desperate for sandals you dirty little bastard."

February 11th 2005

I am extremely stressed due to my sheep at the moment as there is very little money from escorting coming in and I have endless bills to pay, namely the abattoir, butcher, tannery and hay supplier who charged me £6 a bale, knowing it was for sheep, the thieving git. £6 a bale is what the horsey people pay because it's top quality and is the energy equivalent of rocket fuel. He was the only small bale hay supplier I could find so will have to stick with him for this year. I have 120 sheep in total including lambs, it's far too many for me with no tractor or quad bike so as from next tupping time I'm scaling right back to a number where I am once again able to enjoy it. I've really done the whole thing ars about face and instead of buying a trailer first, I bought the sheep and planned to have the trailer by the time I needed it. But with so many sheep, the feed, equipment and medicine costs increased, which meant I couldn't afford to buy a trailer in time for when the lambs had to go to the abattoir. I'm waiting to see if the finance I applied for, for a new trailer, has been approved. Fingers crossed.

So I'm now in a state of comparative poverty, unable to buy milk for tea, having just spent £600 on something very beautiful but which could have waited; I had a huge slab of seasoned oak given to me a couple of years ago; a long slice of trunk about eight foot by two foot with a wonderfully gnarled edge which was the bark side of the tree. I had the idea of having two blanket boxes made from it using the oak as the lids. The clever carpenter I found used cheap wood for the sides which he distressed and painted a delicate off-white. I chose pewter handles and hinges and the resulting boxes are gorgeous! Well worth two months of living on boiled potatoes *and water. No room for them in caravan of course but they're stored in old dairy for now.*

Paul is here tomorrow to crutch the lambs. He's getting a bit past it and keeps losing his grip on them. When he was last here he lost control of a huge Romney wether and ended up on his back like a furious beetle, still managing to keep one hand on the scrabbling 80kg sheep that was lunging for freedom, and the other on the whirring shearing machine. For a minute I was transfixed at the comedic Tom and Jerry scene playing out before me. The spell was quickly broken as he roared,

"Turn it off! turn it off!."

At one point I had twelve goats and eight cattle, plus the sheep. This is all very lovely but you have to think it through, as in how will you feed and shelter them throughout the winter and where will you store all the feed? Wherever it is, it has to be completely weatherproof and rat proof. How do you plan to keep getting them annually in calf/kid/lamb?. Are you going to buy a bull/ram/billy of your own or hire in?. All three males of the species are potentially very dangerous and if a bull goes lame, do you have a cattle crush to restrain over a tonne of very cross bull.

Cowardice has kept me, thus far, safe and unharmed. I am very pleased indeed to have been born a coward. I bought two, exceedingly handsome, pedigree rams a year ago; one was Gerald, a Border Leicester and the other, Jack, a Kerry Hill. A lot of rams

give you the eye and you know it's time to get the hell outa there. But Gerald and Jack were ok, gentle characters who quietly got their ladies pregnant and returned to grazing peacefully. One day as I enjoyed the June sunshine, calling the ewes as they trotted along behind me, Gerald's expression changed from benign to menacing, and within a few seconds, he'd accelerated, head down towards my kneecaps. I legged it Usain Bolt fashion from the field, flinging the gate shut. I don't care, I still love Gerald. Rams can kill and injure easily, they possess immense power and speed and once you are down and knocked off balance, they just keep coming at you until you are human peanut butter.

My eight cattle were collected by a farmer back in the autumn, who kept a Belted Galloway bull. They have all returned home pregnant except Sunny, the Guernsey, who was empty. The vet examined her and it turned out she had an abnormally small vagina, so small the bull couldn't insert his penis. Lucky old cow, I'd pay good money for a vagina like Sunny's, a sound medical reason to never have to have sex again.

'Gerald and Jack; handsome but deadly'

February 12th 2005

Had to endure extremely tedious, doggie-style intercourse with a little Chinese man this afternoon, having lectured him on the merits of using a teaser ram on ewes to encourage a shorter lambing period. I was sucking mindlessly away on his little oriental willy, my thoughts amongst the sheep and muttering something about my winter feed bill. Before he left he produced an extra £10 'for hay.' Sometimes clients can be very kind. Also saw an ancient old man who said he was 77 but looked 97, stick thin and wheezed continuously. After he'd ejaculated with the aid of my faithful friend, the mains operated vibrator, producing what looked like diluted Colman's mustard in the condom, he said he hadn't come in nearly two years. Oh my good God, how I managed not to be sick I'll never know.

February 15th 2005

Hm, seems I've got to push the boat out a bit. The last chap I saw strongly recommended I stop advertising in the local paper, get some decent photos taken of myself and put them on a proper escorts website. So I Googled, 'glamour photographers,' booked a train to London and a photo session costing £300 bloody pounds! I am not looking forward to this.

February 19th 2005

Here we go...
"Hi Delilah, I have a fantasy that I was hoping you might consider. I'm about 40 minutes away from you today. I'd pay you £80 to do this: I walk in and pay you. You then go off to your

bedroom and I walk in after two minutes to find you wearing black tights and very slutty high heels, heavy makeup and tits out. You're bent over and being a naughty little fuck, toys all over the bed and I come up behind you and spank you all over your tights. When you're ass is nice and red I tear a hole in them and push my cock through so it's rubbing between your tights and skin. I finger you at the same time. Then you turn around and give me the wettest and sloppiest deep throat I've ever had. You rub my wet cock all over your face and you gag making your eyes water and mascara run. I grab your tits and finger fuck you hard concentrating on your G-spot until you gush for me. I cum all over your tits and watch as you rub it in.

Just need to do it now!

Nigel x

(Sorry Nige old boy..no can do)

February 21st 2005

Drove out of area for a change of scenery to walk dogs today and to try and exorcise some demons, thereby hopefully reducing tendency to grumpiness. I just checked out the exact meaning of 'misanthropy:' 'a general hatred, distrust or contempt of the human species or human nature.' That describes me perfectly. I am proud to be able to call myself a misanthropist. Emily Bronte described the aspect of Wuthering Heights, the farmhouse, as, 'a perfect misanthropists heaven.' I need to live in Wuthering Heights.

After my dog walk, I decided to splash out on chips in a pub on the way home. The pub used to be owned and run by a wonderful old landlord, Albert, who'd been a dairy farmer all his life up until taking over the pub. My last visit was when Albert ran it, about five years ago; bangers n mash for six quid, perfect. No frills, just good beer 'n grub and a roaring fire in the inglenook. My visit today revealed the pub to have changed a lot; Albert had long since retired, all paintwork was now 'eau-de-nil' and Farrow and Ball's 'elephants breath,' with shabby chic tables and waiters and waitresses in long black aprons.

"Hi, could I have a portion of chips please?," I asked a good looking lad,

"Er, I'll just check the chef has chips, he is expecting a busy day today."

(There's two people in the pub. Check the chef has chips? Isn't that like asking a gardener if he has a lawn mower?)

Young man returns,

"Yes that's fine. £2.50 please,"

"Thank you, and a hot chocolate would be lovely."

This produced a suppressed flurry of anxious mixing and stirring and conspiratorial exchanges between the two bar workers, one of whom proceeded to slosh Tesco semi-skimmed milk into a disappointingly small mug. Two teaspoonfuls of Options low calorie hot chocolate powder were added, stirred and placed under the milk heater nozzle. The barmaid handed it to me, beaming, pleased as punch with her efforts, as I looked down at my £2.75 worth of drink, actual cost £0.20.

"Do you have any cream please, and could you heat it, it's tepid."

Five minutes later she reappeared at my table with a warmish hot chocolate and disappeared once more to find the cream. This arrived followed by the chips.

"Did you want salt?,"

"Well, yes, and vinegar and a fork too." Jesus.

February 23rd 2005

Yesterday I went to London for the photo shoot. Tod came with me and slept soundly throughout, bless his heart. Now I have to say, just the mere notion of me, of all people, having a glamour shoot is just the most ridiculous thing. Mainly because I am without doubt one of the least interested women in glamour that you are ever likely to meet. But if I'm to stick with this escorting malarkey, at least for the time being, then I must as a prerequisite look as alluring and drop dead gorgeous as possible.

The whole thing was a hard, very hard thing for me to get my head around. I am you see, from head to toe, quite literally, the antithesis of all things womanly and sexy; stout work boots and a boiler suit with multiple holes in, mostly inflicted by barbed wire, brambles and goats. But I'd made the decision to fiddle with willies professionally, therefore the photo shoot had to be endured. Having invested in a plentiful supply of lacy underwear and sparkly hair accessories from Ebay, I arrived at the studio, feeling as much at home as a vicar in a massage parlour, and trying to mask my nervousness by chatting and making unfunny jokes. The studio itself wasn't too bad. He clearly was a reasonably professional bloke and the spacious room was equipped with ornate, fake gold chairs, mirrors and swathes of purple and pink chiffon with which to toss about my person.

I'd paid an extra £50 to be made up professionally, so sitting in the dressing room, looking sadly at my browless and lashless reflection, (I'll explain the facial hair thing later) cruelly illuminated by far too many 60watt bulbs, the makeup lady arrived. I watched with interest as she began layering up my face with an assortment of black and candy coloured paints, glitters and pigments. After about twenty minutes I actually looked quite attractive and had she stopped there I would have been happy. However she continued painting, concealing and daubing, with my eyebrows ending up as two, very thin black lines, my cheeks like those of a Pelham puppet and a big painted on beauty spot the size of a five pence piece. I looked like a cross between Betty Boo and a pantomime dame but forced a smile, thanked her and began to remove my size 20 Tesco pants and bra in order to force the size 16 ones on. Some of the underwear I'd brought was the stuff I used to squeeze myself into for internet dating when I was several stone lighter, hence I'd been compelled to starve myself for two weeks prior to the shoot. But it was still impossible to stretch the ridiculously flimsy bits of lace and silk around my middle. Eventually I forced an item around me, and the photographer, grown impatient by now, arranged my limbs into various grotesque come hither positions, at odd angles and shapes,

"If it's not uncomfortable it won't look good," he'd said. Not the words I wanted to hear. Anyway, two hours later and I was shown the photographs. Appalling, just appalling. Christ I wouldn't have shagged me for free let alone part with cash. He whizzed through the photos on his computer and muttered something about 'looking for an agency that deals in larger ladies.' He was however very keen on editing me down to a size 12 with the aid of clever technology. I couldn't resist and disappeared off to a tea shop for pastries and a pot of Earl Grey for two hours whilst he performed his instant weight-loss surgery. When I returned and was shown the new pictures, I was stunned! I looked amazing, and apart from the transvestite makeup job I was sure to be in hot demand and be a wealthy woman before Christmas. Turns out I had a lot to learn.

Feeling like I'd survived three hours on the rack when I finally lumbered out into the daylight, Tod and I returned to the train station and slept for the entire journey home.

February 24th 2005

So, I now have a proper profile on a proper escorts website, in order that all manner of lusty men can tug away till they can tug no more. My glamour photos have been uploaded to the profile, it all feels terribly debauched and surreal.

'Technology eh!'

'The before'

February 25th 2005

Bloody hell, phone and inbox are flooded with inflamed men, all desirous of my body. Saw a guy today who'd raved over my pics. I opened the door to him and he turned right round and drove off...hmm.

February 27th 2005

I saw an older gentleman this morning, completely normal chap until he laid down whereupon he began to twitch and judder about in ecstasy as if in the company of Venus herself. He kept saying sorry for no obvious reason, laid a cold hand on my breast and in a state of extreme arousal, he popped the funds for dog food into a condom within seconds. Bloody marvellous I say.

February 28th 2005

I have a condition known as trichotillomania, This means I have an irrepressible urge to pull hair out, my own hair. It is caused by stress, a lot of stress. Consequently I have very thin head hair and have no lashes or brows, and bare a striking resemblance to Gollum. I therefore rely on dark brown crayon to prevent my shocking the poor men that have wound their way across moor and heath to see me. I've been plucking out pretty intensively lately so my hair is now reduced to a little topknot, in no way resembling the thick, luscious tresses portrayed in the glamour photos, they were actually clip-in hair extensions. A client I saw today was curiously inspecting the sad little Jack Russell tail on the back of my head and clearly perplexed as to how such a flowing mane of chestnut locks could be contained within a tiny elastic band, sprouting a whippet tail of greying wisps.

"I'd love to see your hair Delilah, could you let it down for me?,"

"Um, well, it's having a not so luscious day today, do you mind if I leave it up?."

I've seen a couple of psychiatrists about the hair-pulling but it didn't help at all. Syrupy, overly kind ladies, sitting cross-legged, folder and notes on lap, nodding sympathetically at me over their glasses.

"I see Cathy, I see. And how did you feel after you'd pulled your hair out this week? How did the pulling make you feel afterwards?." It made me feel like shite of course woman. What a load of old cobblers. Once, during an exceedingly crap period in my life, I started pulling at my hairline, not a good area to be plucking at. Within days I began to resemble Bill Bailey as the hair line moved back and back. I was terrified at the thought of what I could potentially end up looking like and managed to stop pulling at that particular area by shifting my focus to food. This resulted in my troughing through an entire walk-in larder in a friend's house I was looking after at the time. I gained two stone but kept my hairline.

I met a man for an escort booking a couple of days ago who said he'd been deeply unhappy for years to the extent he'd been regularly ringing the Samaritans, such was his pain and anguish. My therapy/escort session ran thus, whilst he lay there clothed in a very neat and becoming lilac twin-set from M&S; a knee-length skirt, broderie anglaise blouse, thick tights and flat, sensible shoes. It all seemed perfectly normal and he rather suited the outfit;

"So, are you married?,"

"No," he replied, sounding utterly dejected.

"I was but we split up about five years ago, I've been struggling since then with stuff." (I'm thinking 'stuff' has to do with the ladies outfit)

"Stuff?,"

"Yes I've been so low and desperate I've been ringing the Samaritans."

"You poor thing what's the matter?,"

"I'm confused, just very confused." (He doesn't know if he's into men or women is my bet).

"Well, I always used to really fancy women but I really struggle to get turned on by a woman now."

"Ok so when was the last time you were aroused by a woman?,"

"About five years ago."

"And have you ever been aroused by a man?,"

"Yes about three months ago," he said with a sheepish little smile.

"Ah!," I exclaimed triumphantly, "you're gay! go and have a ball, have twenty balls!."

"Well yes but I'm so ashamed Delilah. My family would never cope with the shame of it, my cousin Paula might understand I suppose, she's very broad-minded."

"Ring cousin Paula tomorrow and say you need to see her for a chat. Just do it, it's your life. So what if you like men, I like the Wurzels. Even went to see them in concert, how bad can it be?."

"You know, you're right, you're damn well right. I'm so glad I came here today, you're an amazing woman!."

So off he went, having changed back into men's clothes, a lot merrier than when he arrived. He rang me the next day to say he'd spoken to Paula who threw her arms around him, put the kettle on and said she'd suspected he liked men years ago. Imbued with confidence he then rang and told the rest of his family, including his ex wife and grown up children. No one was in the least shocked. Two weeks later he rang me to say he'd met a man online and was having the most wonderful time and when he was married I was to be invited.

That little episode was a most satisfying one for me. I cannot honestly say that seeing two men holding hands fills me with a natural 'ahh how lovely' sensation, but keeping up the pretence of liking women when you actually like men, must be hard work.

February 29th 2005

Up at barn today, wind blowing a hooley. Phone rings and a guy says,

"You look amazing in your green panties in picture."

Meanwhile I'm putting calamine lotion on a goat. I really shouldn't answer the hooky phone when on farm. Very little money in bank, I'm starting to worry now. My mind is in constant fret mode, knowing I'm but two missed direct debit payments away from destitution.

I've registered with a care agency to bring in a bit more money and have been doing the occasional job for them, no personal care, just home help. So this was today's experience, helping an elderly couple in Peaseholme for two hours.. What a filthy pair of old crumblies. They are about 90 years old and pretty well out of it mentally which is a bit draining after a while. The wife, who is very gentle and sweet said to herself whilst tottering about the kitchen,

"That's a bit sticky, that won't do," referring to the work surface. She faffed around with a cloth and I left her to it. Later, I found the cloth laid neatly on the draining board and gave it a quick whiff to check on its freshness, reeling back at the smell of stale, pungent urine. She must have brought it in from the toilet where it had been used for some ghastly purpose. I shudder to think at the state of their underpants, as to my knowledge, no bathing went on under that roof.

One day, the husband peered at me with his rheumy old eyes as he sat down to the lunch I had prepared him. In a wobbly Scottish accent he croaked,

"Doont git any fatter! Doont git any fatter!".

Then, pointing at my stomach and dribbling, continued,

"Ree juice, ree juice!."

Jesus, even a stones throw from the grave, they still like 'em thin n shaggable. Anyway, a bit late for reducing thought I, having eaten from their fridge an assortment of items which were a day out of date; their son had said to me when I began working there, to help myself to food, a foolish gesture on his part had he been aware of my capabilities. I responded to his generous offer with a fake, dismissive wave of the hand in a 'oh you're very kind but I've had my two Ryvita today.' Once I was alone and the elderly couple were ensconced in the dining room, I set to with gusto, powering through the fridge contents like a pregnant sow; a whole quiche, a pack of seven hotdogs, a pot of most toothsome crayfish, two Cornettos and a bar of Dairy Milk.

March 3rd 2005

Jemima, one of my Southdown ewes looked close to lambing so I decided to stay up tonight as falling asleep spells disaster for me; I go into a hot chocolate and toast induced coma and wake up six hours later with disastrous consequences in the lambing shed. I'm at my absolute best when busy. Free time is not good, I eat loads, sit for hours, get rampant indigestion and then hate myself for not having achieved anything, a bit of pressure is good. Whilst waiting for signs of contractions which involved bi-hourly trips on foot in the dark, (she was too imminent to watch from beneath my duvet) I practised for hours on the bosses Steinway grand piano, as he's away this week, what an instrument, beautiful!

She began pushing in earnest at about midnight. By 12.45am she'd produced the plug from the cervix. By 1.00am there was a water bag and at 1.30am the first little lamb appeared. Thirty minutes after that she gently pushed the second one out. I watched the whole process clad in five thermal layers with a bottle of obstetric lubricant in my hand in case she needed help. March can be a cruel month to be born in when you're a sheep and damn cold for the shepherd too. But something takes over when it's a tiny life at stake and you go into practical mode, roll up your sleeves and temporarily forget your own discomfort, whether that be tiredness or cold or both.

Ideally, no intervention is best when a ewe is lambing. Premature pulling out of lambs by the well-meaning or impatient shepherd can result in the mother rejecting her lamb/s. The pushing part is part of the bonding process so unless she really does need help or just some gentle easing out, it's best to leave well *alone and keep an eye on the proceedings. I learnt this the hard way a few years ago and dived in too early to help a ewe. She consequently rejected both lambs and began ramming the little things in their ribcages and would have killed both had I not whisked them away quickly and put them under a heat lamp in the orphan lamb pen. This is not a case of the sheep being stupid, it is nature's way of rejecting one lamb so the other is more likely to survive in terms of her milk yield or any other number of reasons. But in my case I had interfered and being a first-time lamber she would have needed the bonding process even more. So she had a year of idling about, eating and sleeping and not rearing babies and I had two months of bottle rearing her twin female lambs. Both were so adorable I kept them as pets. See what I mean, I am hopelessly non commercial.*

'62z Lambkin's Sister, a much loved pet sheep'

Anyway I let Jemima lick her lambs clean, towelled them both as it was -2 degrees tonight, and dipped the umbilical cords of both in iodine which dries out and disinfects the cord. Mum had no colostrum at all in her udder so I mixed up some warm powdered replacement. By 8am she'd started to produce her own milk so I made my way back to hut for breakfast.

Colostrum is vital for a newborn lamb, without it, it will die. For six hours immediately following birth, the lamb's gut lining is permeable so the antibodies in the mum's colostrum are its first defence against infection. This transference of antibodies ceases at about 36 hours, so you can't hang about. It is also very high in fat and protein and is a laxative to stimulate the lamb's digestive system. All being well, a newborn is up on its feet and feeding within twenty minutes of birth.

Correctly presented, a lamb is born nose and front feet first, hooves pointing outward with the nose resting on top. The worst presentation is the 'head back' position, in this situation you have to reach inside and bring the head round but often it springs back again against the lambs side. I find it harder to lamb a head-back than a jumble of triplets. Remember you are working blind and so you do become experienced in what a back leg and a front leg feel like.

One also instinctively knows when a lamb is presenting as a breech because the mother is not stimulated correctly enough to want to push. In this scenario the lamb needs to be born ASAP as there is a risk the umbilical cord could break, the lamb will start to breath whilst still inside its mother and drown in the fluids. The best way of gaining lambing experience is to help out with other much larger flocks. You end up a stammering, incomprehensible wreck at the end, but it's worth it.

'In the thick of it'

March 6th 2005

A polite enough email from an older gentleman:

"Good morning Delilah, I have just come across your profile." (not literally I hope) "Can it be true? A real woman at last! Just honest and sensual and not a slave to the assumed male preferences. Perfect photos: red heels, lips, lacy lingerie and a pussy to die for, that's not been attacked by a Gillette. (I think you'll find you've just listed male preferences) I may have died and gone to heaven. A quick read through your blogs also had me smiling and a lot more informed on all matters rural. I need to make contact with this lady methinks.

So I will introduce myself; I am an easy going, white professional in my early 50's. Am often told I don't look my age and am of slimmish build. I am in a relationship but like so many of us, it is not perfect so from time to time I seek the pleasure of a different experience with another partner whilst recognising the need for careful planning and discretion for such a liaison. I am a man of the world and happy to go with the flow sexually. I do like sensual kissing and massage. The pleasure for me is the pleasuring of each other. I am not into the one sided approach taken by some of the male species! I am unfortunately based over in Hamthwaite," (hmm, could be handy, that's near the abattoir. He could collect the last batch of lamb joints I had done) "so it could take a bit of planning to get to you but it's do-able. When the coast is clear, I will give you a call to firm up details.

Malcolm xx"

March 8th 2005

Attempted to help the fanciable contract fencer today but I was of no use at all and followed him round like a pet hamster all afternoon in torrential rain, slipping on the leaf litter and impaling my knees on spikey horse chestnuts. However I was invaluable in offering my truck as a platform for him to stand on whilst cutting overhanging trees. Waited for the inevitable, "my girlfriend," reference, which came as I was reapplying my extra pouty lip gloss. Who cares, she can suck on his dodgy teeth.

March 10th 2005

The ever generous gardener agreed to sharpen his axe, in order that I may merrily set about the task of chopping up a tonne of chestnut for Archibald's wood stove. Not a hope did I have. Raising *arm in untypically girlie fashion, and letting the axe fall hopelessly on a log with all the force of a bread knife into a tea cake, I discarded said tool with a condescending 'pah, who the hell uses a bloody axe these days anyway, medieval.' Made mental note to ring tool hire company about a wood splitter.*

March 12th 2005

Met a proper old gypsy called Reginald, he was camped up on moorland by road in a bow top Romany caravan. Had a goat which he kept for milk. Offered me a tea so I asked for it weak with no sugar. Was strong enough to burn warts off and hideously sweet.

March 15th 2005

Shropshire Down lambed, not an overly big single but both front legs back at the shoulder so had I not been there to pull the legs forward, it would almost certainly have died. She timed it perfectly for choir practice and I was able to scurry back to hut, grab Beethoven's 9th score and motor off to the mad conductor. He seems to be becoming increasingly frustrated at our amateur attempts at learning and memorising timings, diminuendos and crescendos. I am genuinely afraid of finishing phrases because if one of us is a fraction of a beat out, he bloody well hears it, throws a furious look at the offending chorister and throws himself round the church with much vexatious phlegm. That said, he is a very gifted if rather tetchy musician and has the unenviable task of getting us to a high enough standard to perform the piece at City Hall in Kingston-upon-Hull in three months time.

Back from choir practice, two more logs in stove so it stays in all night, curl up in bed and check for any escorting texts. I am now, as you will read, more versed in the ways of men who have worked themselves up into a sexual lather and am better equipped to deal with the eyebrow lifting messages I receive on a daily basis. Hence..

"I want you to have my baby inside you."

(Don't be so bloody ridiculous)

"I'm interested in a 15 minute appointment, what's included?,"

"Hello, protected oral on you and boob play, all semen stays in condom."

"Do I get to touch your pussy?."

"No."

"Is your pussy shaven?, can I put fingers inside?."

"I'm not an oven-ready chicken, go away."

"Good evening, I can't take my eyes off your amazing pictures. What times are you available please? I'm hoping you're available! Thank you, Paul."

"Hi Paul, what time were you thinking?,"

"Is half an hours time too little notice?,"

"Can I ask your age please?,"

"I'm 47. Do you offer a cheeky little prostrate massage?,"

(No but I can offer a cheeky little boot up the ars)

"What? Good god no."

"Hi I from Leeds n saw profile impressed so wots your nearest station? Are you dd cup or e and do yu kiss wiv tounge pete."

"You need to be able to drive, I don't accept taxis."

"Wot you mean don't accept taxis?."

"I don't allow clients to arrive by taxi."

"Very strange y not? No diffrunt to a car if u want bizniz how far from station arl walk."

"20 miles. It's a valid reason. Taxi drivers gossip and are local to the area."

"Ok I don't mind a walk I'm fit wots nearest station?."

"Orkney."

"Orkney, never erd of it is it near Leeds? Are you d or e cup?,"

...and so it goes on, a mind numbing, steady lava flow of illiteracy and filth.

March 16th 2005

Farming, even on a small scale as I do, can still be difficult, particularly in the winter. Freezing rain and wind on a late February night, on your knees lambing twins, hands raw with cold and the lure of hot tea in a warm kitchen, can be testing for the spirit. But the familiar rustle and soft plop of a newborn lamb onto the straw, the first shake of its head and the first tiny bleat, its first breath in this world, is a heart-melting moment. I will never cease to be bowled over at the first birth of the new year.

A beautiful spring day today, up at 7am to bottle feed the orphans. The smaller of the two who had pneumonia seems improved after the injection I gave her. Tried to persuade Archie to start using Clik on his flock in the summer. When sprayed on the shoulders and back of the sheep, Clik migrates invisibly as if by magic, to cover all the woolly parts, thus protecting the sheep from the potentially devastating effects of the common bluebottle or blowfly as it's commonly known, which if left unchecked will lay its eggs in the fleece, the eggs then hatch and the maggots eat the sheep alive. This condition, known as fly-strike, is the biggest potential threat to life for an adult sheep, the risk being present from April through to October, depending on weather conditions. Often referred to by the peasant as, 'the maggot' or 'eez struck,' the victim will die a horrid death which is eventually caused by the toxins excreted by the maggots, entering into the sheep's bloodstream.

Many hundreds of years ago all sheep naturally shed their wool in May/June, but selective breeding has produced sheep that retain their wool indefinitely until man intervenes to shear it off. Certain breeds called 'primitives,' still shed wool naturally such as the Soay and Wiltshire Horn. Wool used to be a hugely valuable commodity, sadly the industry needs some reinventing if farmers are to get excited at the prospect of shearing off such a low value product, sadder still that shearing is one of the most skilled and respected jobs within agriculture.

Possessing the business brain of a beetle I kept the wool from ten Dorset Down ewes last year, carded it, spun it on my spinning wheel and knitted it into a kingsize Aran blanket, imagining I could make some much needed revenue. However if I'd factored in labour costs, the blanket would have had a retail value of roughly £2000, can't see 'em flocking at the farm gate at that price. It is beautiful though and in pride of place on my bed.

I am desperately in need of a turnover crate. This isn't a big wooden box for keeping fruit pastries in. It is a large, sturdily constructed metal crush that contains a sheep safely and comfortably, enabling the shepherd to invert said animal and trim its feet or any other procedure that can be carried out whilst sheep is upside down. Turning a 70kg sheep manually is a knack but that said, the job was a lot easier twenty years ago when my BMI wasn't the equivalent of a Kune Kune pig. Aside from a sheep's hefty size they are wise to the being caught, turned upside down and injected business, and upon seeing my approach, laden with sprays, clippers and syringes, dip their heads, plant four feet solidly on the ground and remained rooted to the spot like the Eiffel Tower. I have had to admit defeat on occasion and persuade a client who has visited me for the relief of sexual tension, to climb the hill and wrestle a sheep.

March 17th 2005

Has been fairly steady with regards to men these past few days, although yesterday and today the phone hasn't rung at all, slightly worrying but also bloody fantastic. Last guy I saw was a Scottish chap, 53 years old, very well spoken, smartly dressed, smelt lovely. Married for ten years, had regular if not frequent sex with his wife and fancied the occasional change. He'd not seen an escort for 15 years. As it turned out, he relieved himself via my speedy hand movements. Praise the Lord, it is a happy day indeed when I get to keep my pants on.

March 18th 2005

Escorting calls have dried up. Three men in succession have made a polite excuse upon their first clapping eyes on me at the hut door, and cleared off. I'm nearly up to my overdraft limit and I'm so worried I'd give this all up for a bedsit in Hackney if it meant a full bank account. I'm joking of course, I can think of nothing worse.

Have made important decision: remove all glamour photos, take some selfies and put those on profile instead.

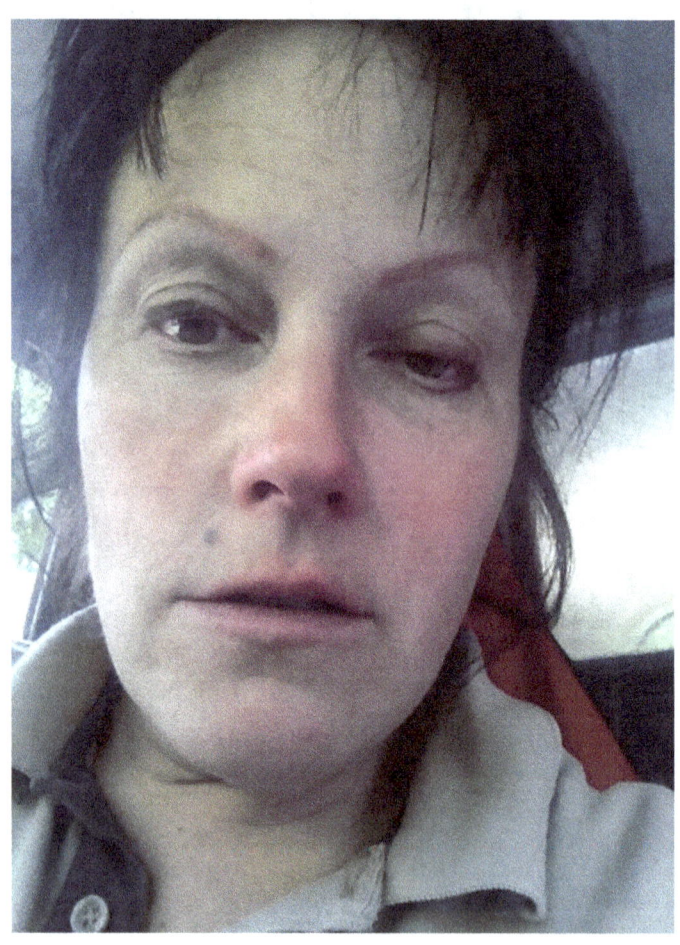

'The after'

March 19th 2005

Text just in:

"Fancy giving me a blowey, ow much?,"

"£30 what time?,"

"Ow many times can I unload?," (at this point I am well used to spotting a tattooed Sun reader under 25 years of age)

"Once."

"And can I fuck your ass for £60?,"

"You are clearly a sewer rat, go away."

"I want to fill your cunt."

"And a very angry young man, may I suggest counselling."

"D'you want my cock between your tits cos you don't sound very keen,"

(This one's a tad simple methinks)

"I am not available, you sound appalling."

"So arv gotta be a toffee nose ta shag ya av oi?,"

"The phrase, 'can I fuck your ass for £60,' wouldn't evoke an erotic response from any woman, be she escort or archdeacon."

"Ya done ask ya done get, bet your finkin bout me doin it to ya int ya?."

"No."

"So why you an escort then, you must be skint."

"Correct. I need ewe feed and a quad bike."

He stopped texting, presumably grunting his way back to the hole he'd been digging before he texted me, wondering I'm sure what on earth the words 'ewe' and 'quad' meant. The mention of these typically unfeminine things usually silences the over zealous texter.

Saw a 35 year old man today. He was an engineer in the Navy and suffered from OCD, insisting I wear latex examination gloves, which he'd provided, before I was permitted to touch his willy.

Another text..

"Hi Delilah are you free?,"

"I can do 6pm."

"Do you have any friends?,"

"No."

"Well could you possibly handcuff me then?,"

"Is that a sensible substitute for having friends?."

"Oh well never mind."

(At least he was polite)

March 21st 2005

Up at 5am today, took Nellie the collie across fields to open gates for Bill, a local chap who very reluctantly came to my aid this morning to move a load of haylage bales. They weigh about 400kg each, so why on earth I decided on big bales when the tractor here is out of action I've no idea. I thought it would be possible to cart sections of the bale to the sheep and cows with a wheelbarrow, which it was and I did, though it was hard bloody work.

Haylage is the stuff inside the huge, black plastic-wrapped bales you've probably seen in the fields and are sealed by shrink wrapping them to allow the damp grass within to ferment just slightly, thereby producing a product that's dust free and higher in feed value than hay, perfect for the delicate lungs of horses. Hay however is different and has had all the moisture removed by drying it in the sun for several days before baling it in the traditional way. Finally, silage is grass that has barely been left on the field once cut, for anytime at all, and therefore has a higher moisture content before being baled. It is strong stuff and mainly fed to cattle. Most dairy/cattle farmers are identifiable by carrying this smell about their person, regardless of how many baths they may have had or cans of Lynx used. This isn't a criticism, it's a compliment. I love the smell of silage, indeed I smelt of it for years. It's a rich, earthy, of the land smell.

I worked for a dairy farmer in my slender youth called Nobby Plowright, a bad tempered old git who hailed from Yorkshire. Permanent grumpiness aside, he was an excellent farmer and had the novel idea of channelling off the liquid grass juice that was produced by silage making. Its correct name is 'silage effluent,' and it is as unpleasant smelling as the name suggests. It wouldn't be my first choice as a green smoothie ingredient but it is highly nutritious and the cows went mad for it.

Anyway, Bill shifted the bales for me with his old Massey Ferguson so that was one job out of the way. It was cold last night so I'd put little lamb jackets on the smaller lambs and took them off this morning. Will put them back on if it's due to be cold tonight again. Sprayed the feet of two lambs that had scald, wormed Boo the Border Leicester and let Nellie drive sheep for a change instead of gathering. Always more of a challenge for a dog, but she's a champ and has it off to a fine art.

Have decided I quite fancy the bank manager, even though he looks about fifteen, is intimately acquainted with my bank balance and hence my penniless state and hopelessness with money. Vibrated the semen (fracking) out of another middle aged married man today with my vibrator. A marvellous appliance, powerful as a juicer and handy as a weapon of self defence should the need arise. It achieves the same result as sex, which I avoid at all costs.

March 22nd 2005

Well, there's a surprise. My newly uploaded fat photos onto the escorting website have not deterred men at all, am still getting plenty of enquiries. Funny that, if I put a fat photo (clothed) onto a dating site, not one response.

March 23rd 2005

Mabel the Golden Guernsey goat had twins today. Herdwick shearling needed help lambing, first lamb was backwards, second lamb had a front leg back but I didn't hang about pulling leg forwards because tongue was purple. First lamb fine but second one was lifeless even after swinging it. Did the usual of gently poking the nostrils with a piece of straw. Nine times out of ten the straw trick produces an intake of breath but not on this occasion. So I covered its entire mouth and nostrils with my mouth and blew gently till I could see the lungs inflate. It gave a gasp and began breathing, I was chuffed to bits.

Transported 150 bales from local shooting estate, back to my barn. Trailer only carries sixteen bales so was a bit of a mission. Hay poking through leggings and sticking to the sweaty crotch of my Tesco pants, was wistfully imagining how glorious it would be to skip in weightless fairy fashion from one easy task to the next. A hay bale is not particularly heavy, between 20kg and 35kg depending on the state of disrepair and stage of dilapidation of the *baling machine and the competence of the operator back in the hot balmy days of the previous summer.*

Having never met the baling machine in question or its operator, I cursed each time a four foot long bale, heavy as lead was followed by a two foot long hobbit sized bale. Still, the barn is now solidly filled to the roof with hay, which I find myself casting smug looks at. Whilst loading, a well spoken lad rang asking if he could see me in the next thirty minutes which was an absolute no no as I'm completely covered in hay, with smelly armpits and crotch and a painful hip that's rendered my gait to the shuffling limp of the witch in Hansel and Gretel. I feel very much like a witch these last few weeks; it would feel completely natural to wear a black cloak, striped woolly stockings and pointy black boots, hissing at anyone who crosses my path. I took a reluctant look in the rear view mirror today, to see how I'm faring against the ravages of time. The results are disappointing to say the least.

March 24th 2005

It's 9.30am and a guy rings....

"Ohh hi iz thiz Deelayla?," in a dark, syrupy voice that portended the arrival of some foul request.

"Yes, this is she, how may I be of assistance?," deliberately putting on my NatWest online Chat Help voice.

"Yiz Deelayla I want to give you massage wiv ma bodee, iz dat orkee Deelayla?,"

"Yes that's fine," (I'm sounding less cheery now as his voice seems to have lowered and the sure signs of 'I want to do something to you even the animal kingdom would baulk at' are apparent in his voice.)

"Yiz Deelayla and I want you to massage me wiv your bodee, iz dat orkee?,"

"Yep." (I'm only staying on the phone out of curiosity now and for the purposes of additional book material)

"So I'd like to bring some scented sheets, iz dis orkee Deelayla?,"

"Yep yep carry on," (my toast is burning so let's have the finale)

"Deelayla the sheets will be scented wiv da rose and da lemon, iz dat orkee Deelayla?,"

"Yes!!! Fine!!," (Gritted teeth now, hurry the fuck up)

"I'm going to put something on the sheets to relax you, dat orkee wiv you Deelayla?,"

(I'm thinking he's not referring to Comfort fabric conditioner)

"Ah, ok, yes I'll stop you there. Something to make me comatose before you slip your cock up my poor old backside is it? What IS the matter with you men?

"How did you know dis Deelayla?."

Phone call ends.

March 27th

I'd quite like bigger nipples, it might increase phone calls; a set of National Geographic teats, the sort you see on tribal Africans that have multi suckled crèche loads of kids since they were twelve. Might be a bit eye-catching in cold weather though.

Had an irritating call early this morning whilst enjoying a sunrise walk with my dogs. It ran thus, in a small, terrified voice with a strong Indian accent,

"Ah.. um, are u dwing thee vawterspots?."

"No I am not."

"Oh, uh kaykay, so.. um, ah, are u dwing thee humillyashin?."

"No, I am dwing thee dog walking."

March 29th 2005

It is midnight and as usual my inner clock is nowhere to be seen as I fry meatballs, onions and mushrooms at this indigestible hour. It's been a tough month with my overdraft tiptoeing on the edge of its limit. I meanwhile continued with my fruitless attempts at satisfying the occasional male visitor. Last night I waddled off to bed, adopted the usual starfish position and reached out in the darkness for the little bottle of Otex, an ear-wax softener, and promptly poured Otrivine nasal drops into my ear and over the side of my face. No harm done so I can only assume the two products are interchangeable.

April 2nd 2005

Busy day today, up early to walk collies, straight back to mucking out sheep shed then to vets to pick up antibiotic. The veterinary practice is on a large, pedigree Aberdeen Angus cattle farm and whilst sat in my pick-up, I foolishly took an escort call on my mobile. Listening to the guy on the other end enquiring after fantasy role-play and high-heel domination, his diminutive and ashamed little voice overpowered by the thunderously loud roaring of 100 cattle being turned out to grass after six months inside, he promptly hung up, despite my reassuring words of,

"Sorry about the cows, how can I help?."

Now here's a gruesome truth. Doggie style when you're 100% not into it, hurts. I tense my fanny up, pull some involuntary lemon-sucking expressions, bite the duvet and pray to God (sorry God) that he relieves himself as soon as possible. Big willies are obviously the worst, (it's true what they say about black men which is why after two experiences I refuse to see them) I simply couldn't do this job without KY Jelly and am frequently asked, 'so what turns you on?,' which irritates me as I'm stupefied as to what reply I can give that won't send them running for the hills. The honest answer would be 'absolutely nothing,' but I dilute it a little to 'I can't remember.' Doggie style though, for all its discomfort and degradation is actually the best, because I don't have to force a smile and can screw my face up while he grunts away like a sow in an apple orchard.

"It feel good babe?,"

"Mm," I reply unconvincingly, deciding which project to put the £60 towards, a new exhaust or hen-house.

April 5th 2005

Perfect timing as needed £60 for two singing lessons; saw a tiny little Moslem guy. He was so petit, it was farcicle to see my chunky frame next to his.

As luck would have it, he laid on bed, propped up on a pillow wearing a teeshirt and shorts and said he was 'happy to just talk.' Oh how I loved the tiny little Moslem man. He asked if I slaughter the lambs myself,

"No, I take them to a licensed abattoir, as is the law in this country."

"When lambs are killed properly," he continued, "they stretch their necks out to offer themselves to Allah." (Yeah right)

At this I earnestly wished him gone and so complained of a fictitious sore throat. He cordially took his leave of me and as he left, handed me a tiny bottle of bee propolis 'for my throat.'

Not one for following directions, (five drops) I sloshed some in a glass of water and gulped it down.

April 8th 2005

Had what I thought was going to be a perfectly normal fart, and a litre of orange liquid with bits of bee in, came out.

I went to see Handel's Messiah in London this week, ticket cost was £50, which I could have spent on hiring a carpet cleaner. Now let me state here that Verdi's Requiem leaves me completely breathless with wonder, and having performed it myself, I find it an incomparably stunning piece of work. And Beethoven...there are no words to fully express the sheer majesty and complex beauty of this man's musical output. I have listened to his 9th Symphony at least one hundred times and have and never will, tire of it.

But Handel's Messiah? I found it as emotionally stimulating as hoovering. My backside was unbearably numb and what with the constant mucus build up in my throat due to acid reflux and the ineffective shifting from one buttock to the other in an attempt to relieve the pressure of the unyielding wooden chair, I fucking hated Handel by the time 9pm finally arrived. Furtively coughing and gulping in Gollum fashion, I was desperate, desperate to go home and sprawl in my delicious bed. I closed my eyes for long periods and imagined childish words to replace the incomprehensible stuff I was hearing; 'this spider is rejected' and 'we love sheep,' were my only moments of release from the mental torture of two hours of Handel. Never again.

April 10th 2005

Just received a call on this crisp, beautiful morning;

"Yeh, ello, that er..Delilah?," whispered in a dark, troubled, guilt-laden voice and sounding as if he'd just emptied his granny's teapot of her life savings for three hours with a hooker.

"You about this afternoon?,"

"Yes I am!," I replied cheerily.

"Er, just one question, you got er..boots?,"

"Boots? You mean welly boots?,

"No I mean like..knee-length,"

I hung up.

I've just waited up until midnight for a bloke driving from Sheffield. He arrived here and parked directly in front of Archibald's house, headlights on and engine running. He may as well have banged on their door and asked, 'hello, is your prostitute at home?,' bloody cretin. Anyway he had brought with him a bottle of red wine which I'll turn into mulled for sipping on my own one evening, much nicer. I'm not good with grown up things like alcohol, shame as it would be great to show off a love and knowledge of wine, alas anything stronger than Ribena and I wake up with a head like a hornets nest. We chatted, he said I was a woman of good taste and could tell this by the goats cheese I had sitting in my kitchen.

Lying on the bed looking slightly startled as the hut swayed to and fro in the wind, he announced,

"I don't think I can go through with this, I feel a bit guilty."

He was married with two kids. I suspect the truth is he didn't fancy me because I have the sexual aura of Benny from Crossroads. Oh well £70 for talking nonsense for thirty minutes.

April 12th

Do astronauts take their iPhones to space? Do iPhones work in space? Now there's a cool text to receive, "home soon dear, just leaving Saturn," mind you, compared to some of the whoppers you guys tell your wives it sounds pretty feasible. Knapsacking weeds today, it was bloody hot and I feel slightly odd after inhaling herbicide, nothing a cup of Earl Grey can't cure. A ewe turned on my collie today protecting her lamb, dog is scared of sheep now and hides under truck, she's fine with weaned lambs as they scuttle about and do her bidding. She'll be right as rain tomorrow.

April 15th 2005

Saw an odd Irish fellow, wanted to watch me on the loo, having a wee. Then asked if I wouldn't mind stealing a pair of worn panties from my lady employer. WTF.

Jesus why am I not in bed yet, Ive got to be away at 7.30am for a sheep show. I just can't be normal and have a fixed daily routine, yet half of me craves the comfort and dependability of routine, the other half hates it. The only routine I have imposed on me is the mind meltingly dull, fixed series of polite questions I ask the poor blighters that turn up to see me. I am ashamed to admit that I have stopped all pretence of behaving and looking like a respectable escort and shuffle out to greet men in a bewildering, drab cocktail of bleach-stained and goat-chewed leggings, a Christmas pudding jumper and purple crocs. I am so relieved I have stopped allowing oral sex on me. It is an odious and often odiferous chore which I was only able to suffer by placing a pillow on my belly to hide the face of a woman who looks like she's watching a football match in the rain.

April 17th 2005

Text from someone calling themselves 'SissySlutthe23rd.'

"Hey are you looking for a kinky sex slave for whatever you want? If you want I can do your domestic cleaning, laundry and everything. Also I love to get dressed as a slut with ladies clothes and undies and then to get fucked with dildo with strap on. Also if you want you can pee in my mouth and whatever you want Miss, so can I serve you Miss? If you are interested please text me. Only

text never call. I would pay you to serve you so please text me Miss thanku"

(What the?...)

April 19th 2005

Woken early this morning by my text alert beeping. I reached out an arm in the dark and blinked, bleary eyed at the screen,

"Hi Delilah I'm Martin, a 45 year old, slim-built white guy from Manchester. I think you look fantastic and I'd like to book you for two hours face-sitting please. Yours respectfully, Martin."

Well this was a new one on me. I would have said it was pretty much lacking in self respect on the part of the sitee to have an 11 stone woman with piles and wind sit on your face, but fair play to the bloke, he did ask very respectfully.

"I'm afraid I don't offer that service."

"That's a shame cos you've got a lovely bum that's just perfect for face-sitting, however I respect your wishes and won't ask again. Goodbye and good luck to you. Yours respectfully, Martin."

I sighed a deep sigh, a sigh that could only come from a woman at 6am who'd been asked respectfully to sit on a man's face.

I have been escorting for a few months now and it conerns me a tad, that instead of being in a state of permanent shock that I should have stooped to such a level, I simply find it all so tortuously dull. However I've mentioned this before and I'll say it again; having suffered all my life with various brain maladies, ranging from horrendous depression, pulling my hair out, self induced starvation and wholesale laxative consumption, through to monstrous and super rapid weight gain, escorting has cured the lot! All my life I was convinced that meeting the perfect man would make everything better and that love would replace iced buns.

Any wise person will tell you that's it's only when you've sorted your own head out and are not living the daily psychological equivalent of bungee jumping, can you ever hope to meet and be happy with anyone else. The viewing of many willies up close, has, to put it simply, burst the bubble of imaginary romance and fantastical happiness. Heathcliff wasn't a raven-haired, passionate, bodice-ripping, gorgeous vagabond, beneath which lay tender, loving, husband material. He was an uneducated farmer's son who beat women and dug up the ten years dead, love of his life, Cathy, and cuddled her skeleton. Mind you, given a choice, I'd choose Heathcliff over a nice guy any day.

Escorting then has cured me of the black demon that has shadowed me all these years. I'm certainly not advocating that shagging for money is a cure-all for every drug-ridden, self-harming, bulimic teenager. But for me it has done the trick.

Had an email from the tannery to say my sheepskins are ready for collection. I must stop keeping them for myself and try to sell them, as my home is looking like a Flintstone film set. And what with the bags of carded wool from last years shearing which I need to spin, it's getting full in here.

I saw a man today that told me he was a spastic, poor chap. He was all bent up with tiny shrunken arms that paddled about in front of him like a little T.Rex. He was rather bad tempered and unpleasant but I forced myself to be nice, inflicted as he was by his dinosaur appendages.

The mental pressure of leaping between the two occupations, farming and prostitution, has rendered me incapable of behaving in any way seductive, hence,

"Will you be requiring oral sex?," is delivered with the mundanity of,

"Would you like some help with your packing?."

I saw a Chinese client yesterday called Andy, a serious young man in his mid thirties whose English was virtually non-existent. He was an odd chap and kept popping his head towards me in a chicken-type, pecking movement, repeating,

"Kees kees I wan kees. I wan you be my go fwen."

After what seemed an eternity of listening to him and dodging his pecking, he went to use the nice Victorian water jug, bowl and clean white towel I always provide in my gypsy caravan. During his strangely wild ablutions he ended up throwing water everywhere; floor, walls, and finished by dropping the sopping towel on floor. The hut looked like he'd been pressure washing an elephant's enclosure, rude fucker, he's not coming back that's for sure. Andy had brought with him stick-on tattoos of the Chinese year of the something, gaily coloured gaudy looking things. Anyway he insisted my bottom was the loveliest thing ever and had me roll over whilst he stuck them to my buttocks and sat back admiringly, ruminating on the view as if he'd painted The Haywain on my ars. I had a hell of a job removing them with facial scrub when he'd gone. He texted me the next day and for several days after that, telling me he'd learned to play Scarborough Fair on his acoustic guitar and that he would very much like to come round and serenade me. Hmm...no, you're alright thanks, I have the Simon and Garfunkel recording.

April 21st 2005

Sweep the collie took fright at thunder and dissappeared all last night, was worried but he turned up today looking very bedraggled. I am officially old, I only listen to Radio 4. Seen a few cocks this week, some miniscule and others chunky. Saw a barrister today, who, having been told by me to keep his voice down as we had workmen in the yard, boomed out during the act, "I say old girl just whip the jonny off and rub some gel on my naked old man." He made odd staccato "ah ah ah" noises like a baby after a good dosing of gripe water. I'm mentally shot due to the number of clothes changes I make everyday, from toiling peasant to rustic slut. It's pretty much like Robin William's Mrs Doubtfire, apart from the plastic face, well not yet anyway.... Have found a bull hopefully. Tomorrow must trim goats feet.

April 23rd 2005

I managed to skilfully slot a client in between two lambing ewes this evening, figuratively not literally. The experience was not a good one and was the only time I've ever felt in danger. Having raced back from the lambing shed and Imperial Leathered the afterbirth off my hands and arms, enticed Nellie off the bed and removed dog hair and straw, I awaited his phone call. Normally a well developed sixth sense provides me with enough information to put a rough picture of the client together and as a result there are many texts and calls I ignor. Contrary to the old saying, 'never judge a book by its cover,' in escorting I always judge a book by its cover. For example:

"You working today?,"

It is with almost absolute certainty that the composer of the above text is under the age of 35. Or if he is well past that age then he is most definitely not worth bothering with because he is incapable of stringing a polite text together. Whereas:

"Hi Delilah, are you available today at all?,"

The above individual is ok; polite and with a good grasp of punctuation and grammar, which in turn seems to produce a polite human being. However in this case, I hadn't seen any clients for several days because I simply couldn't face it. But being now in the midst of illuminating a new calligraphy commission, I was in need of a book of gold leaf and so was compelled to see someone. Thus my antenna were not fully extended. In hindsight, all the signs were there of someone 'odd.' He'd said he was 38 on the phone, in a strangely quiet, barely comprehensible voice. Also his texts were neanderthal;

"U free I need to cum see you."

I must have been mad to follow up a text like this. So when he stepped out of his car into the darkness, I was apprehensive. Suffice to say if it weren't for Nellie who can be very aggressive with male strangers, I think he would have slung me some punches. He never made it as far as the gypsy caravan as I concocted a concrete excuse to get his weird aggressive person off the place ASAP. His actual words were:

"You never said it were a shitty farm on a mountain. I'd get real angry but I don't wanna get bit by that dog."

Thank you Nellie thank you, you saved my bacon.

I saw a regular this afternoon, he makes the journey to see me about once a month, is a pleasant enough chap and drives a sporty mini that is always immaculate so I don't imagine the muddy, rutted track up the hill can be very enticing for him. He is another fan of the clothes peg scenario, not something I can quite get my head around, but then I'm blessed with the heightened sexuality of a 60 year old nun. He places a peg on each of his nipples and I sit there looking at him, waiting until the increasing pain somehow results in semen at the other end. It's all marvellously quick and devoid of any interaction on my part.

All semen stays in the condom with every client. The stuff repulses me. I don't know why but it evokes an instant gag reflex if I so much as get a whiff of it, a strange reaction to something that brought about my existence. But then blood and entrails and mucus are essential to life, doesn't mean I have to enjoy the smell, taste or texture of them.

During the act of mouth on willy, I find myself fixing my attention on their feet, simply because I'm bored to the point I could scream, and lying there, my head amongst their baubles and bits, comparing the differences in their nail lengths, toe length, instep height, bunions, callouses and general foot care, all helps to keep me awake. I did fell asleep once; I was tired, having had two hours sleep during lambing, and the guy had a huge stomach that very handily obscured my head from his view. With my mouth on his willy and my head resting on his upper thigh, it was very comfortable indeed and I slipped into a delicious snooze. I was awoken by him calling my name repeatedly, wondering why I had been motionless for five minutes.

A client did an extraordinarily kind thing today, to this date no one has ever gone to such trouble, particularly as he was a stranger. He'd spent half an hour in the hut, and was preparing to leave as I bewailed my sorry circumstances, also including my mother in the wailing as she'd run out of cigarettes and bread and had asked me to take her some round. Hand on heart, I was not intentionally squeezing charity out of him, it hadn't entered my head, I moan to anyone who'll listen about my inability to budget. Quite unexpectedly he gave me an extra £40 as a gift, asked where my mother lived, and on his way home, dropped cigarettes and bread round to her. May he live a long, happy and prosperous life, wherever he is.

A couple of ghastly texts arrived today. It is astounding that for the last forty years of my existence, from my beginnings as a single cell, an unknown parallel universe has existed alongside me, a universe of men who send texts such as,

"I'm quite tactile and like to kiss, is this ok with you? And I was wondering how wet you get. Also do you squirt, gush and cum?. Is there anything that you definitely wouldn't do?."

(Well, the five things you've just mentioned for starters)

"Fuck you, you fucking scumbag, you're a fucking prostitute."

He seemed a bit wound up, so I left him to it.

"Do you do any animal related stuff?."

(Oh – my – god)

"I'm looking for a woman who I can watch on the toilet having a shit, is this a service you can offer?."

"Nope."

And finally, before I turn in with my cocoa,

"You shud be a model!."

"I look like I'm wearing the fat suit from Little Britain and I'm 38, don't be ridiculous."

April 24th 2005

My anxiety levels rose alarmingly a couple of weeks ago and I found myself with a seemingly incurable and compulsive urge to nod my head. Yes yes I know, go ahead and laugh. It gave me a horrendous headache and foul temper and was totally exhausting. I went to the doctor who feigned interest in my odd condition with a series of suppressed yawns and with a dismissive wave of her Bic, referred me to a nodding head therapist. A day and time was arranged for an initial telephone consultation and having driven to my local village pub in order to get sufficient mobile signal, for such is the way of things in medieval Yorkshire, I sat in my truck awaiting her call. It is an odd and depressing situation to have a stranger, a woman in this case, speak the following words in a hushed and sympathetic voice on a gloriously sunny day;

"And do you, or have you ever had, any thoughts of ending your own life?,"

"A couple."

Even more hushed and caring now,

"I see, and have you ever had any need or desire to harm yourself?,"

I realise the young lad clearing moss from the cobbles outside the pub has probably been listening to our entire conversation.

"I pull hair out of myself, does that count?,"

"I see, and can I ask you Cathy, do you consider yourself to be or have you ever considered yourself to be, a danger to others?,"

(Only if I haven't eaten for two hours)

"No, I don't believe so."

And so the conversation droned on, until in the end I made some excuse about farm work and bad her politely goodbye.

Sitting here looking down at my enormous breasts, I notice they have become more and more pendulous and that I am no longer able to see my nipples. As I have gained weight, they seem to have rotated and the nipples now point downwards, like a dairy cow.

April 25th 2005

Gorgeous man on farm today servicing tractors, just perfectly delicious. Don't think he had similar thoughts, seeing my lunar module sized ars in a farm boiler suit.

April 26th 2005

Number 52 ewe had the beginnings of a waterbag out of her back end today, kept a close eye but after three hours with no signs of her wanting to push and still happily munching away on hay, I decided to take action and suspecting either a breach or ringwomb, as both these conditions don't trigger the pushing urge, I discovered to my dismay that it was in fact ringwomb. Diagnosis is simple, when a hand is placed inside the vagina for examination, it cannot move beyond the cervix because it hasn't dilated, even though the lambs are ready and waiting to be born. I learnt from the vet afterwards that there is some evidence to suggest that the condition may be a mineral/trace element deficiency. There used to be a highly effective drug available, that when injected, with some gentle manipulation, caused a ewe to dilate successfully. It has since been removed from use, so the only treatment is endless patience by manual dilation, something I wasn't confident enough to do. It is not always successful and the skill lies in knowing when to stop and perform a Caesarian. Either procedure entailed calling the vet which I did. He was here within thirty minutes, striding leisurely up the hill, bucket of equipment in hand, whistling away, with me hopping around watching him approach, hissing to myself,

"Hurry the fuck up, she's going to lose these lambs!."

After giving her an epidural he manipulated the cervix for well over half an hour until I was convinced there were now two dead lambs in there, (she'd been scanned so I knew how many to expect) and all the time giving me sound advice on potato growing and bee keeping.

To my amazement he delivered two big, healthy lambs. For once I didn't care about the bill and was over the moon. I returned home a very happy shepherd to be greeted by the first text of the day,

"Hi I'm Ryan, 23 years old and wd love to meet. I love a mature lady, it's my fantasy. You have a beautiful pair of tits if you don't mind me saying."

"Actually I bloody well do mind you saying, I've just had twins and you've spoilt the moment, please go away."

He went away, probably confused as to why a woman would offer escort services so soon after giving birth, especially to twins.

And another,

"Hello, what a beautiful body you have. I like the fact you work off your home, that will make it more relaxing. Do you offer domination and hardsports. I will like to be your toilet slave for a session, what time suits you best for that?."

"You clearly haven't read the profile."

Not sure which pissed me off most about this text; the fact he's into faeces or wincingly bad grammar. "Work off your home," indeed.

By the way, 'hardsports' is sexual activity involving poo. I know, me neither.

April 29th 2005

Was very silly and agreed to see a man after 8pm. I don't like late evening bookings as clients that are available at this time of day tend to be on the dodgy side (why aren't they at home emptying the dishwasher and watching Match of the Day?). Many of them are a bit thick and a tad rough around the edges. Put it this way, my endless chattering of choir activities and the magnificence of Verdi's Requiem doesn't sink below the surface of these wretched creatures. You think I sound cruel and presume too much? Read on..

He sounded quite normal and nice on the phone, although I thought I detected a hint of, 'I'm still looking good at 50 with long hair,' tone in his voice. He drove into the farmyard and emerged from his van looking like the brother of Catweazel on a lifetimes free supply of marijuana, complete with long, greying Gandalf hair and reeking of hashish. My heart sunk, this was not good. 10pm and a whole tortuous hour lay before me of feigned pleasure with an ageing hippy who had no detectable whiff of soap about his person.

Where do I begin? The man was perfectly horrid, all sinew and angles and odd erratic behaviour, presumably as a result of drugs. Throughout the hour he pulled some awfully theatrical expressions in an attempt I assume to look every inch the porn star, which included putting one finger between his teeth (his own finger) and biting it, in what he hoped was a look of sexual abandonment, he looked a bloody idiot. I decided the best way forward would be an hours intensive comedy entertainment in a desperate attempt to get away with no sexual activity whatsoever.

After 45 minutes he was incapable of an erection, became extremely annoyed at me and blamed the soft equipment problem on my Dawn French capers. Me being a bit concerned at this point for my safety, I offered half his money back whereupon he instantly sweetened and took his polite leave of me.

It can't buy you love but it can buy your way out of a flogging from Catweazel.

May 2nd 2005

Text arrived at 7am, 7am! How can these blokes be thinking of sex at this hour?! I'm thinking of tea, just tea.

"Bet you woz well fit wen you woz 25 wiv a fitt figur."

I think he'd gone beyond 'lazy' grammar with this one, no grasp of the English language at all.

May 15th 2005

"Hello Delilah, Dr Andy here again. I've got to do an emergency list tomorrow so cannot make my session, however I have managed to swap for Monday morning off, so if it's ok with you, might you be free next Monday at 10am? As it is, the erection in my scrubs whilst looking at your profile is very unprofessional. I'm sure someone will notice it! Sorry about tomorrow. Cheerio, Dr Andy."

Of course, he didn't turn up the following Monday or any other day. I suspect he was no more Dr Andy than I am Chief Superintendent Waterhouse. Men really are most odd. Made myself a vanilla Chai and opened some more texts;

"Hi I would like to play with your pussy to see what I could get up you, toys, cucumber, fingers, maybe see how many fingers. Your thoughts on this please?."

(My thoughts? You don't want to hear them.)

"Hi there naughty perfection, need a sex slave or toy this evening?."

"Nope."

"Can I fuck you in you pussy hole with condon mind me asking."

(Terrible use of English, terrible, get thee gone)

Thank god, I've seen two clients today; I was in the severe doldrums this morning due to a large overdraft, and was sat in the dairy eating hobnobs, envisaging my new home as a shelter made from birch branches and heather on the moors, when my employer walked in,

"I say! There's an appslootlee huuge dawg's mess on the front lawn, could you deal with it please, thenk yor."

My first client of the day was a chap called Tony, 58, a butcher from Colne in Lancashire, who had been messaging and emailing me constantly since he first discovered my profile and had no doubt been masturbating furiously between furtive peeks online while his wife cooked supper. He must surely have been salivating over the thought of meeting me in person, the poor buggar.

After trivial conversation for as long as I could string it out, the dreaded moment arrived and he came at me, poking his tongue around my mouth. This with someone who you find as visually stimulating as a washing-up rack is just, well, bloody horrible. Try as I might to conceal my disgust, I instinctively pull back my head. It's like having a live eel in your mouth except that on balance I'd prefer a live eel, at least it can't leave negative feedback on my profile for not returning the gesture. Anyway, thank heavens he ejaculated reasonably quickly after five minutes of concentrative grinding while I kept my eyes closed and gave some thought to the latest DEFRA cattle passport regulations.

The second chap was David, a thoroughly nice man in his early 70's, who only required quick relief with my vibrator, five minutes work.

May 16th

Email:

"I am 25 years old and haven't been with many women. Does this put you off? I need to be completely honest. I was born with Achondroplasia which is a type of dwarfism. I stand at 4ft 11" and naturally have confidence issues. The reason why I am looking online is to try and find someone who can teach me a few things but also be comfortable in doing so (if that makes sense). I saw your profile and it stood out. I just think by getting confidence this way, will help me overall. Does this make sense? x."

Oh I just couldn't, dear little hobbit man.

May 17th 2005

Molly's lamb who was born three days ago, has a nasty and very worrying stomach infection. Gut problems in young lambs are never good. I noticed it several days ago and gave him an injection of antibiotic and Loxicom which reduces inflammation. He improved for a while but seems to have worsened again, so I've stomach-tubed him with electrolytes which rehydrate. According to the vet, it's not the infection that kills the lamb but the dehydration. Also the Southdown ewe who had twins has a bad case of mastitis, I knew straight away because when I let them all out for their morning feed, she stayed sitting there. I had a look and sure enough, one side of her udder was hard and hot to the touch; gave her antibiotics and Loxicom.

May 18th 2005

Molly's lamb is not looking good despite having given it every drug in my medicine cabinet. As he tottered out to the field this morning, I noticed he was lame and on picking him up I saw his little hooves had blood on them and nibble marks. A rat had been chewing at his feet. Rats are wily little fuckers and can sense when an animal is not right and a meal might be on the cards. They smell infection and decaying flesh, yucharty bloody yuch. The only thing I could think of was to paint his hooves with coal tar to discourage the rats.

May 19th 2005

Shocking news, the lamb was dead this morning and had been half eaten by rats. Even worse, the Southdown ewe that has mastitis was sat in the corner with blood on the ground surrounding her udder. The rats had eaten half her udder away, leaving the barn looking like a Stephen King movie set. I chucked the dead lamb in a bag, ready for the livestock incinerator guys to collect, gave the poor ewe antibiotics and painkillers and sprayed the whole area with Terramycin spray. Amazingly, once I'd helped her to her feet, she staggered out into the field. Rang the pest control man there and then, he was out here within the hour and laid bait points in the barn.

So Molly is childless but doesn't seem bothered over the loss. She'd known the poor little thing wasn't right for some time and subconsciously distanced herself, maybe sensing it may not make it, in the same way the rats sensed it. Had Molly been a woman she would have needed hundreds of hours of counselling and would have shunned the sexual advances of her husband for evermore. My ewe toddled off and began grazing with an 'oh well there's always next year,' wag of her tail. On the subject of sheeps' tails, did you know they wag them vigorously when happy?. Just like a dog, when I give the sheep a scratch, I get a full blown wagging session, very sweet.

May 20th 2005

Result, got the bastard! Huge dead rat at the same spot I'd found Molly with a chewed udder, the bait had worked. I found this rat episode chilling, gruesome stuff. The ewe is doing fine but I'm keeping an eye on her for maggots because her damaged udder could attract bluebottles. Have jabbed her again today with antibiotic and resprayed her udder, she should be fine although I'll never be able to breed from her again. She'll spend the next ten years in retirement until she dies of old age, costing me in hay and straw and generally loafing about enjoying life. I'm happy though, bless her.

May 23rd 2005

A man rang me today and asked if i would consider performing sexual acts with his dog. I replied with a string of expletives, none of which are repeatable. The man needs help, preferably from a Rottveiler with a temper. Saw a thoroughly nice man today, having sucked his willy, he changed one of my ceiling spotlight bulbs and helped me stack firewood.

May 27th 2005

Text conversation:

"Good evening Delilah, how are you? Would you be available for a dinner date on Valentine's Day evening with me and a possible stay over with you? Love your profile. Hope to hear from you soon. Love and kisses. Jay xxx."

(Valentine's day? It's nearly June!)

"Hi, I'm sorry I do not offer overnights." (Christ one hour is hideous enough)

"I'm very interested in making a booking with you for Valentine's day evening for a special hour with you. Love and kisses. Jay xxx."

"Ok great."

"Once I get time for a booking hun I will let you know. Is there anything you would like to do when we meet hun? Love and kisses. Jay xxx."

(Well you could cut the love n kisses cobblers for a start)

"I don't take advance bookings especially when they're months off as in your case, because such clients are almost always living in a fantasy world, where they have no intention of ever seeing an escort, and are merely playing around texting. If you would like to

pay me a visit, ring on the same day with a couple of hours notice. Thanks. Delilah."

"Ok will do."

"Guarantee you won't. May I suggest contacting an escort who offers text chat. This would probably be more suited to your needs. All the best. Delilah."

"I will make a booking with you on that day, I've never messed anyone around as I don't do that. I have respect for people and always keep my word and promises."

I didn't hear from him on Valentine's day.

'Gather ye rosebuds while ye may.' Shakespeare was of course referring to making the most of our youth. I am referring to sneaking out whilst the owners of the farm are away and dead heading a lot of roses that are not actually dead yet, in my quest for making moist potpourri. I have three enormous Kilner jars, laden with compressed rose petals, salt, brown sugar, spices and a few drops of brandy. After two months I will have a rose petal 'cake' that I'll add essential oil of rose and gum benzoin to. Benzoin lends a sweet, vanillary scent. This moist potpourri as opposed to the dry sort, keeps its scent for years. I have found a company who produce the most fantastic and unusual fragrances for perfumery; banana, cucumber etc, can't wait to get experimenting.

June 2nd 2005

It's been three months since I met the married man I've been seeing occasionally, he's not a client, this liaison was as nature intended. For a couple of months after we'd first met I felt like I'd been whacked over the head with a piece of wood, dazed and amazed how anyone could have found me attractive enough to chat me up in the first place.

It began with me sat in the foyer of the Royal Albert Hall, with only one visible eyebrow remaining. It had been a long train trip from Yorkshire and I'd fallen into a deep, dribbling, listing hard to the left, sleep, on the train, face wedged hard up against the upholstery, which was now smeared with the crayon of one eyebrow. Having at last arrived, I was now sat happily drinking a frothy latte with a huge chocolate Flake in it, very much looking forward to seeing Carl Orff's Carmina Burana, and chatting to members of the choir who were all smartly dressed in black and enjoying their pre performance refreshments. Our choir had performed this piece some months back, it is a fantastic piece to sing, and in the same way as Verdi's Requiem, it has a wonderfully purging effect on the cluttered mind, such is the power, drama and sheer volume required of the singer.

After banging on endlessly about Orff to endless choir members, who all seemed to finish their coffees very quickly, another male chorister sat down next to me and darted me a shifty look. I wasn't sure at the time whether he was shifty or shy. To be honest, I didn't really care as I was so excited about the impending performance that the only thing I remember about that initial meeting was that he had enormous hands and weird hair.

To cut a long story very short, it turned out Anthony was a married, womanising troll who must have driven his wife to the edge of madness with his addiction to flaunting his wares at any opportunity. His 'wares,' I discovered later, were a set of impotent testicles and a flaccid penis, all rather depressing seeing as it was the first time in years a man had found me attractive, who wasn't clutching a £50 note in his hand. Six weeks after meeting me, he was performing the same tricks on a middle aged blonde, the choir chairwoman. Inexperienced in the devious ways married men adopt to ensnare unwary females, I fell for the well rehearsed lines, then subsequently couldn't handle the trickery and deceit and became dreadfully depressed for months. But I am bored analysing the experience now, having analysed it constantly to the point I thought I was going to need medical help. Clearly an individual who struggled to accept his age, he initially told me he was 52. An hour or so spent Google-stalking him, revealed his actual age; I found his profile on a financial investment company's website, who he'd left two years previously, which stated:

'At 65, Anthony's extensive financial experience has been of invaluable...' Bla bla bla. Oh Jesus thank god he was impotent, I nearly willingly shagged a pensioner. I fantasised about wedging a kipper in the radiator of his BMW and emptying ten tonnes of cattle manure on his front lawn but I haven't got a tractor and trailer. Fingers crossed he catches genital warts from the choir chairwoman.

I have discovered an excellent way of speeding up the recovery time after a crappy relationship. Bake, just bake. Having had little or no interest in self-raising flour and baking powder, I am now producing tea breads and lemon drizzles on an apocalyptic scale. Was up till 4am this morning watching YouTube instructional videos on Eccles cakes. What the hell? I'm secretly a little embarrassed over my married man fuck up and baking OCD, but then a year ago I became obsessed with Great White shark YouTube videos. It all became rather silly and the washing up remained undone for three days in my quest for the perfect shark *attack. Oh and another thing, Anthony didn't floss and I could see a build up of meals between his fangs. Why doesn't everyone floss? Food gets stuck between your teeth and rots and makes your breath smell.*

June 8th 2005

Had an email from one of Archie's townie friends, about to move to the country and wanting sheep advice. Well, you did ask.

"Watch for any number of problems during lambing, it could be that the sheep's not lambed yet/aborted/not in lamb/won't accept it's own effing lamb/pinched another lamb/gone lame/got mastitis/flystrike/pushing its back end out/on it's back/bloated/had triplets/got one teat/no milk/hard bag/no teeth/lost a tag/swayback/pulpy kidney/watery mouth/had too much beet/got twin lamb disease/lice/worms/fluke/got out again/needs feeding/difficult lambing/got an infection/poaching my field up/blown up on turnips/and still died anyway after we spent a fortune on it. Foot bathing, injecting, preventative fly treatments, weighing, grading, scanning, shearing, (usually on the hottest day of the year) dagging, belly clipping, tagging, looking at carefully twice a day. Strimming or spraying under electric fences, changing fencer batteries, permanent fencing, hay/silage making, putting up lamb pens, lambing em in Spring, bedding, watering feeding mucking out pens, ringing and turning out, stomach tubing, bottle feeding, creep feeders topping up, shelters in fields, hay racks, water butts and troughs, water laid on, turning troughs over before and after each feed so birds don't shit in them, topping paddocks, growing and feeding fodder beet, putting stubble turnips in, strip grazing moving the fence every day. Don't buy culls, go easycare, permanent fencing if possible, saves a lot of hassle with electric fences, lamb outside not too early, get a lightweight portable handling system and weigher. Talk to a knowledgeable vet about a health plan. Heptavac and foot rot vaccinations worth it. Footbath

a must. Don't buy in with lice/scab, biting their wool or big, fat, over meaty ewes for breeding, nor over prolific lambers as no ewe has more than 2 teats and although some can rear triplets they need a lot of feed and bag will probably be wrecked for next year.

Just my opinions. I'm no vet, just help out with sheep a bit."

June 10th 2005

At last! After three days of earning no money, I had a one hour booking with a polite but slightly strange, middle aged chap, very much in the Boris Johnson category lookswise; lots of floppy yellow hair, mustard coloured corduroys and a tattersall shirt. He was infatuated with my weight,

"So how much do you weigh Delilah?,"

"Hm, not sure, about 11 stone."

"Are you sure you're not 15 stone?,"

"Bloody hope not, I don't own scales."

"Come on tell me you're 15 stone,"

(Whatever, as long as he goes home soon)

"I'm 15 stone."

"And again, it turns me on,"

"I'm 15 stone."

"Would you be able to sit on me?,"

"No sorry."

"It turns me on watching a big woman sit on things and break them."

(God to think he would have wanked whilst watching Shallow Hall)

"Have you got a chair you would be prepared to sit on and break?."

"No."

"How strong were you when working on farms?,"

"Strong as a bloody ox."

"Really?! But how strong? Could you have lifted me?."

"Shouldn't think so, I carried a 50kg bag of Nitram once, only for two metres though."

"Ooh wow! That's amazing! Can I feel your arm muscles?,"

"Nothing there now, I only turn sheep upside down when absolutely necessary and handle bird feed deliveries in 20kg sacks."

He went on and bloody on. In the end I agreed to sit on his lap to keep him quiet, afterwards he pulled on his mustard cords and returned home, having never had an erection or seen under my clothes. Funny old world.

June 12th 2005

'Unexpected item in bagging area.'

Today has been an exceptionally shitty day. Nellie has a growth on the underside of her paw, on the main pad. It began to bleed and she has trodden paw-shaped bloodied imprints over the whole caravan. I whisked her to the vets and she's booked in tomorrow to have it removed.

Whilst scurrying around with a bottle of Vanish and a cloth, I accepted an escort booking in one hours time. He arrived and settled down on the bed which I'd covered with a clean throw to cover up stubborn paw prints, Now look, I'm not wilfully moaning about every bloke I see, in fact the vast majority are very nice indeed, but this guy was bloody awful. It began with me finding him mildly irritating then quickly escalated to the point where I wanted him to buggar off asap. He was bulky and clumsy and kept kicking my beautiful cushions off the bed whilst thrashing around in fake blissful abandon. As he writhed around on top of me, he would exhale loudly, constantly, producing the most noxious breath that was poisonous enough to turn red tomatoes green again. The worst part was he kept removing his willy and plonking it back inside me like a sink plunger, thereby creating a vacuum which not only produced the most unfeminine and monstrous fanny farts (there is I'm sure a proper medical term for these) but managed to suction the bloody condom off, which deposited itself, empty thank god, inside me. Now for someone who finds the idea of an inserted tampon an alien invasion, the knowledge of this small plastic bag nestling within my tubes like flukeworm in a sheep, filled me horror. However before I realised what had happened I was still subjecting myself to his ghastly grinding and sink plunging technique complete with gasworks breath. Eventually I was forced to say;

"Look are you planning on coming anytime soon?,"

He agreed to stop and as I sat up, he grunted,

"Ere its come off."

Well, holy mother of Jesus, the following situation was just, well, unspeakably wretched; as I sat getting dressed, stressing as to how I was going to get to the doctors before they closed, (I'd spent five minutes guddling around myself but couldn't feel it inside me) and though he was fully aware of my predicament, he continued to masturbate! unbebloodylievable.

Eventually the foul creature sloped off and I raced to the doctor and lied eloquently about the unfortunate mishap between my boyfriend and I (boyfriend! Can you imagine! I'd rather date the Antichrist). She removed the condom very quickly and I returned to the farm pronto to check sheep and shut the hens in for the night. Once in, I lit the fire, made tea and slept. Thank god today is over.

June 15th 2005

My exceedingly posh employer's wife, Henrietta, having spent her entire life being waited on by a stream of cap-doffing servants, decided she would experiment with the ingenious invention known to all as the washing machine.

Having purchased a bright, cobalt blue tunic in a far flung land whose inhabitants have yet to hear of dye mordant, she, at the end of a long sweaty, summers day, removed her tunic to find her entire upper body dyed a vibrant lapis lazuli. This is no exaggeration because as I went to clean the bathroom that morning, the bath interior was blue, very very blue, including all the once beautiful white, fluffy towels. It was everywhere, she'd even left a big blue ring on the toilet seat. Henrietta then decided to put the offending garment in the washing machine, a fairly sensible move I suppose. What wasn't sensible was to put it in with a yellow silk, embroidered evening dress. I tried everything on the shelves in Tesco to remove the blue, including undiluted bleach but nothing worked. The dress is now a lurid, algae tinged green and all the towels an odd shade of mottled toad.

June 20th 2005

Text this morning,

"How long will I need to be with you for you to give me a sore red ass with a slipper or belt."

I didn't reply.

"Hi Delilah I'm 45 and Italian, I've a passion for feet and high elegant heels if that's not an issue, Luca."

"I'm afraid that is an issue."

"Ok thanks anyway."

"Hi arduous available for blowing only today? And is it without condom."

"Sorry I'm not available."

Can predictive text get it that wrong?

Just in the nick of time a guy rang for an 11am appointment, £70 which will buy me Footvax, a vaccine which prevents footrot in sheep.

The client was 'musical,' he said, and taught blues guitar. He bore the ofttimes ashen complexion and greying teeth of musical people who spend very little time out of doors and smoke. (Not classical musicians though. For some reason, they are in an altogether different class) He was very nervy with shaking hands and kept smiling every thirty seconds for no obvious reason, a twitch I presume.

Also saw a youngish chap today with a peculiar willy that when suitably excited, poked down and between his legs, a very unnatural shape and not anatomically matched to the shape of a vagina, so it bloody hurt. Was mightily glad when he'd gone.

June 22nd 2005

7am start, brush cut brambles in marsh field because sheep have been getting stuck in them. To country supplies store for ewe feed blocks then Tesco then further brush cutting. Saw a Rastafarian bloke, a thin DJ, said he tried to do his first mugging at ten years of age, but couldn't bring himself to do it. He had rushed out at a couple with the intention of nicking a wallet or two but instead looked a bit sheepish and asked for the time, kinda sweet that.

June 23rd 2005

Saw a barrister today who said he loved wearing the compulsory peculiar wig for work. Also saw a policeman, who, upon entering the hut, asked if he could 'do a line of coke.'

"No you cannot."

His willy remained stubbornly floppy and unresponsive despite my half hearted mauling, another easy £70.

June 24th

I have to laugh when a man texts, "can I worship your feet?."

A more unsavoury act I cannot imagine. Both Achilles are torn, plus collapsed arches and bunions. You can begin your act of worship by booking me a session with a private podiatrist. A complete foot transplant is what is needed.

I was utterly despondent this morning when after hobbling round Guildford for four hours, I finally purchased a pair of hiking boots for the stroke inducing price of £165. 15 minutes into my dog walk they were killing me. Each weighed as much as a small fridge freezer and upon catching sight of my reflection, I was reminded of Jack Nicholson staggering round calling "Dannyyyy!" in The Shining.

July 20th 2005

No diary written for a month or so, no real excuse, just lazy and disorganised. Saw a man today who asked if I would accept an invitation to dinner, no sex. This I jumped at! Stuff my face on *someone else's debit card and no hairy old scrotum for afters, fantastic!*

I've at last managed to get the chap who grazes his cattle here, to top the fields. Thistles and nettles are running amock which is great for butterflies and other invertebrates but I have to keep things a little under control; cattle and sheep don't fatten very well on thistles. Archibald lets me use a few acres of his estate, rent free which is great and I'm very grateful. But it is not my land and my idea to sub-let it to a local cattle farmer was one of my more sensible ideas. The land needs fencing, ditching, hedging, subsoiling, liming, fertilising, harrowing, rolling, reseeding and tree canopy clearing and unless you have your own kit and can do it yourself, it is just not financially viable.

My first winter here was pretty hard going as I'd made the mistake of having huge haylage bales delivered for winter feed. My only form of mechanisation being a wheelbarrow, I would totter precariously around the buildings through rampaging sheep who were mad keen for their breakfast, with me trying to stay upright on the icy scaffolding boards that I used as pathways across the deep mud in winter.

That first season, though tough with heavy snow and freezing days and nights, I really enjoyed. The barn at night, was like a scene from the Bible; cattle, sheep and goats all lying down, cudding contentedly.

'My first two cows'

August 2nd 2005

Performed Mozart's requiem yesterday with the choir, at a venue in London, long long coach trip but oh boy...I'm on a glorious high. Once home, I plucked up the courage to open my escort email inbox;

"Hi Delilah, I just had a look at your profile and I would really like to meet up with you. The problem is I do have a bit of an odd request. I would like to tickle you, sounds strange I know but I have a tickling fetish where I enjoy tickling and being tickled by beautiful women. So the questions I have are. Firstly are you ticklish? Secondly where are your ticklish places? And thirdly would it be ok for me to do this? I completely understand if not and bear no grudge but it would be awfully nice to hear from you. If you do not wish to be tickled for an extended period of time perhaps you could tickle me also if that would be OK? I am very ticklish.

Love David."

(However many times did he use the word 'ticklish/ed?.' And no, I didn't take him up on the tickling thing).

"Hi there I can't stop looking at your pics, trust me your breasts are so gorgeous, been thinking of you all the time love your pics. By the way I would love to go to Tesco to get chunky chips instead the bowl of chips in front of me."

(Huh? Tesco? Chips?)

"Ahoy Delilah!! Did one escape from heaven? Just wondering if you'll ever be passing through Heathrow? Love to meet. I'm Keyzer Soze, the greatest trick the Devil ever played was to convince the world that he didn't exist and just like that he was gone. There is no Keyser Soze xxx."

(W.T.F ??)

"Hi have you done them on below mentioned

I just want to watch you pee fart and poo for me

No sex

No dirty thing

I am 23 Italian

Thanks Michelangelo."

(You are a dirty thing Michelangelo)

"Hello Delilah, slightly off the wall request. I have a fetish in my mind for hardsports/brown showers which I think is wrong and I think a session with someone may help get rid of the fetish. Is this something that would interest you? Apologies for any offence caused.

Best wishes, Andrew."

(You **think** is wrong??)

"Hi would you be interested in playing out incestuous role play? It would be mother and son."

(Jesus)

Hi Delinquent, are you available next Saturday for an hour? I'm looking for a massage bee X."

(Spellcheck..turn it off)

(This is a big one reader, here goes..)

"Hi Mistress, I was wondering if we could arrange a session, with you in control dominating? I thought I'd include everything as regards to my interests and try and give you an insight into what turns me on. Hopefully from this you can then take charge and dictate how the session goes and control it, as you will be in charge. What I would love would be for you to take control from the moment we meet. You order me to strip to ensure I'm naked and vulnerable with you taking all of my clothes and putting them into a bag. You then make it clear that unless I do as I'm told I won't get them back and will be thrown out the door. This will ensure control is in your hands from the start and I will have to follow your instructions to the letter. Maybe after the initial control taken by you, you could explain to me that I'm your slave and I will do as you want or else. To maybe add further control/humiliation to this, you could dress me up in a bra, panties and stockings. This would be even more humiliating to be thrown out of the door dressed like this, if I do not follow orders. I want you to be authoritative but also secretly delighted that you have your own plaything which you want to use for your pleasure. The fact that you get turned on by the power you have over the slave, should come across, that you will use your slave for your pleasure, whether it's to lick you out, use to face-sit, use to thrash with your whipping stick etc, means he is worth something to you but at the same time you will throw him out of the door naked if he doesn't agree to everything you want. You would

take great joy out of dominating me in any way so I really need to go out of my way to please you, and do anything you want, to avoid this from happening. I think once you initially have control over me with you fully dressed and me naked or dressed as a sissy as my mistress has now taken them and everything I own is now her property. You will then have a hold over me to ensure I do as you wish. I would then love the following activities to be included in the session:

Tie up my balls

Boot and foot worship (please can you paint your toenails red)

Water sports directly into the mouth (maybe also fill up a glass with some to force me to drink later on in the session)

Face slapping repeatedly throughout the session to maintain control, not letting me forget for one moment who is in control

Spanking over your knee with my cock and balls squeezed in between your legs

Rimming, huge turn on if verbal humiliation could be delivered whilst forcing me to do it, that would be great

Strap on with a reasonably sized strap on

Sissy play, dressing me up in girlie clothes

Could you let me know if you can cater for this request

Regards Jeff."

(Jeff, you are a very strange man, I understand nothing of what you have written)

August 10th 2005

Having been to the hospital to have a camera inserted down my nose to investigate the cause of my permanently sore throat, Mr

Patel announced that my vocal chords were very healthy but that I had severe acid burns resulting from acid reflux. So I am now on a course of tablets for six weeks. Following his advice, I have tried in my own, not terribly serious way to reduce meal size and leave several hours between meals but I have the self discipline of a five year old and after two days of unsweetened porridge and no butter, gave into a 20oz jacket potato, a chunk of butter the size of a satsuma and a whole 16oz can of baked beans heaped with grated cheese.

The flatulence this produced was evil and now my throat is burning like a blow torch, though this could be the industrial size bar of Cadburys earlier or the pasta and cheese at 11pm last night. I am indeed weak, wretched, fat and greedy and doubtless will die alone in my sheep shed having inhaled a Minstrel or some such foodie sin.

Saw a guy today that looked for all the world like Chris Martin fallen on hard times. An attractive chap until he smiled, to reveal a missing tooth.

Yesterday saw a man of 35 years of age, very public school and attractive. I used my vibrator on him and he went instantly into paroxysms of intense pleasure. It was very easy money and he writhed and moaned, eventually ejaculating with the energy release of a racehorse from its starting box, although it was rather off putting at his calling out 'mummy!' at the moment of orgasm. I didn't react to his strange incestuous outburst though, and he left me after twenty minutes. Bizarrely he rang again ten minutes later and asked if he could come back, stepped up into the hut a bit sheepishly and declared,

"Im a sex addict."

Fine by me, I thought as I pocketed another £30.

August 12th 2005

Email:

"hey i no your an escort but iv been looking at your pictures for some while an i think iv fallen for you so if you fancy a fall time boyfriend who wouldnt stand in the way of what you do message me back maybe x."

Bless.

August 15th 2005

Text just in:
"Jesus I'm 23, sat here looking at your pics, you have big tits."
I don't reply.
"My cock is throbbing looking at your pics."
I don't reply.
"Please text back just once cos you're sooo fit please please."
I don't reply.
"Wow unbelievable I'm 23, your tits are huge, my cock is throbbing."
"Yes you've made your point. I do not see clients under 30."
He doesn't reply.

August 20th 2005

The locksmith who fixed my ignition barrel back in the summer, had mistakenly driven off with the automatic gate opener to Gallows Farm. I have a spare but it's still very annoying as they're not cheap and I'd like it back, not great for security either. Episode was my fault entirely because I'd left the opener in his van whilst hitching a lift with him up to my stranded truck. I rang immediately he'd left and explained that the gate opener was on his dash board,

"Ah yeh, yep I see it, no probs I'll post it back to you if you text me your address," which I did, straight away. Two months and several texts and phone calls later, he still hasn't returned it;

"Hello it's Cathy, it's been two months, did you manage to post the gate opener?,"

"Ah yes! It's on my microwave, I'm going to the post office in the morning and will definitely post it to you then, sorry about that!."

Two weeks later, nothing in post.

"Hello, it's Cathy, what is your address? I will come and collect it."

I drove to his house some 25 miles away and knocked on the door. His wife answered and smiling, retrieved it from the top of the microwave. What the hell?! I'd even offered to post him the stamped envelope with which to post it to me in. I mean the man is obviously a complete and utter knob.

Washed very thoroughly this morning knowing I had a bloke booked for mid morning. Went to barn to check sheep first and scattered diatomaceous earth over the straw bedding. This is a very fine, soft powder, the ground up fossilised remains of millions of animals and is a superb desiccant. It kills lice and mites by dehydrating them to death. Thing is, it was raining and blowing a gale and the fine white powder clung to my clothes, hair and face, giving me a strange, pale, ethereal look. Removal of my bra released a cascade of straw and crumbly white paste. My client stepped into the hut, noted the odd appearance with a quizzical glance but was too polite to say anything.

Had a man booked for 2pm today and at 1.55pm I'm scurrying round the barn sorting out my bird feed delivery which involves the handling of live mealworms, a kilo of them. He drove in, got out of his car and I apologised for the task I was in the middle of doing and had to finish,

"Sorry, gotta do this or the mealworms will die."

He looked on in horrified disapproval, revulsion and disappointment as I picked up handfuls of wriggling worms. My job completed, we made our way to the hut where I washed my hands and attempted to behave a bit more 'escorty.' After ten minutes of me pulling at his unimpressed willy, he said,

"You know I'm just going to go." He dressed in silence and drove off. Oh well, must have been the mealworms.

Text just arrived;

"Hey, my name's Louise, my husband keeps asking me for a threesome so I thought the easiest way to find a willing girl would be on an adult site. Would you be interested? I am 26 and he is 27 xx."

I didn't reply to this one. A long time ago when the world was young, when T.V's were two foot deep and Amazon was just the name of a river, this idea may have intrigued me. Now it all sounded rather too 'busy.'

Have a read of this poor buggar's email:

"Hi, may I ask if you are single? I am unattached, no kids, working, tall, white, non-smoking gent. I'm told I have lovely eyes (this means he is not a looker) and I miss that someone special. I'm looking for romance, kissing, sleeping in together. I am genuine. I can send you a picture. Can we try? I'm blown away by your pictures. Jon xx."

"Send a picture via the website if you like." (you never know, he might be partially sighted and gorgeous with a 200 acre farm)

"I'm not registered properly on there, maybe I could call you, we could get to know each other. I miss romance/nights in. I live in Derbyshire, not too far. When free? We could meet?/stay over. It's romance not paid fun I'm looking for xx."

"You're on a prostitutes website, if you hadn't spotted."

"May I give you a quick call just to say hello? Then send pics."

"No point ringing if I don't find you attractive, send a bloody picture!."

"I want to call, can I stay the night tonight?."

"Stay the night?, are you mad? I've never even met you. I'm an escort. Please arrange a booking if that is what you require. If you're after a partner for life, may I suggest a dating website."

When I started doing this a few months ago, in the days I used to make an effort, I went to see a man who lived fairly locally, about eight miles away. I got out of my pickup in heels and a skirt, a skirt! Can you believe it! He was a married, professional guy, high up in the security business. Very tall and impressively built but strangely awkward and lacking in confidence in his manner and gait, as if he'd been subject to beatings from his wife. She was out at work, and we had sex in their marital bed. God how awful that a husband could do that, she would have been devastated, though he did say their marriage was at an end. He came incredibly quickly, almost immediately which cheered me up no end. I saw him in town a month later and dashed into the nearest shop to hide, a car parts shop, peering with fake interest at gaskets and big-ends.

Dang me if I didn't see him three weeks later in M&S, stood at the entrance to the lingerie changing rooms with a woman. Both looked extremely downcast, another divorce on the cards. I was sweating, red faced, makeupless, and laden with thermal vests, long johns and heavy duty reinforced bras. I hid until he'd gone.

Another out-call I'd made at the beginning of my escorting 'career' was also to a married man and once again involved carrying out the accursed deed in the marriage bed. I found it very troubling, surrounded by make-up, clothes and other wifely things. He then suggested the idea of his 18 year old son joining in. Thank fuck I never married or had kids.

August 21st 2005

"Hi there Delinquent (turn the bloody predictive text off!) Sorry to bother you, may I say your profile is great and some lovely pictures. I have spent many hours wanking over them. I'd luv to cum see you and I'd like to contact you to arrange a booking. I'm very particular about underwear and lingerie (oh dear) I hope this is not a problem (it's a huge problem). If you haven't got what I'm looking for I'd like to purchase the underwear for you, would this be ok? Love Jon x."

(I declined his kind offer)

August 22nd 2005

"Hello Delilah, I am new to all this stuff but my love of bigger women and big curves led me here. Love your pics. Could I ask one thing? I know you shouldn't ask a woman's measurements but as I am such a big bum lover it's actually the bigger the better for me, so was wondering if you knew how many inches your bum is?

Hope to hear from you, James xx."

(I don't own a tape measure)

And another real beauty now...

"Hi, I have a fantasy I'd like to fulfil. I really like the idea of going down on you knowing you have had a busy day, seeing a few clients and all the tastes that go along with that. (Sweet Jesus, the dirty little fucker) I would like to be used for your pleasure or to clean where they have been. I would like you to be a bit of a bully to me. My ultimate fantasy would be me waiting in the car while you see someone. They come over your ass, pussy and tits and leave, and you get me to clean up their cum. I hope that's not too weird (not too weird?! I was grimacing just writing this stuff down) Please let me know if you would like to do this. It would be really best to do after a busy busy day.

Regards,

Keith."

August 24th 2005

Three emails I received today:

"Hi babe, I would be very interested to meet with you today around lunchtime. I have a very large cock so please let me know you will be ok with this. Also do you have any uniforms you could cross dress me with?

Let me know so we can arrange to meet.

Kind regards,

Nigel."

"Hey there, you good hunnie? How's you been? I live in Crossholme. If you fancy a regular fuck bud with a massive big black dick, I'm up for it plus I'm very hot and know how to fuck good! Roy."

August 25th 2005

Two blokes today, really sore fanny, awful. First client pain in ars, ages to cum, came with machine and it shot out 50mph all over wall n pillow, arrived on motor bike, worryingly loud. Second a good looking pikey, 25 yrs old, arrived in big pick up at 11pm. Christ I can't wait for this all to be over. Three lame sheep today damn it.

Emails:

"Hey there. I have a job that you maybe interested in. It's a real job. I own a photography company and I'm looking for a manager of the studio. There are two receptionists, a cleaner and me and the other photographer. The hours are 10-3pm, Tuesday to Saturday.

I'm looking for a naughty manager who I have sex with in my office or suck me off. U can wear slightly naughty things. I need total discretion as my other staff can't find out. You will be paid monthly or weekly. You can work full or part time.

We can discuss wages and benefits if you're interested? I promise you this isn't a joke or a wind up, this is a genuine job. I just fulfil a few fantasies.

I'm Chris, please call or text on: 07403 ...."

"Hi Delilah,

Thank you for this morning. I enjoyed meeting you and had fun. You are a very sexy and beautiful woman and I was a lucky guy to spend some time with you.

Hope we can meet again soon. You mentioned that you're due your period soon. I would like to come back again when it's here. Remember if you happen to mess your knickers during your period or other times I would like to know, just drop me an email.

Robin xx"

Hi Delilah,

I would like to come and see you for an hour's incall session.

A somewhat unusual request for you.. Are you happy to include ballbusting? Mainly kicking me in the balls, also some crushing with your feet and maybe with heels if I can take it, maybe you have some cruel ones to use! How hard are you willing to go with the ballbusting? I would like to finish either with sex or a footjob.

Frank xxx."

"Hello Delilah, would you be interested in giving me hardsports. basically I'm after you to poo on me and wank me off with it after. If so, how much would it cost?

Cheers

Bertie."

Bertie, you dirty dirty man.

The email below has me dumbstruck. What, just what, is he prattling on about?..

"My name is Henry and I'm a virgin. I like to book a mature and experienced lady because I have some concerns and like to see a lady who is honest, friendly and detailed. BUT to know if you really are an EXPERIENCED lady and HONEST, I like to ask you two question:

1. In my profile you will see a picture of my cum and that picture shows THREE of my cum loads. I waited for a week and after a week I masturbated three times with time gap of 2 hrs between each cum. My female friend who is 31 says that I cum very less and also said that I should call my cum 'seminal droplets' as its mere few drops of semen. She said that if I cum after a week it should be a lot and very thick but mine is less and watery. She

further said that my balls are smaller therefore due to their size I cum less.

So you can see my three cum load amount, and kindly if you can tell whether that's average amount for three or you think less and KINDLY if you think less then how less you think my cum amount is. I know some cum more and some less, but I need the comparison with AVERAGE/NORMAL size cum. So please just dont say some cum less and some more. Kindly compare with average amount you see.

2. Secondly do you really find my balls smaller than other men balls?? And if they are then how small are they from other men.

Please love it would be a great favor if you can tell me your HONEST and BLUNT views about my cum and balls. Rest of my questions I'll ask you in booking.

Regards and I wait for your reply. Please be honest with above questions because I like to know few more things from you during the booking so I like to see how honest and detailed you are.

Regards and please let me know if you are not interested and not answering my questions.

I'm all clean. Can provide STI certificate on arrival".

"Hi sexy how are you?

Can you offer me this things?

69

Kissing

Swallowing my spam."

Spam! Ha ha bloody ha.

"Hi Delightful. I know you don't get to check your mails that often but I'm not in a hurry and think this will be easier to explain by mail. I'll be looking forward to your reply when you get the chance.

Can I start by saying I am a massive fan of yours. What man wouldn't be with the most amazing boobies I have ever seen and a gorgeous curvy figure.

I have been reading your blog posts with great interest. You seem to really love your way of life and it certainly seems to keep you busy. I actually share your love of the rural life as I myself live and work in the countryside. I am a farming lad working in a lovely valley a few miles from you and I love the freedom and witnessing the beauty of nature on a daily basis.

My name is Pete, I'm 25 and have been a farming lad for the last 7 years. I'll just be completely honest and say I'm not really the best when it comes to sex. I have always struggled with self confidence and this has affected me in the bedroom. I even think it probably cost me my last relationship. I would love to find someone understanding who can help put me at ease and show me a thing or two. I think being able to get some practice with someone who could put me at ease would really help me.

I really don't want to offend you by asking this and I hope I don't. As a farming lad I'm not exactly what you would call well paid. A trade off for having such an enjoyable way of life I suppose. As you can be so busy I was wondering how you feel about having an extra pair of hands to help you out on occasion. I am a hard worker with the right backgound and have access to strimmers, brushcutters and chainsaws. I would love to help you out and you could in turn help me out. It's just an idea and I certainly understand if you're not interested.

Love Pete X."

"Hi I was wondering if you would try a lift carry fetish session where we try to carry each other around and give each other ponyrides, piggybacks etc. I'd like to try it.

Thanks."

Truly...men are from Mars and women from Venus.

"Hey, is there any chance of 30minute session tonight? I would like a quick blowjob and then doggy style. Could I cum on your bum and lick it up?xxx."

August 28th 2005

Damn good day today, seen two men to the tune of £140. Drove to Allerton farm supplies to buy 25 feed blocks for sheep, am now prepared for winter. Bumped into a sheepdog trainer, Paul. He had seven collies in the back of his pickup, all perfectly behaved, how do these people do it? A year or so ago he'd helped me out training Fly and was rather aggressive and bad tempered towards us both, with much arm flailing and roaring;

"Come bye!..Stand!. I said fucking **STAND!!**. Keep moving! **KEEP MOVING!** Show her you're the bloody boss!...**LIE DOWN!**."

I couldn't keep track of who he was roaring at most of the time, myself or Fly, and found myself following the commands of 'away to me' and 'stand,' when he'd been instructing the dog, such was my fear of him. I put up with it for a couple of sessions but decided I was far too flower-like for his SAS training methods. It reinforces how jolly glad I am I didn't join the army/navy/police. I lack the discipline to water my house plants regularly, never mind traverse moorland with 50kg strapped to my back, perish the thought.

Ok, and with an almost seamless transition from dogs and sheep, to prostitution, I shall now briefly sum up this afternoon:

The first of two men I saw was West Indian, he was very tall and confessed before he removed his trousers that he was ashamed of his small willy. I suspected otherwise in a tall gentleman of his ethnicity and so as I poked my head between his legs, I affected mock surprise at discovering he was indeed of donkey sized proportions. If you have ever wondered how much truth is in the expression, 'hung like a donkey,' I shall now enlighten you;

Several years ago I worked as a livestock manager on a farm that was open to the public. At certain times of the year we were very busy, up to 1500 people per day. One day as I scurried about between jobs, Eric the donkey who lived permanently with Penny, his donkey wife, decided some conjugal relations would be just the ticket on a busy Sunday afternoon. The two donkeys were stood contentedly pulling hay from their manger and munching away happily in their sunlit pen, the public moving as one cloud-like mass, with synchronised 'awws' and 'ahhs!' as they gazed upon the various farmy occupants in the barn.

The sound of the cloud shifted from awe and amazement to mild shock followed by sniggering, then full on hilarity as hundreds of impressionable children and their parents watched on as Eric and Penny went at it like a professional porn film couple; Eric's tongue lolling, eyes wide in carnal bliss and Penny vigorously champing her mouth as lady equine tend to during these activities. And yes, donkeys are very well endowed, enormous in fact, given their overall body size. Clearly a very happy donkey couple, one could almost hear the internalised thoughts of husbands, 'lucky sod,' and their wives, lucky Penny.'

Anyway, back to the West Indian chap; I applied a condom, not easy given his Eric sized girth and tried to get my mouth around his enormous appendage. Sex was surprisingly easy and quick as I'd heaped on the KY like gravy.

The second man was an unattractive but colourful character; late 50's, married, wealthy and a fund manager for a firm of Arabs. He was bowled over by my agricultural charms as I fed him tea and toast and sold him half a lamb for his freezer. I was given £80 for 45 minutes of my time which comprised of nothing sexual whatsoever. He'd watched me as we stood in the kitchen, shovelling down four doorsteps of thickly buttered toast and a pint of Lady Grey. He then took his leave, saying,

"You are obviously very busy, can I visit you Thursday and take you out for a meal?."

I didn't take him up on the offer. For the umpteenth time I heard him say what many men have said, that if it weren't for escorts, it is very unlikely he would still be married. I would say about 95% of the married men I've seen, all agree that because either a/ the wife isn't interested in sex or b/ it's very rare and dull, the being able to see escorts keeps them sane and reasonably content. About 80% say they are happy and love their wives and wouldn't have affairs, hence they see escorts because it is anonymous and emotionless. Many said they have tried Relate with no success.

Sep 2nd 2005

The pneumonic lamb has improved! Non stop dogs, sheep and penises today. Saw a chap whose wife has manic depression. He hadn't ejaculated for six months and hadn't had sex for two years, and bounced around on top of me with much enthusiasm, threw back his head like a billy goat and put forth six months worth of frustration into the condom.

Plodged through endless mud to feed neighbour's horses, caught up one of her ewes that was lame on front left with foot rot, gave it 6mls Alamycin, trimmed hoof and sprayed between digits. She also has a huge infected growth on her ear which the owner was supposed to have got the vet out to look at. The ear burst while I was wrestling her into a sitting position to carry out hoof treatment and I was sprayed from hair to knees with pus and blood.

Having just arrived back at Gallows Farm, the bloke I had to delay because of the poorly sheep, texted me,

"Hope you're good n wet babe, I'm soo ready for you."

Jesus Christ, not what I wanted to hear. I cancelled him. Managed to scrub pus and blood from face, hair, hands and neck before another bloke I had booked, turned up. Blessings on the creators of perfumed body sprays. I am also indebted to whatever mechanisms within the human body are responsible for premature ejaculation which resulted in him relieving himself uncontrollably within seconds, at my having revealed no more than a glimpse of elbow.

My mum has coined the phrase 'hooky blorks,' referring to the devious, randy little fuckers I have to entertain on an almost daily basis. 'Hooky' as in 'hooker.'

The beautiful Border Leicester ewe lambs I have, are also known affectionately as the 'hooky theres,' so named because their noses are very aquiline and well, hooked.

Sep 10th 2005

My only hooky blork today was a gardener, another deprived husband, who announced smilingly, as he sat on the bed,

"I like your gypsy caravan because it doesn't smell of mens' anuses."

A call today from a woman. Uh oh, she's found his second mobile phone, hidden in the boot probably. This conversation, like all the texts/emails in this book are absolutely as they were sent to me,

"Is this Delilah?,"

"Yes how can I help?,"

(Shrieking hysterically) "You're a fucking marriage wrecker! My husband had sex with you didn't he!."

"Yes probably, I couldn't say for sure, I don't recall who your husband was."

(More hysterical now) "You don't remember?!!,"

"I've seen several men, and they tend to give false names anyway, I can't help you I'm sorry."

(Sparks spitting out of phone now) "Did he or didn't he have sex with you?!!,"

"Probably, but if he didn't he certainly will with someone else at some point."

(Sobbing uncontrollably) "I can't believe he did this, I thought we were happy."

"Listen, calm down. He isn't leaving you for a 19 year old, he's just bored and sexually very frustrated and I'm certain loves you very much. You have to separate the two, they are not related, not to a guy anyway. Sit down with him, with a cuppa and a whole pack of Hobnobs and get it all out in the open, everything, no more secrets, and discuss fun ways to liven up your sex life."

The sobbing had reduced to snivels by now,

"I'm so glad I've spoken to you, you sound so normal. Would you come round for a coffee? It would make me feel so much better."

"Er, ok." (She'll have changed her thinking by the time I arrive and be wielding a bread knife and a fire extinguisher)

Remember readers, it's not escorts approaching the men. The men go searching for them and if it weren't for escorts, affairs would be rife, and they are a damn sight more devastating to deal with. When men see an escort purely for sexual relief, there's no constant secret back and forth texting and ringing. No dodgy nights and weekends away on 'business.' No open ended promises and most importantly, no emotional connection, which is where the biggest feeling of betrayal would seem to stem from in women.

Sep 15th 2005

Called into a neighbour's house this evening to say hello and enjoyed several drinks and the most delicious nibbles. Managed to reduce them to tears of laughter with my bawdy re-telling of past dates gone wrong.

Met with an unbelievably attractive 35 year old today, I mean JESUS, off the scale TOTALLY RIDICULOUSLY GORGEOUS. He'd never met with an escort before and was very nervous, hence we talked for ages before I managed to coax his terrified willy out of its lair. Dazzling white teeth, thick and adorable dark brown hair laced with grey, a body to die for and THE most amazing eyes I've ever seen, pale blue and dark irises. My god it's at rare moments such as these that the desire to be 25, stunningly beautiful and with a professional career is overwhelming. Reality smacked me hard in the face as I caught sight of my bloated self in the bedroom mirror with its half cropped hair. Half cropped due to the DIY removal of glue-in hair extensions. I had become impatient with the nail varnish remover and pliers, which is an effective but slow method of removal. So I'd resorted to kitchen scissors.

Sep 18th 2005

Another intoxicating day of cleaning, controlling errant dogs and penis amusement. Began the day with Archibald, who, having ridden into the yard after a mornings hunting, mentioned very politely,

"I say, there's a rather enormous one by the stables, looks very much like a dog's to me." He is far too posh to say the word 'poo' and so refers to it as 'one.' Having handed his horse over to the groom, who began to remove the animal of its riding paraphernalia, he toddled off inside to partake of his customary glass of port and a perusal of the morning papers.

I am well prepared for these dog poo discovery situations, as me and my dog poo bucket cannot be all places at once. I traipsed after him into the oak panelled drawing room,

"That Archibald, is a fox poo!," I said jubilantly, as if I'd discovered a new planet.

"Oh rarely, are you shooer?,"

"Absolutely, you see fox poo..."

At this point the attention of husband and wife drifted away. Someone once told me that this is a peculiar trait to be found in the upper echelons of society, a case apparently of 'too posh to listen,' although I worked for a farmer who would also stop paying attention to me 60 seconds into the conversation, possibly due to his partial deafness after 40 years working in a grain dryer with no ear protection. But the 'too posh to listen' lot, I have to fight like a terrier for their attention if I dare to rise above my station and talk for more than three consecutive minutes.

It is not difficult to understand why I have to battle to make myself heard to Archie and his wife. To them I am 'below the salt,' a minion, an underling, a hireling, a bootlicker, a dogsbody, a lickspittle, a lackey, a henchman, a vassal, a fawning subordinate, a labouring peasant, a ploughman, a peat digger, a milkmaid, a stable lad, a greasy Joan keeling my pot. Anyway, I was determined to continue and ignored their expressions of 'time to leave us now dear,' as they dipped their heads once more to the Telegraph crossword. I forced the subject matter of animal faeces upon them;

"Ah yes you see fox poo is very dark, nearly black in fact and is full of fruit stones because foxes eat the windfalls off your plum trees. My dogs don't eat plums."

"Oh rare-li, you **are** a country girl aren't choo,"

I couldn't resist it and replied,

"Yep, I know my shit."

At this they both laughed, despite themselves.

Sep 27th 2005

Jesus Christ what a nightmare of a day;

Current life devoid of all cheer, horribly overdrawn, hut full of straw, dog hair and horribly cold because I've run out of firewood, plus the boiler in yard has broken so no hot shower in dairy. Local blacksmith is under my hut as I write this, fixing the axle on one of the wheels. I hate hate hate him as desperately need to see this bloke that's just rung, but there's a fucking blacksmith under the hut. Ok ok Cathy keep calm; bend down and speak to the man who is hammering and welding and doing god knows what. I'm in my normal filthy farm attire thereby extinguishing any suspicion of what I am about to do. Fortunately he is a trusting and uncomplicated soul, so telling him I was interviewing a man for lambing help next March was easy.

Shut myself in hut, wash fanny with wipes as no hot water, put on clean knickers and hope to god he doesn't want sex as period hasn't quite finished, think this must be the last of these bouts of womb haemorrhaging as I've not had any ovarian activity in months, fingers crossed it's a sign that my menopause is imminent. Wish earnestly the NHS offered hysterectomies to 14 year olds, would have saved a fortune over the years

Anyway, back to the problem of escorting with only a distance of two feet and wooden floorboards between me, the blacksmith and unemployment (Archibald and Henrietta would not look kindly on my activities, however genuine the need). Put overalls on, grab my routine black eyeliner, red lippy and can of Impulse and dash across to old dairy building, where we store all the crop chemicals, silage wrapping and lambing sundries. There's an old sofa in there where the boss puts his spaniels at night-time, it'll have to do. Layer on eyeliner and lipstick and don clean leggings and a tee shirt. Open farmyard gate and beckon to the approaching client from dairy door, eyes darting nervously twixt client and blacksmith who is still hammering away. Yank hessian sacking across dairy windows once he's inside and it's bloody **freezing**, *no heating at all. Fuck fuck fuck I left condoms and KY in hut. Apologise in advance to client for what I am about to wear, pull wellies on and woolly jumper, nip across to hut and return to dairy, flushed.*

Sep 28th 2005

Explained to blacksmith who was still working underneath my home, that for a second day I was interviewing men for lambing help…

The chap that drove in to see me was very cooperative and as per my instructions, after extremely brisk and hurried hand relief, demanded loudly of me at the open door of the dairy:

"So what date would you like me to be here for lambing!?," and "how much are decent ewes fetching now!?," which all helped to disguise my illicit activities.

Oct 15th 2005

I made mulled wine tonight despite it being October. Whilst on my third glass, pissed, and well into the second stage of quince jam-making, the phone rang. An extremely well spoken, quite elderly man;

"Hellair, is that the lovely Delilah?,"

"It is."

"Is there anything you don't doo?,"

"If you'd like to look at the 'enjoys list' on my profile please."

"Yes but there doesn't appear to be much **on** it,"

(That's because I don't enjoy anything)

"Could I ask, doo yoo lake rimming?,"

"No."

"Oh, oh rait, that's a bit of a shame as I've discovered I'm rather sensitive a

rind that area.

"I can't help you I'm afraid."

"Well, what a bite a spenking. Do yoo doo spenking?."

(Suppress deep sigh) "yes ok." It's highly likely he can't get an erection at his age so should be an easy session.

"Splendid splendid! And do yoo lake to be spenked first or do yoo lake to begin the spenking?."

I suggested he go elsewhere to practise his spenking.

Oct 17th 2005

I had the odious task of a trip to town today, in order to replace my phone, having left it on the bumper of my pick-up whereupon it slid off and I reversed over it. Also in town, to acquire a set of rugged lace-up boots, perfect for a spot of hiking in the Cairngorms but actually needed to keep my crumbly old ankles from twisting whilst working. Last on the list was to pronate myself on the dentist's chair and bare my gnashers to Mr Patel, so he can apply filler to my top teeth to stop them crumbling away. Apparently I have been grinding away like a Hereford cow for decades and have paper thin *teeth that are set to fall like confetti from my open mouth in Tom and Jerry fashion.*

I have become very unsociable lately, with my life following an almost identical daily routine of dog walking, sheep care and willies.

Oct 20th 2005

Saw a 25 year old builder tonight, terribly common and rough, squeezed my boobs mercilessly and kept squashing my shoulders with his graffitied upper body. He had a tiny little willy and was, I should imagine, very much aware of the fact, judging by the way he pumped up and down like a nail gun, awful business. Thankfully he ejaculated quickly.

I have discovered I have a gift for yammering away so as to put extremely nervous men, completely at their ease. It isn't something that comes naturally due to my warm and giving nature, on the contrary, I am a bad tempered and ornery old harridan, but I do find it easy to switch characters. It is instinctively triggered by the fact that I have no interest whatsoever in sexual matters, and so by absolute necessity I transform into this engaging, warm, fascinated by all they have to say, chat show host, in order to save a potentially unpleasant situation developing. Should they realise I am no more suited to the profession of escorting than oil rig construction, they would almost certainly demand a refund. However, the majority of men leave refreshed and happy despite having received a very stingy amount of sexual shenanigans and little or no entangling of genitalia. Yet they are often immensely relieved at having found someone to talk to about their relationship problems. Bravo I say, bravo!

Oct 23rd 2005

Have put the poorly piglet who has been living in my shepherds hut for over a week now, in one of the calving pens under a heat lamp as I'm never going through a morning like today again:

I was woken up at 6.30am by the most appalling smell of diarrhoea. It was everywhere, how the hell one tiny piglet could produce such foetid and evil smelling liquid in such quantity is quite amazing. I had a man booked in for 9am and so with a heart as heavy as lead, I set to on all fours with kitchen towel and a bin liner, gagging as I went. Once the chunky bits had been removed, I opened my brand new, only delivered yesterday, well researched and pricey Bissell carpet cleaner, confident in its ability to completely remove all evidence of evil piglet motions before my 75 year old client arrived.

Upon unpacking the thing, which had cost £150, a disheartening and flimsy pile of plastic mouldings, presumably plonked off the end of a production line somewhere in China, greeted me. None of the parts fitted together properly and once assembled, painstakingly I might add, and with the gnawing suspicion the thing wasn't going to be up to the job, my blood pressure was on the up. I filled it with hot water and chemical and turned the thing on, whereupon it set up a humming and a whining, reluctantly stirring into feeble action, with barely enough suction to vacuum up a pixie's pubic hair. With the mounting panic of knowing my client was due in 30 minutes, I lost the plot and hurled the thing into the air, swearing and roaring violently. Angry at my own loss of self control, I gave the pile of polycarbonate shite the hiding it deserved, and kicked it clattering and crunching down the steps of the hut. For three days before I could get to the tip, it received another swift kick each time I came in of an evening, futile and pointless but it made me feel a whole lot better.

I had ten minutes before he was due and so frantically scrubbed and rubbed and scrubbed some more with hot water and disinfectant. My client didn't seem to notice any malignant odours as he walked in, there was no discernible wrinkling of the nose. Very often the anticipation of carnal activities renders them immune to their surroundings. He was well dressed, tall and thin, with a dodgy hip and walking stick and reeked of pipe smoke. After stripping off almost immediately upon entering and hitting his hairless head on the low door, an orange PVC thong was revealed. It was a tragic sight.

He whipped the thong off, stuffing it into the pocket of his tweed jacket that was hanging on the door and washed his bottom, drying his anal area overly thoroughly on my clean white towel. He was gone pretty quickly, after about half an hour or so, his elderly willy remaining in its button mushroom state throughout. I had a hot bath in owners farmhouse and washed all bedding and towels.

'Nice work little piggie'

Oct 28th 2005

An extremely attractive chap by the name of Kyle, came to see me today. Alas he was 27, so a decade younger than his chosen escort, but very dishy with tousled, mid brown 'I work in the City,' hair, and a lovely nut brown chest. Anyway it was the same old same old, in as much as he was married with two young children, said he hadn't had sex in years (I don't believe that for a minute) and this was to be his first indiscretion involving his willy during that time (I don't believe that either). He wasn't including minor office party incidents such as tongue in other peoples' mouths and breast brushing.

*After a lengthy discourse on the for and againsts of decapitation versus hanging during the Tudor period, I'm serious, I'll talk about **anything** rather than be meddled with, I wacked a condom over his didgeridoo and applied light suction with an almost instant result which was utterly fabulous news. I then made enquiries as to his marital problems. My advice as always, was abrupt and direct,*

"You have one life, your children will cope with a split absolutely fine if handled correctly, and you will have your life back. The question now is can you handle the financial burden of a divorce?."

This he said was the only issue preventing him from making good his escape. He was hugely impressed by my advisory skills and suggested I train as a counsellor. I'm not sure, a vision of a queue of po-faced, miserably married men and women seeking a cure-all at my gate, doesn't fill me with glee. The advice dispensed would be swift and harsh, very Thomas Cromwellian:

'Deliver the break-up line. Lie low whilst the wreckage settles and it will all be ok in the end.'

Anyway, Kyle really didn't seem to want to go and chatted for ages whilst lying on my bed. At last, once dressed, he asked me if he could come and shoot some rabbits next week. This may well have been a euphemism for, 'I'm coming back Tuesday for another blow-job.' I like to think not though as my pink princess girlie girl side (apparently I still have one) likes to think he is returning for my quirky humour and charms. Failing that, the rabbits would do. The reality is surely that he just wants nookie. Would it be too much to ask just for **one** attractive, intelligent man to want to see me with my breasts inside my clothing and his balls not out. Eventually he drove away, still banging on about rabbit shooting. God it is a wearisome business.

The routine I now follow as I welcome each client into the shepherds hut, is eroding away my sense of normality and place in this world. I am always pleasant and polite and make every effort to ensure they each and every one, feel relaxed and welcome. The veneer is very thin however; millimetres below the surface is the face of a woman regarding the aroused man stood before her, as one might gaze despairingly, metal pan scourer in hand, into a blackened oven interior.

My other client today was a 67 year old called Rodney. Admittedly he was not overly easy on the eye and only just managed to fit his enormous stomach through the hut door, but in actual fact he was very nice and I quite enjoyed his company. When I say 'enjoyed,' that doesn't include the ten minutes of sweaty pulsating flesh pounding away behind me as he stood on the floor with me crouched on the bed, praying to the god of prostitute salvation that he would be done with ASAP. He was about 25 stone. Mercifully, most of the hour involved him explaining in great detail the method of producing concrete staircases for blocks of flats and shopping malls.

Oct 30th 2005

The boiler, as mentioned previously, has broken, so have been boiling kettles in order to wash, subsequently the feet have been a little neglected during strip washes. Well actually it's been a week since I washed them. Did my best with wet wipes but it's impossible to get everything out from between your toes and nails unless you can soak them properly in a bubble bath.

Saw a poor unsuspecting man today, who, and I have to say it came as a bit of a surprise, proceeded to lick between my toes with the singular concentration of a cat washing behind its ears. I was horrified and counted the seconds until he backed away from my heinous feet. He didn't react much, maybe he'd had raw onions for breakfast. I can only think that with shed loads of testosterone and a full scrotum, men on a mission to see an escort become a bit punch drunk to such trivial matters as dirty toes.

A man in his late forties gave me a serious pounding from behind today, my poor poor foofoo. I really do think that I just don't have the neurological pathways in my brain and the necessary nerve endings in order for my vagina to be able to leap up and dance with delight when a client arrives. That makes me asexual doesn't it? like a unicellular fungi. Anyway thank the gods and pharmaceutical companies for KY Jelly, he ejaculated like a priest after 20 years of celibacy, roaring and panting and gasping as if an anaesthetist had miscalculated before an appendix removal.

A sheep belonging to a frateflee well awf neighbour, had to be put to sleep today, the one with the growth on her ear, it was cancerous evidently. The vet sedated her then injected a measured lethal dose of anaesthetic into the vein, totally humane and pain free, a great way to go.

Took a neighbouring shepherd's young dog, called Cap, out around my sheep today to give it some experience. I used a small group of ewes that were used to being dogged and slipped a long string on Cap so I'd have some control. He picked it all up quite quickly by the end of our session so we'll keep at the training. Separated out my older sheep and gave them their own special pen in barn with hay and molasses, happy ladies.

Nov 2nd 2005

Put new Herdwick ram, Robert, in with Archibald's Herdwick shearlings, gorgeous looking sheep, can't wait to see the lambs next spring. No idea why he named him Robert but he's a fine looking chap. I checked his feet, teeth and bollocks, then wormed him and he trotted off to be amongst his harem, wouldn't trust him though, reckon he'd happily break my knuckles and kneecaps given a sufficient run up.

Saw a bald Middle Eastern chap this evening whose breath resembled boiled cabbages more than boiled cabbage smells of boiled cabbage. He was a huge, corpulent businessman, very full of himself and had brought with him a tiny phial of a strange and potent smelling Arabic perfume, probably distilled from the opium poppy and some poor caged monkey's pancreas. I threw it in the muck spreader as soon as he'd gone, worried that it may have Holy Grail properties and I'd be tracked down by an irate hoard of bearded Indiana Jones style Middle Easterns. During the booking, he insisted I offer up my private parts for the licking thereof. It was at this exact moment when I realised I'd forgotten to change pants after sitting on a deliciously potent, open bale of silage for half an hour this afternoon, enjoying sandwiches and tea whilst filling in the sheep medicine record book. His head rose like a great chocolate egg from within my thighs and looking like he'd sucked a lemon, he croaked,

"Plizz to have wipe, plizz, plizz!."

I handed him a wet wipe, poor buggar.

Phone rang today,

"Is this Delilah?,"

"Yes."

"Would you be interested in a fantasy? It's quite a big one. (eh up, here we go)

"Yes come on then let's hear it," (more book material, it's all good)

"Would you be interested in doing stuff with my dog?,"

"Jesus fucking Christ mate, you have serious problems."

Saw a second chap later on, whilst wearing my Tesco Xmas pudding jumper. Is this wrong? I suppose I should try and at least look feminine even if my lady parts have long since retired. But honestly, men don't seem to notice my clothes, they are in an erotic mist, having wanked until blue in the face, over my deceptively attractive photos. Anyway it's far too cold to make an effort. He'd requested a tantric massage on the phone but having no idea what on earth this is, I began pushing my fingers into his back. After about ten minutes he turned over and I realised he'd soaked the new duvet.

Now, as mentioned before, and sorry to buck the trend but semen arouses the same feelings in me as a bowl of week old, cold tapioca. I am not a fan of the stuff. I ushered him out ASAP and put all bedding in at 60 degrees with some disinfectant thrown in, to be sure all nasties were killed. The good news was he'd arrived with a box of Milk Tray which made for a marvellous evening of eating chocolate and spinning the wool from the Dorset Downs.

I'm reminded of an outcall I did during my first month of escorting. I think it was only my third or fourth experience; I received a call from a very polite, respectful sounding chap (lord knows why, I don't think I'd have much respect for a bloke who shagged women for a living) with whom I arranged an overnight stay at a hotel in Torquay. The journey took me eight hours! But the job was paying £700, vital cash. I'd set off in the morning in my pickup after feeding the livestock, having left Nellie with my mum at her home in Haycastle. Unaccustomed as I was to driving beyond the five miles to Asda and the agricultural supplies store, an eight hour drive had emptied my brain of all normal decision making capabilities, and I arrived at the seafront hotel with one mission on my mind, to find food. I was tired, stressed and in a strange town, about to spend 24 hours with someone I'd never met and who I was almost certainly not going to like. I needed to eat, on a big scale.

Given that he was paying a goodly amount of money I decided to ditch the Christmas pudding jumper for a day and don a Cotton Traders 5XL tshirt and a freshly washed Bushman's shepherds smock. I was four hours late and blamed it on sheep on the road, feeble but the best I could manage at the time.

My mental problems regarding food had not abated and within twenty minutes of walking into his hotel room I'd polished off two small bowls of sugar cubes. They are delicious, the roughly hewn little brown jobbies, like sugar boulders. Ive always had a passion for sugar cubes.

"Christ, you can put it away!," he politely exclaimed, nibbling away on a complementary hotel biscuit. He was from the West Country, and spoke like a genuine Wurzel. In his early 40's, with a narrow bendy cock like those flexible heated things you use to curl your hair with, he was one of those irritatingly active sorts that I wanted to smack. Notwithstanding, I devoured the delicious meal he'd had delivered to the room, followed by the remains of his, then had to fight off his tongue, probing around my mouth and throat like a triffid. Listening to his incessant Bristolian ramblings, only bearable through the haze of half a kg of sugar cubes, I collapsed in bed, dog tired and about to burst through overeating. Fell instantly asleep, awoken by him rattling and jerking up and down on top of me, making my teeth knock together. He came in minutes, praise the Lord. Couldn't sleep as the bed was ludicrously soft, so slept in bunk bed that was in the same room. He offered very politely to leave me alone to sleep and said he was going back home to his home in Torquay, fantastic news! His immortal words were delivered in perfect Wurzelian dialect,

"Reckon it were oy that were fucked nod 'ee."

I awoke at 10am after eleven hours sleep and upon discovering he'd generously left the bill open for me, I enjoyed a breakfast of sugar cubes, bacon, sausage, mushroom, cereal, croissants, plus biscuits and chocolate on the drive home. Compulsive eating and escorting are really not compatible.

Nov 5th 2005

I've literally just opened this email:

"May I ask Delilah, when is your next period due and what sort of bread do you like?."

(Am very much hoping these two topics are not connected in any way)

"Mercifully I am enjoying an early menopause and make my own bread. Good day to you."

Agreed to a booking with a guy who sounded polite and professional with a subtle Yorkshire accent and just a tinsy bit familiar. At 1pm he drove in, in his Discovery, climbed the steps of the hut, and I, horrified, exclaimed;

"Ah!, it's you."

"Aye, it's me," he replied. Several minutes of awkwardness followed. He'd been at the farm the previous week taking blood samples from our bulls; Big Business and Oliver. I was confused, should we discuss the best wormer for Nematodirus outbreaks in lambs, or do I whip his you know what out and get to work ASAP. In the end I did both, ensuring I got an hours free veterinary advice before lamely guddling around with his clever veterinary willy. He didn't return and a different vet appeared at our next farm visit.

Nov 8th 2005

Saw a bloke tonight, yuck yuck yuck, smelly balls, sucked his horrid cock till lockjaw set in and in desperation to have him leave, said a ewe was lambing (in November? he didn't twig).

Ear tagged all 250 lambs today with no disaster, it was a good job.

Have seen a client called Barnaby a few times now, who pays me to stay overnight at his farm. He's clearly very taken with me and the last time we met, made me a supper of French onion soup and brownies as a seal of his undying devotion. I was most definitely not in love with Barnaby or his soup, in fact I found him bordering on the repulsive. He told me one evening that his ex partner had left him because he 'breathed too loudly.'

"Can you believe it?," he cried, "I mean fancy dumping me for breathing, the cow."

After three hours spent sitting on the sofa watching repeats of Countdown, I too wanted to leave him. His breathing was of the advanced Tuberculosis variety, a cacophony of snorts and burbles and quick inhalations, followed by long exhalations that sounded like a punctured tyre. I wanted to kill Barnaby, to stuff a dishcloth into his burbling mouth.

We went to bed that night and when he had completed the disagreeable business of his putting his willy in my private parts, he wheezed off to the bathroom. The bedroom was filled with a very distinct smell, it didn't smell human or if it was, it was a rotting infected part of a human. It really was awful, though nothing was said, and at the time I genuinely blamed Barnaby's back passage (as in rectum, not his utility room). I sprayed some Lynx about while he coughed and rattled away in the bathroom, and didn't return.

A week later I saw another client and again the appalling smell. It turned out I must have had some sort of womb infection because a brown, viscous discharge appeared in my pants that smelt like a decomposing rodent was in my uterus, God it was a savage honk. Thing is there was no discomfort whatsoever and utter coward that I am, I was too scared to visit the doctor in case he diagnosed me with the first case since the 15th century, of syphilis. I have always used a condom and if I'm now sterile, well that's fabulous news. Why couldn't I have contracted decomposing rodent in uterus disease years ago.

I had a text enquiry from a mature gentleman today, about 70 years of age. We arranged a suitable day and time as he sounded a nice, well bred sort of chap. His final text before he set off to meet me was,

"Looking forward to meeting you. You sound very nice and pleasant, your pics are great. I do like giving oral and receiving and like 69 as well as doggy, hope you are up for wearing stockings and suspenders."

Breaking this text down into its pertinent parts, I can safely sat that no, I like none of the above. I know it's only one hour and it's good money but this time the thought of a long long hour with an old man and one odious task after another was just too much to poke up with. I cancelled the appointment. I know I have plumbed new depths of asexuality in the last year or so but why the hell would two people want each other's smelly privates and bum holes in each other's faces? Having had to undergo this ordeal a few times before I removed it from my 'enjoys' list, the short straw must surely be held by the person trapped beneath.

Nov 10th 2005

My goat Heidi died of acute toxic mastitis, tragic as she was the sweetest gentlest goat, I can't quite believe she has gone. She'd had several doses of antibiotics but the infection had entered her bloodstream. Heidi had given birth to two kids, ten weeks ago who by now will be fine on cereals and hay. When the death collection man came to collect the mother, it was fortunate that Archie's wife, Henrietta, was away for the day, she being a squeamish and sensitive soul. The death man is a simple, smiling chap who gurns a lot and whom I could not bring myself to look at for longer than necessary today, owing to the blob of mucus dangling from his large red nose. Having piled the goat into a barrow, he wheeled her down the hill, across the immaculate garden and through the gravel frontage of the Manor House, leaving a trail of blood from her lolling head. Like it or not you do become somewhat hardened to farm deaths, it is an inevitable, sad and costly part of farming. But also a lamentable state of affairs when folk who are working in agriculture have to tiptoe around the wealthy Londoners living in their country farmhouses, for fear of offending them. The mere mention of mastitis and a dead goat would have had Henrietta reaching for the smelling salts.

Nov 15th 2005

Had sexual intercourse with a 67 year old. Poor bloke had had a hernia operation a few months back and his abdomen looked like he'd wrestled a shark. He was pleasant enough but I found him just a tincy bit revolting, his groin area was safe enough but his armpits whiffed like a marathon runners, twenty miles in.

"Can we kiss?."

"Er, ok but I had Pesto with extra onion last night", a lie of course. I would have eaten sheep droppings, fresh warm ones if it meant not having to endure his wet old tongue roving around my mouth. Did I ever like this human breeding nonsense? I assume I must have done years ago, but even in these day of endless dental hygiene products, a lot of people have dodgy old teeth, plaquey gums and awful breath. I have a very good nose for these things and can pick up in seconds, a suspect mouth interior.

Prostitution is truly an abominable way of paying ones bills, harken reader, harken...

Wanked off a 6'4" bloke in the woods at the risk of being beaten to death with a rock but he paid me £50 so I was happy. I think farming has relaxed my outlook on men and their bits.

A couple of texts:

"Hi, your blog about the straw delivery is hilarious! Seriously made me laugh out loud!, in fact I had to move seats on the train as people were looking peeved at my raucous laughter!."

"Thank you! That's good to hear."

"Yes, amazing, I loved it."

(I have the above man to thank, because it was his text that sparked the idea of collating my experiences into a book).

"Hi Delilah I'm 99% sure I came to see you a few months ago. You were older, voluptuous and well spoken. You lived in a really nice old gypsy caravan and teased my balls and Bell End with a vibrator, have I the right lady?."

I didn't reply to this, always a bit wary that it's the wife, attempting to catch me out. Anyway I'm even older now and much more voluptuous. He also seems to have given 'Bell End,' street name status.

Nov 20th 2005

Major outbreak of Haemonchus Contortus in sheep and goats; the whole face and jaw doubles in size, apparently it's the protein cells leaking fluid as the blood is devoured by the worms in the intestine, quite disgusting. As soon as it's light tomorrow I shall let the goats out of the field to 'browse,' ie; feed from the trees and hedges. The reason the goats have got Haemonchus is because I had to shut them in that field rather them letting them roam and browse as the blighters were treading on and destroying all the fences, and so they were forced to graze. The grass is where the Haemonchus resides. Goats evolved to feed upwards from hedges and trees, not downwards, so they have no immunity to this particular worm. Will medicate everything tomorrow.

I've sold my old quad bike to Percy, a neighbouring farmer. It was a pile of old shite and would conk out at least once per day.

Nov 26th 2005

Saw a guy today for a two hour booking who looked very similar to Dickie Strawbridge, it wasn't of course, he didn't have the green credentials and the moustache was too small. £200 worth of delectable little notes.

Nov 29th 2005

Saw a bloke tonight, after dark. Now bearing in mind my profile says 'no blacks due to personal reasons' (it's the willy thing, it's just too much), he turned up and well, you couldn't have had a blacker bloke walk through the gates. He was a pleasant chap but I was mightily relieved when he'd gone.

Saw another city guy today, he said a very true thing,

"As soon as they (women) know you're in banking, they look at you like they want to harvest your organs."

Charming comment made by a man today, who was lying on my bed at the time,

"You're attractive, but you do look your age, those wispy bits at the side of your head add a few years." (Wispy bits? Wispy bits?)

I am overdrawn by several hundred pounds and I owe the vet. Went to agri supplies today for two gate hinges and sander pads. Was on way home with sensible, if rather unfeminine purchases and then impulsively, with surprising speed and suddenness, I swung into Hemingways, the over priced tat store, full of tat you had no idea you really wanted till you walked in. I bought a big plastic goat for £95. Am I bloody mad?!!

Ten minutes previously, having stared long and thoughtfully at a £75 fence battery, in order that Archibald's donkey, May, can't destroy my veggie patch, I was moved to misery at the thought of spending so much money on something so mundane. So I bought a plastic blackbird, a small plastic Friesian cow and a two inch high terracotta pot. Sod the battery, artificial livestock would be sure to come in handy.

Nov 30th 2005

Once more, I managed to pluck up the courage and open escort emails, something I dread. Sat down with a cider this time, here we go..

"Hi there, I'm a clean, kinky young man, hoping to book you this Tuesday for a half hour in-call. During this meeting as part of the booking, I'd like rimming both ways. I am 100% smooth. I use Veet regularly and will do so on the day of the booking. Looking forward to speaking to you. Love Puss-in-boots."

(I had no idea men used Veet)

"Hi there! Just looking at your pics whilst stroking my cock, wud love to cum visit and spend a few hours fucking you every which way and watch you cum lots. I bet you get super wet n slippery (nope, dry as an old JCloth). I'm in Halifax, miles away so I'd need a day trip there to see you during the week and I'll tell wife I'm having a long day at work. I'm 45, good looking, with a nice cock."

(Your poor poor wife)

"Hi there, do you see British born Asian guys, 39 years old, if not very sorry to bother you. Do you do 69 sex, cd I lick your pussy and lick your bum. Do you rim or not? I wash and am clean down below. I only like white women, sorry, it's a preference, I am married to one and see others on the side. You have a very nice beautiful sexy body, nice boobs esp nice looking tasty ass, love to be suffocated with that wow absolutely beautiful. My dick not that big but women say my girth pretty big. Thanks v much!."

Occasionally a text arrives that bears no relevance to escorting whatsoever:

"My Chinese mate had a girlfriend called Lorraine, but he was cheating on her with another girl called Claire Lee. Unfortunately Lorraine died. At her funeral he stood up and sang,

"I can see Claire Lee now Lorraine has gone."

Another text from same person, a few minutes later,

"Morning Jimmy, I'm back to work so using work phone for a couple of hours. Found a photo of your ex on it!."

"This is Delilah, you have the wrong number."

"So sorry, is this Delia the chef?,"

"No, Delilah the prostitute."

"What the fuck! I've well got the wrong number sorry!."

"No probs."

(Long pause lasting an hour)

"So are you as fit as that cook on TV?,"

(I had no idea Delia was 'fit')

"I am not Delia Smith. I have limited cooking skills, leave me alone unless you want to book me."

He left me alone.

Dec 2nd 2005

Another particularly debauched text from a semi literate twenty something, with, I suspect, tattoos covering at least a quarter of his body and either on benefits or a building site, or quite possibly, both,

"Hi do you do cock sucking without condom, come in mouth, swallow, rimming and dress like a filthy slut?,"

"No, no, no, no and no."

An interesting text:

"Could I take you shopping for shoes?,"

"Why shoes? I'm not interested in shoes,"

"I like shoes, which sort would you prefer?,"

"Waterproof hiking boots and wellies."

"Great! I'll buy some. Do you mind going shopping with a young guy?,"

"I'm not into shopping, can we make it quick,"

"That's fine, how much are the boots you want? I bought my mum's friend some leather boots today. I only have £400 left."

"Why do you want to take an old lady shopping?,"

"Bcoz I like older women especially when they like young guys spending money on them. I'm 16 so a lot of women don't like that but I have taken my mum's friend shopping secretly a few times and she then let's me smell her feet as a reward. Would you reward me or just give me the honour of spending time with you?."

"Er yeah, sure, sniff my feet lad, can I sniff yours?," (is this kid for real?!)

"Hee hee, if you want. It's nice to find ladies who don't mind letting a 16 year old smell their feet as long as they keep it secret, (I wasn't planning on telling anyone, just publishing this book at some point) would you let me do anything else or just smell your feet?."

"If you pay me the set rates I provide a set service."

"Mum's friend (who the hell **is** this woman?) snogged me and let me suck her tits, before peeing on my chest."

(This kid has an adventurous imagination for a youngster)

"It's so dominant to have an older woman pee on me. Have you ever peed on a 16 year old?."

"Can't say I have."

"Would you be willing to pee on my face or in my mouth then?,"

"Mm, no." (I'm after a £200 pair of work boots, not urinating down a virgin's neck)

"That's ok, I guess you wouldn't want to have sex or intimate service?,"

A vastly overgrown, fifty acre field on the farm springs to mind;

"Actually, what I'd find enormously arousing is to have a lad toiling in the fields for no payment for two weeks, can you use a chainsaw and reverse a tractor and trailer?." (Long shot but worth a try)

"I've always wanted an older woman to make me work for free!."

"Best get yourself a stout pair of steel toecaps if you're going to be walking 50 acres for a fortnight."

He didn't text back.

Have just come in from going through boss's flock, doing pre-tupping checks for teeth, udders and body condition. Does anyone out there understand the following email? I don't, it's nonsense, he must surely be a few sausages short or am I a total prude?,

"I don't think I've tried to meet you before, and maybe sissies like me are not your cup of tea but you sound so lovely and right up my street, so I had to try, sorry if I'm being a pest. I was hoping that you would agree to see me this week and take charge of me in my frillies for a while to see if you would consider taking me on, on a regular basis for corrupting and sexually dominating. Please Miss, **plcase** could I come to one of your parties?," (parties?, the last party I can remember having was when I was five and my mum made me a chocolate Smartie cake and bought me Stickle Bricks) "I'm not into big pain but do like to be forced feminised, cuffed and sexually abused and corrupted whilst truly powerless. Sort of a cross between domination, girlfriend experience, adult baby minding and sissy rape." (Blimey, no idea what any of that means but it doesn't sound very wholesome) "I am happy to attend a party or any other suggestion/command that you make. I'm not sure I'd be much good as one of your studs though. I am quite shy, rather small and love to be tied up and corrupted sexually so I'm not butch at all, sorry! I love party girls so am happy to reimburse all expenses in that area." (Does lambing vaguely count as a party? He could reimburse all veterinary, feed and medicine costs) "I don't party but used to and miss the atmosphere and am very happy should you wish to instruct me to see and pay another mistress as well as you, in fact two of you or more would be wonderful. I am very genuine Miss. Please will you consider a 'Sissy Trial' for me mistress? I'm happy to come to you or book a hotel, lots of love, Slutty Baby Lucy."

Nope, I've re-read this email but my simple, rural mind simply cannot piece together this fucked up sexual jigsaw. He must have had a troubled childhood, surely no one is born this way? Ok, I'll open one more email before I head out again,

"Hi Delegation, do you offer OWO or CIM," (this means 'oral without' and 'cum in mouth') hope to see you soon."

"I do not drink semen, preferring instead Assam with a little honey. I do not approach penises without a protective covering on them as they weep an unpleasant slimy substance prior to ejaculation, and many possess a sour smell, similar to that of a busy fishing port.

Best wishes, Delegation,

PS; you may be wise to check your predictive text before hitting the 'send' button in future."

Re the sissy email, I did actually see one in the flesh a few months ago. As usual, a pressing need for income had me agree to an outcall at a hotel to 'service a sissy.' God only knows what this means but I must have sounded convincing enough on the phone in order for him to book me;

I knocked on the door, and a bald, forty something gentleman answered; over six foot tall, with a hairy chest and extremely buck teeth, clad in a Barbara Cartland get up: baby pink frilly negligee, bra and pink ballet pumps. I had to tie him to the bed and pretend to be dominating, bloody ridiculous carry on, bouncing around for a while on top of his flaccid appendage, making polite conversation for ten minutes about the new Chip and Pin legislation and my bad lambing percentages, before he realised I was utterly incompetent at servicing his needs and asked me politely to leave.

Another time, I'd arrived at an address I'd been given, knocked on the door and a doddery old lady answered, looking most confused as I greeted her with,

"Hello, I'm Delilah, you booked me." Much sniggering was audible from behind an adjacent hedge as I climbed miserably back into my pick-up truck. Just kids mucking about.

December 4th 2005

I have at last begun cooking proper meals, so far beef and red wine stew and a moist fruit cake, the caravan smells divine.

To add to my feminine allure I am going on a chainsaw course in Feb. Quite how I am going to fit into the safety trousers I have no idea....

Looked at £3 a bale hay at Treetop farm down road, musty and rubbish. Had a bloke booked at 10.30am. I drove in 5 mins late and he looked me up n down, obviously majorly dissappointed, declined the offer and drove away. No surprise really as I was in striped Wellibobs, Leiderhosen, a Xmas jumper and a woolly hat. He had requested, "something striped with big pants to accentuate my curves."

Saw an old boy with foul breath. If he'd been a plane, the vapour trail would have stretched to Cornwall. It's getting really hard to fake any sort of pleasure now. I'm really really hating it. Have to try hard not to be rude on the phone to them.

December 6th 2005

Reserved two Kerry Hill ewe lambs today from a breeder near Haworth, forgot to get a connector cap for worming gun at agri stores, so I now have to individually worm 200 lambs with a 5ml syringe, plonker.

Saw a client who worked as a pest control man, so asked him if he could put some fresh rat bait in orphan lamb shed, before relieving him manually. Escort phone rang whilst I was crutching the lambs out today, why oh why do I take calls when I'm on farm, it never works,

"Could I pop in for a quick BJ?."

"No, I'm crutching," I replied over the din of 400 baaing sheep. He hung up.

At the end of today I had a wonderful hot soak in the farmhouse bath, Henrietta's very good like that and often her and Archie will invite me over for supper and a chat. Tonight's bath was a deep, herbal foamy one, I felt like a new woman afterwards, having exfoliated, moisturised and talcum powdered every crevice, but then went and spoilt the moment by seeing a man whose toenails were so disgusting I had him put his socks back on. Finally settled down with a Tia Maria on ice and watched Castaway, I would happily have Wilson for a friend instead of a person.

December 7th 2005

Had to take PC in to be fixed today, I thumped it a couple of days ago for playing up, not very intelligent of me at all. It objected. Christ, they'll see the pics of me draping my naked rolls over furniture for the photo session I had.

When I first began this appalling sideline, being very naïve, I used to give blow jobs without a condom, which was foolish and very risky health-wise, but I genuinely had no idea it was unsafe. I wouldn't do it now if I was offered £500 an hour. I'd rather give mouth to mouth to a TB infected badger.

December 9th 2005

I saw two guys today, a grand total of £140 for about eighty minutes work, sounds great and it is great but yesterday, for example, not a single call or text so I have to grab the opportunities when they occur.

One of the guys was a chunky 42 year old married man, reasonably content he said but had been with his woman for ten years and they hadn't had sex for five years, same old story. He confided in me that he loved to spank women and in particular to be spanked himself by older women approaching their sixties. He thought Helen Mirren was gorgeous. The kinky buggar also told me that when he was first spanked at school for being naughty, at about five years of age, he distinctly remembers enjoying the sensation and also said that being lightly kicked was a turn-on too.

I don't understand any of it, plain Jane me. He emailed later to say he found watching me pull on my farm boiler suit and wellies afterwards, a turn on. (Eh?) He had gone to visit an escort another time to discover she was a chain smoker and so subsequently reeked like an old jazz club carpet when he left her flat. His wife would have suspected immediately so he had to go to Asda and buy an entirely new outfit before travelling home. The things men do for rumpy pumpy.

December 11th 2005

Scald in four ewes this morning so have invested in a foot pad; a big sponge filled mat that you soak in a bacteria killing solution, and then it's a case of training the sheep to walk across it. It took me three hours to tempt 20 sheep using sugar beet nuts and cooing sweet words of encouragement. I did it eventually. Another week or so they'll be fine. Contrary to the commonly held opinion of them being stupid, they are in fact, extremely bright. A stupid animal would run across it, giving no thought to potential danger. As far as they were concerned, it looked very suspicious indeed. I love my sheep.

Saw an Indian chap today, I could smell his pooey bottom and there were poo smears on my white duvet afterwards. Jesus.

Sneakily wormed cows today by mixing Fasinex, a fluke wormer, in with soaked sugar beet. They decided to rip open a bale of haylage themselves and had a good scoff, so will start feeding them from now on. Archie bought a new teaser ram today. A teaser is a vasectomised ram that stimulates all the ewes to ovulate and therefore makes for a more compact lambing, because once ovulating, the ewes tend to become synchronised, in the same way nuns do. I can vouch for this having spent ten years as a devout nun.

Saw a tall, trendy bloke with a bright ginger beard, who'd shaved his entire upper body, but had two days growth on it, was like touching a big pan scourer.

December 15th 2005

Teaser ram seems pretty docile, Archie named him Flash. Ewes are ploughing through their energy feed blocks, they all look in really good condition. Must get into town at some point for a new bra, my bust is sagging like a bag of lemons. Saw a chap who's £80 paid for much needed brake pads on the pickup. Sat in hut at lunch time, enjoying a salad of spinach, Mozzerella, tomatoes and balsamic vinegar, and a glass of rose petal wine, bought from the local winery, who pick the roses and make the wine themselves, it's divine. Mistakenly opened my hooky emails during lunch:

"Fuck you, you fat dirty whore, ur just too fat, fat girls sweat and smell a lot."

I decided to let him continue through life under the misguided knowledge that all overweight women smell. Saw a horrid little man this afternoon, he had a front tooth missing and what looked like a glass eye, smelly armpits and clammy hands. He then got up and left a big poo smear on bed, that's two smears in as many days. Upon seeing the deposit he'd left, he said,

"I do apologise, I had a chicken tikka masala at work."

I was lost for words. All bedding was stripped, windows opened, lavender essential oil sprinkled generously over mattress and carpet and thoroughly vacuumed. Re-made bed, fresh flowers from local florist on table and all memories of ghastly men exorcised until tomorrow. Listened to Rachmaninov's Piano Concerto No.3, in its entirety, complete bliss. Up at 6am tomorrow, as Galloway bull is being delivered.

December 19th 2005

Bloke today grunted from behind,

"Joo wannit harder Delilah," as he thrust away manfully.

(No, I want you to finish whatever it is you are trying to do, go home and leave me to my pasta and Brokeback Mountain.)

My bra smells strongly of onions, I must have put it in with a load of kitchen tea towels. Didn't enjoy today, endless texts and calls on hooky phone, up and down hill to check on progress of ground workers who are laying chalk around barn entrance and water troughs. Met with a second hedging guy who'd I'd sourced locally, showed him the hedges that needed laying and left him to it. He tapped on my door twenty minutes later, and whimpered,

"I just can't, I've got such a headache, it's too much, I just cant."

I was speechless, another moron? Sent him home with a verbal kick up the ars. Bull arrived, lovely chap, woolly and compact. Rung and arranged session of lamb cutting with butcher, rung abattoir, took calls from the usual aroused men and was acerbic with all of them. In bed by 9.30pm, shattered. Just before I turned phone off, two texts arrived in quick succession;

"Hello, (huskily) is that Delilah?,"

"Yep."

"I've got a fantasy,"

(Jesus here we go again)

"I want you to watch me eat my own cum."

(That's no bad thing, if he's eating it, he's not breeding, and that is good news.)

"Firstly, why on earth would I want to watch you do that? Secondly, why on earth would you want to do that anyway?."

And another text asking if I 'do bareback,' this means sex with no condom. These are the same individuals that throw their litter out of cars I'm sure.

Then a call;

"I think you should bend over, touch your toes and I give you six of the best."

"I think you should bend over, touch your toes, and I'll give you six of the best, with my steel toe caps."

Turned phone off and wished, not for the first time, that I'd paid attention at school.

December 21st 2005

Separated out another scanned group of ewes into twins, singles and triplet bearing ewes and offered adlib feed blocks to multiples.

Client gave me roses and Baileys today and showed me all the pictures of the women he'd bedded, fascinating. He was fat and unattractive, very wealthy and squeezed me constantly like a bloody cheese press, I could have punched him. Another after lunch, ejaculated via hand thank God whilst convulsing and writhing about like a road kill deer.

Text from a bloke asking if I did 'ball bashing.' Apparently being kicked hard in the testicles was a turn on for him. The world has gone mad. Had phone call this evening, gruff East End accent;

"Ello zat Diloyla??,"

"I'm sorry?,"

"Yeh am I speakin' to Diloyla?,"

"Speaking, how can I help?," (I know exactly how I could help, by assisting you in talking properly.)

"Yeh wots your availabiliee and do ya spesher lize in anyfink?."

"Yes, chocolate and chestnut refrigerator cake."

(Stony uncomprehending silence)

"Oy mean loike, do ya do fant asee role play stuff?."

"No I don't, goodbye, and thanks for the book material."

Went into town today to pay money into bank and decided to treat myself to a coke float in Pizza Hut;

"Hello, what would you like Madame?,"

"Could I order a portion of chips and a coke float please?,"

"I'm sorry coke floats are only available from the child's menu, and you're an adult."

"But, I'm not not asking for an adult portion, just exactly what's on the menu."

"I'm afraid you can't have a coke float because you are an adult."

"But this is madness, I'm not asking for an under 5's admission to Disneyworld, I just want a bloody coke float."

"No sorry we can't let you do that."

"One day, you will look back at this episode in your life and marvel at the sheer ludicrousness of it," I replied.

I left Pizza Hut in a huff and consoled myself with a cream tea in a nice little cottage teashop.

I'm amazed at how much harder I've become over the last year. When I shut my door after waving a faked smiling goodbye, they leave my head. And when I get into bed, I don't recall any of the foul deeds committed upon it, a mental screen comes down when I open the door to them, and just as well or I'd be licking the walls in a mental institution. I had a two hour booking with a black man earlier today, another one who clearly hadn't read my profile. It's an alarming experience, glancing nervously up whilst lying on your back, having King Kong pounding your cervix. I made him tea and kept him talking for an hour beforehand, thus protracting the dreaded deed and only leaving him ten minutes in which to ejaculate.

Men sometimes say they feel guilty sneaking around on their partners, most don't feel guilty. The former are the guys who see escorts regularly and often become addicted to the habit of seeing a different one every month. I can understand the addiction in that if I were a sexually frustrated husband and there was a website offering every variety of bonbon, dolly-mixture and all-sort, I'd be picking and mixing as often as my bank balance would allow. Everyone lies, but men statistically more because the poor buggers are often suppressing sexual desires that mostly involve them having sex with women, and men, other than their partners. They are just behaving as evolution intended, no one gender is morally superior to the other. But having seen engaged men, men married only for one year with pregnant wives, and men of 80 with dead wives still warm in their coffins, as a woman, it is sometimes hard to like them. I have come to the conclusion that they are simply not genetically equipped to remain devoted to one sexual partner. It is in their DNA to reproduce with endless women in order to increase our numbers (like we need it, what we could really do with is another Black Death, it wiped out approximately one half of Europes' population in the 14th century. That would sort out the housing crisis, immigration and environmental issues). But I do genuinely feel sorry for most of the men I've seen. They fall haplessly into the marriage/mortgage/kids scenario, usually because the female half has pressured them into doing so, and spend the next fifty years covertly searching out physical release from the situation they themselves have created. I'm kinda glad I was born female, I'd rather deal with messy sanitary towels and when that's done with after 35 years, night sweats and a beard, than the uncontrollable desire to shag, wank and watch porn till I drop dead at 90. I await the maelstrom of furious emails from happily married men and women to arrive in my inbox. I'm just describing the view from this side of the hedge.

December 22nd

At last, after two years of promising myself, four shiny new BF Goodrich tyres are now on pick up. Finally decided to order them when I ended up in a hedge after sliding down a hilly field with a load of sheep grub in the back. Then lost grip again and slid into metal gate post, leaving deep gouge along side of truck.

Wonderful man brought me Milk Tray today...bliss.

Have a pain in my lower belly, just above the pubic bone, could be the onset of the menopause, a hernia, something terminal, constipation or an exceedingly small child. No chance, unless Archangel Gabriel's been up to his old tricks again. Speaking of which, that special time of year is nearly upon us. If there is a God why oh why doesn't he just pop down once in a while, I mean think of the moral boost it would give everyone if he stuck his head round the door during Midnight Mass at some huge cathedral, turned the water into wine to the tune of 'I told you so' and pootled back up to the starry skies. Oh well it's a damn good excuse for sparkly baubles and mulled wine.

My hair is frustratingly grey at the roots; inner hippy says, "sod it," and proceed as nature intended, while my, "oh god I don't want to get old," inner Jordan says, "Botox and dye and plump everything in sight." A bit like restoring a Tudor building; it's never going to look like the original but the clock can at least be frozen in time.

December 23rd 2005

Wormed all oldies today, the retired ewes who've I've kept on because I'm a softie. Mucked out their pen, 25 barrow loads, anti bacterial powder on ground and fresh straw, happy sheep. Returned to hut, lit stove and got breakfast on the go. Text just arrived,

"Hi Delilah, how ru? Do you sell your bra and panties?."

"No I don't."

The word 'panties' brings to mind impossibly little lacy affairs with all the odour absorbing qualities and buttock support of a disposable doily. Proper pants, the 'fuck me big pants' Hugh Grant sort, now that's pure comfort. Opened escorting email box, always a source of amusement;

"Dear Delilah,

I have paused to ponder and admire your profile many times over the last year. You seem such a nice, (nope) sweet, (definitely nope) country girl (definitely) and a little bit posh?! (Hm yes, a bit) pretty, (used to be) and my god, what a magnificent bosom you possess! (Whatever) You live quite a distance from me, about 100 miles, yet I feel compelled to see you at least once in my lifetime. My real age is 55, yet I am very fit and certainly raring to go (terrific). As you'll see, my feedback on the site is rather good and I am a bit of a naughty boy. (Probably referring to the fact he has a fascination for rectums) Well Delilah I would really like to get very naughty with you! (Stay away from my backside.)

And so I wonder whether you might consider a proposition. I would like to drive all the way to Yorkshire and take you out to dinner, (yes, now we're talking) spend all the meal flirting and talking with you (oh dear) and then go back to yours for a jolly good rogering. But not before I have teased and massaged your glorious body and kissed you all over. (Ditch the rogering bit and leave me at the restaurant) The whole extravaganza might take three hours and you would have to devote your evening to me, poor you! (Telling me) Dinner of course would be on me. May I enquire as to whether you would be happy to indulge in such an escapade, and also, what remuneration you might require for your valuable time? I must stress here that I am in no way rich, I am a man of very modest means.

I look very much forward to hearing from you Delilah, and in the meantime I shall just have to slaver (ugh) over your beautiful pictures, hoping at some point to savour the real deal!

Very best wishes

Adam x"

"Hi. Looking at your profile I think you are perfect to help me play out a fantasy I have. I am looking for a lady to indulge me in being my vivacious aunt who knows exactly what she wants and how to get it; dressed in a skirt, suspenders and loosely buttoned blouse, she parades in front of me before ordering me to ravage her with my tongue as she drops her skirt and bends over to offer both her bum and pussy to me for satisfaction and worship. Is this something you can help me with? (Absolutely bloody not) I'd love to hear from you.

Phil x"

"Hi Delilah,

What a superb pair you have, well done! We had a bumper crop of blackberries in Wiltshire this autumn just gone, was it the same in Yorkshire?

Absolutely no need to reply if you're busy.

Best wishes, Anthony xxx"

"Hi, this is going to sound like a weird proposition but I'm gay and me and my boyfriend have a fetish where we love to fuck with used condoms on. (Oh sweet Mary, I am sat here in the warm, comfortable atmosphere of Costa, writing Cockadoodledoo, there are people sat around, normal people drinking hot chocolate and coffee, and I'm reading emails about 'fucking with used condoms.' May I burn in hell) We had a couple of girls on here that helped us out by collecting them from their clients for a day and then sending them in the mail to us, we will pay for the postage of course (I think the Royal Mail would take a dim view of this). Please let me know if this would interest you, if not, please delete this message. (Delete pressed.)

Thanks for reading

Michael xx"

December 24th 2005

Was up early this morning, changed sheep footbath water and cleaned out three water troughs, back in by 8am for breakfast and checked out escort texts;

"I need a good duck."

"I mean fuck."

"I would much prefer a laying duck."

"Oh so why are you an escort then? Or are you saying I'm a duck?,"

"I meant it literally, I prefer egg on toast to penises."

"What if I cook you a duck egg on toast while you suck me off? I'm a chef and I can cook for you."

"Egg on toast yes, penis sucking..most definitely no, thank you, and good day."

"I need your huge tits all over me and your tongue down my throat. Free this morning?." (Free when Earth and Neptune collide)

At 5pm today I have a gentleman visitor who I very much hope will be a lifesaver in my present money situation. He is quite taken with me, and though he is 80, on his previous visit two weeks ago, tackled the monumental task of massaging my backside and legs and made an excellent job of it. I mentioned my money situation and he said he had a business proposition for me. Hope to god it doesn't involve sex.

December 27th 2005

Well what a tight arsed old fucker he turned out to be. Did I hint at the possibility of a sugar daddy in the last diary entry? Not a bloody bit of it, more like 'flaunt my wealth in front of you, you destitute old prozzy who can't manage her money,' daddy. His exact words yesterday were, 'don't worry Delilah, I have a business plan to put to you, it will be fine.' Turns out all he planned on giving me was top notch management advice to the tune of, 'wear a tighter top and invest in some pink fluffy handcuffs, in order to tempt more men.' Bloody great, thanks. He was sat there flashing photographs of his classic cars for me to see, as if I give a monkeys, was pleasant enough but reluctant to pay me anything at all. Anyway I manage to wheedle four pints of M&S milk out of him and £70 for a half hour booking, even though he'd been here three hours. I'm either very stupid or very soft or both.

Ate a well deserved, family sized roasted vegetable tart when he'd left and headed to bed. Have two care jobs tomorrow for two old ladies. Nothing wrong with either of them, bit vacuous between the ears, perfectly sound in body, but basically bone idle, the pair of them. Many old folks are I find. They sit around watching Homes Under the Hammer whilst they're their joints seize up through lack of movement and become disproportionately irritated at little things. One of the old ladies muttered to me one day,

"That bloody bird hasn't shut up for hours."

It was a blackbird. A bored human was irritated by a blackbird singing. God help the human race.

As I'm sure you will have spotted by the date, it's Christmas and this year, myself, my brother, plus Mum and Dad, spent two lovely days in the Yorkshire Dales, in a gorgeous old manor house near Hawes, belonging to a friend of mine. Tensions rose on Boxing Day however and resulted in my father throwing his toys out of the pram and storming off in a post festive huff, leaving a trail of baubles and confused family members in his wake. He redeemed himself pretty quickly by cooking us all roast beef the following day, so all good. Though Ma and Pa have been divorced for donkeys years, they remain good friends and we all get together as a family several times a year.

Once back at my wee hut, I enjoyed a very pleasant, relaxing and man free afternoon, drinking mulled wine and eating crisps. I watched more TV, slumped in a chair than I have for the entire year, it makes me feel guilty and ashamed, as does a takeaway, hence a Domino's pizza is a twice yearly indulgence. It's nothing to do with the calories, it's, well, it makes me feel so council houseish. Apart from the guilt, takeaway pizza produces an insatiable thirst that has me drinking pints and pints of milk. I'm bothered by the Christmas lunch we ate... celebrating the birth of the baby Jesus by enjoying my roast lamb. I have to try very hard not to think about the fact that I was there at its birth and death, and tended it in the six months in between.

December 29th 2005

Chucked it down today, sheep heartily pissed off with weather, even though they have their nice barn for shelter. I had a good idea and had a sheep sized hole, cut out of the side of the barn that I can close if needs be, so they can troop in and out at their whim, lucky girls and boys. Cows are in for the winter and bored, but if out they badly poach this heavy soil which retards grass growth in the spring.

Saw two men today, first one was a very overweight manager at the Co-op, thought he would never ejaculate, took forever. And the second, a chap that visited last week. A repeat! Unbelievable. Went to AgriStores for Crystalyx for ewes in afternoon. Text this afternoon that read,

"Is that Delilah?, your profile says you're a size 20, oh my god your loads bigger!" (Many thanks for the info)

Had a phone call after breakfast,

"Hi that Delilah?,"

"Yes it is! How may I help you?," spoken breezily and several octaves higher to effect a semblance of interest. Sadly men seem to interpret it as the voice of a woman who is extremely busy and to whom fitting cock in, is an absolute hassle. They are right of course,

"Gotta bit uva fantasy, you inta role play?,"

"Er no, sorry."

"I want you to be my older sister."

This is one of the reasons I've never wanted children and/or a man. Troubling thoughts of incest and fornicating with beasts are to be found in the darkest recesses of many mens' minds, though they may vehemently deny such things.

A man rang several times tonight and texted endlessly in order to arrange a meeting at 9pm, and, far more importantly, offered to buy us a Chinese meal. He rang from the takeaway and asked me what I fancied, great, I was a happy woman and if it had been possible to have him hand over the takeaway, and then leave immediately, perfection. Anyway, he got as far as 500 meters from the farm and rang for directions, (I could tell by the surroundings he described) turned off his phone and disappeared, never to be heard from again. I left a 'disappointed' voicemail that would have left Al Pacino trembling and was reduced to a supper of Marmite on toast. The thought of my chicken and pineapple and special fried rice driving away from me, so nearly within my grasp, was a bitter wound.

Dec 30th 2005

I am sat here writing this on a dark, cold evening in late December, the business of Christmas being for the most part, over. It is cold outside, minus two degrees and I'm jolly glad to be inside in the warm, in front of the fire. Today was not a great day as days go, Fly just did her own thing with the hoggets and would only 'stand' when I yelled at her for the third time. Once the sheep were inside, I noticed one of the hoggets had pneumonia, although sometimes when confronted with several symptoms in a sheep, it's a job to see what the actual problem is. I could see him at the far end of the field before Fly gathered them, that he was laid down and not stood with the rest of the flock, not a good sign. But he got up when he saw the dog and they all came towards me as normal. He had long, thick, vicious lengths of bramble, longer than himself, attached to his wool, which I removed. Then I noticed he had the runs and was breathing exceptionally fast.

So this is the perfect little introduction to sheep-keeping for beginners: you see a lone sheep lying down, it gets up and has a large bramble stuck to it and is breathing rapidly. Was it attached by brambles to the hedge for several hours on a freezing winters night, eventually wrenching itself free at the sight of me and my *dog? Did the sheep consequently develop diarrhoea and pneumonia as a result of food deprivation/stress? Or is the sheep already infested with intestinal worms that also produce diarrhoea? Or does it simply have pneumonia because last night was extremely cold? Or has it contracted pneumonia through a combination of a worm overload and cold? Or is it none of these things? Another problem entirely?. These are things shepherds have to deal with a lot and in almost all cases, the treatment is the same: Loxicom, which is an antiflammatory/painkiller, antibiotic and possibly a worm drench. I gave him all three when he trotted in and when I left him he was munching hay. Fingers crossed for the little chap.*

December 31st 2005

I agreed to do an overnight stay for an elderly client last night. It was a clean minimalist home just outside Harrogate, a wonderful change from my gypsy hut. As usual, the thought of anything involving body parts was too awful to contemplate, so after the polite introductions and declaring myself to be famished, I began to work my way through his fridge. Other people's fridges are very exciting indeed, I could clear fridges for a living very happily. He appeared to be so thrilled to have a woman in his house he couldn't have cared less, even when I pointed out that he bore a striking resemblance to Andrew Lloyd Webber. The Springer Spaniel who loafed about his place, chewed through the only pair of girly shoes I've ever owned, made by Irregular Choice, with three inch, transparent heels and Dolly Mixtures and Iced Gems encapsulated within. God I loved those shoes, impossible to walk in but gorgeous nonetheless. Anyway the bloody Spaniel had destroyed them, and his owner, much embarrassed, gave me £150 for a new pair. The guy produced two monstrously loud farts during the night that woke me up. I was extremely glad to be on my way home that morning.

Charlie the tractor driver here at Gallows farm seems to be getting fatter, a lot fatter, in fact when he drove in at 8am this morning in his little blue Fiat, his huge frame and enormous stomach encased in a tight, blue waterproof anorak, he fairly filled the front half of the car. It looked like the airbag had gone off.

Ok folks, ghastly text time..

"Hi is this the lovely Delilah?,"

"Yes it is."

"Ow grand bit worried I had wrong number he he! I've been looking at your profile and like the look of your lovely big breasts, ow sorry my names Nat."

"Hi Nat, let me know when you have a day and time in mind."

"Sorry if I'm a bit forward I think I've texted you before I really love your blogs, I'm a country lad as well, I drive tractors for work. We might be able to work something out as you're a country lady."

"Where are you based?."

"Haworth."

"Sorry that's way too close for comfort, I have to be discrete."

"Ow I would keep it to myself no one would know apart from us." (and all your agri drinking lads down the local)

"No sorry."

"That's a big shame I was really looking forward to sucking your nipples." (on the contrary, it's a blessed relief to have you nowhere near my bloody nipples) "Ow ok well if u ever need logs I do em for £65 a truck load."

As I sit here on the steps of the hut, looking out across the achingly beautiful moorland, listening to the occasional sheep bleating and the contented clucking of the hens pecking and raking under the hut, I receive a text, reasonably typical in content:

"You're stunning, would you do an outcall, Edinburgh, 5*hotel all paid?."

"Are you rich and famous?,"

"Definitely rich! I'd love to meet you! Questions: party girl?,"

"Country girl."

"Very very intriguing."

(Is it?)

"So tell me, are you up for it? Do you do drugs?,"

"No, why would anyone? Expensive and dangerous."

"I wanted to propose something interesting, I'd love to get high with you, can I tempt you?."

(The nearest for me was sniffing a marker pen aged 11)

"Not a chance, pointless, like 3D glasses. Let me guess, early thirties, successful young achiever?,"

"Yep." (I'm getting pretty good as sussing these idiots out now, not bad for a shepherdess.)

Another text,

"Going to fuck my girlfriend later, can I ring you?." (Ignored that one)

As an escort, I should by all accounts be struck off by Trading Standards for not conforming even remotely, to what constitutes an escort. By this I mean that any client planning on visiting me would fully expect me to be cleansed of farm faecal matter and have at the very least, changed out of the tee shirt and leggings I've been wearing all day. I do smear a little eyeliner on and waft some body spray about, but what can you do?! My heart's not in it. I simply can't bear to be parted from my favourite, baggy Christmas Pudding jumper, I dread to think what has been said about me on forums;

"Do not use this escort, she is the antiserum for all things sexual."

Though the more mature men are almost all, without exception, decent, responsible husbands and seem to me to be very caring towards their wives and children, let's face it, I am not witnessing a particularly wholesome cross section of humanity. Any man capable of sexual liaisons with a prostitute behind his wife's back, no matter how dragonesque the wife may be, is of a decidedly dubious moral character.

January 1st 2006

Wormed and foot trimmed the boss's herd of pygmy goats today. They are tiny and very cute but unfriendly and wild, dispersing like a blown dandelion when disturbed. Their long time husband, Eric, so named because he is anything but idle; when not fornicating, is sharpening his horns on the ash tree and terrifying Archibald's weekend guests as they enter his field to 'play with the baby goats.' Eric, livid at the unwelcome trepassers, shifts from first to forth gear in seconds and hurls himself at the throng of innocent admirers, as they scoop up their wailing children and scrabble for the exit. Surprisingly he didn't mess with me whilst I administered various treatments to his wives, but proudly scrunched himself up and sprayed me with that familiar pithy mix of urine and semen.

One of the nanny goats decided Eric was a poor choice of husband and settled for Flash, the Suffolk ram, not minding in the *least that the two boys were different species altogether. She squeezed through fences and climbed hedges to reach Flash, canoodling up to him in a determined effort to persuade him that she too was a ewe. Initially Flash was up for it, but when he set about jumping on her from the business end, he came to his senses, realising she was no sheep at all and that the resulting offspring would be very very odd, so he turned his back on her. Eric continued to chase her around the field desperate for a bonk, but she refused his advances. Five months later she gave birth to triplets, Eric must have talked her round.*

Lemony, the Highland cow, calved six weeks ago and today I noticed a puddle of liquid calf poo, the colour of Laura Ashley's paint, 'French Clay,' on the barn floor. As a livestock keeper, one instinctively knows when the consistency and colour of animal droppings indicate potential problems, and grey is not a good colour. He was a wild little beast, so I hid and waited until he wandered into the barn with his mum, and nipped round behind to shut the gate. Christ he was a mad fecker, I managed to trap him between wall and gate and having drawn up 10mls of antibiotic, I stuck the needle in his rear, whereupon he leapt like a gazelle, dragging my hand along the breeze block wall, removing a fair amount of skin, the syringe and needle still in his backside. Lord knows how but he then managed to squeeze under a one foot gap at the bottom of the gate, leaving me panting and swearing profusely with a bloodied hand. I rounded him up again with much lunging and nifty darting to and fro, and having assumed the needle was by now lost in the straw bedding, I was relieved to see it was still stuck in his backside. So with all my weight against the gate, I reattached the loaded syringe and pressed the plunger, he's now pestilence free and all the happier for it, though of course I won't be able to get within 50 feet of him ever again.

After I'd been sprayed by Eric, I had a bloke due for an appointment in half an hour, so it was a wash to which I always add Dettol to kill any nasty bacteria, plus lots of perfume sprayed about my person and the hut. I now smelled of hospitals and goats....and cheap body spray.

The man in question was very pleasant and didn't remark on any lingering smells, but honestly, well! I've never seen anything like it. He had the the most enormous testicles. I would say, with no exaggeration, that each of them was as firm, round and sizeable as a gala melon. He clearly had some sort of tumour-like growth down there and I flung my hand to my mouth exclaiming,

"You need to see a doctor! That can't be right?!,"

"No one else has commented on their size," he replied, clearly a lie. He was obviously terrified of the results of a doctor's examination.

January 8th 2006

Took six lambs to abattoir and drove home in a cloud of guilt, how I hate it when they have to die. Forced to make the agonising decision to not buy three extra large MacDonalds Whopper Meals from the drive through, on way home. Nothing to do with my new found aversion to meat, but the fact the bloody sheep trailer wouldn't fit through the drive-through lane.

'More pet sheep, will I ever learn'

I accepted a booking last week via the shameful website on which I advertise my wares. This necessitated flying to Gibraltar, bloody Gibraltar! I can't believe I carried it through, being as my farthest global outpost was Sainsburys. I bought a smart, grey, 'I work in the City' suit, some shiny red high heels which I staggered about in like a new born foal, and now, looking like a podgy, middle aged Virgin air stewardess, I boarded the plane, convinced that every passenger was looking at me; a wicked hooker on her way to a fiery hell.

Having force fed myself like a goose on McDonalds for three hours to calm my nerves, the entire episode felt like an out of body experience, especially since I had no idea what this guy looked like, only that he was a 'doctor in the Navy.' The fact he lived on the great Rock itself lent some credence to this fact I hoped.

Upon my arrival in Gibraltar, after looking furtively around at the mass of people in the airport lounge and hoping my antennae would point me to a randy doctor type, a plumpish, ginger-haired, thirty something gentleman greeted me and I plonked myself down next to him in his very smart Mercedes.

He instructed me to, 'wave your Twix wrapper at the customs man,' as we drove onto the Rock, as 'they never check anyway.' He was right too, it was a Turkish Delight wrapper actually. The scenario in his flat was most odd; womens' clothing and makeup were scattered all over the bedroom, as if she'd just left for work in a hurry, not good.

"Blimey, are you sure no one's going to walk in? Looks like she's just left!."

After mentioning this several times and fearing for my safety should the woman have dashed out earlier and forgotten her lip gloss, he eventually said,

"It's hard for me to talk about but she was killed in a road accident five months ago."

"Oh my God I'm so sorry, how are you coping? I didn't intend to bring that up for you, are you sure you're ok with me being here?."

"Of course," he said, as he hauled out his marrow sized manhood and bore down on me.

I spent two days in Gibralta as per the booking agreement. Happily, he was at work all day, so I had a merry time of it, eating all his Pringles then pocketing the £500 he handed to me at the end of the stay. Some weeks later I had an outcall to Leeds to see a guy who happened to work as a senior director of a company which supplied bullet proof vests to the military. I told him about my trip to Gibraltar whereupon he said he knew of the Doctor on the Rock and would make a few enquiries as to his integrity. Mr Bullet Proof Vest rang me a week later to tell me Mr Rock was a renowned womaniser, married with two children, with no records of a splattered wife on the Gibraltar highway. My my the lengths men go to.

January 10th 2006

Orphan lambs following me everywhere, they ran behind pickup, shot under gate and out onto road the pesky varmints, so pushed them back into field and wedged a pallet under gate. I have three huge bags of lungs, livers and hearts in freezer from the last lot of lambs that went to abattoir. So I lit a BBQ in the field, in January, and cooked them all for the dogs.

Saw a 33 year old today. He was heart broken, poor chap, had just been dumped but couldn't ejaculate with me so returned home fully loaded. Next a 31 year old gardener, married with a 14 month old girl and a house rabbit called Alice. Wanted sex twice, knackered, was over the moon when he'd gone. Fly has sore paw, if not improved within a couple of days, will take her to vets.

January 13th 2006

Saw a pervy 39 year old today who said his most thrilling sexual experience was being tied to a cross and being rogered up the bottom. Kept bucking his teeth like the vicar in the Dick Emery show. Fly has broken her paw so it's a bandage on leg and lampshade on head for six weeks. Had the three black lambs in pick up cab today. One managed to push its hoof into the clock on dashboard which has now disappeared inside the innards of truck, so no more clock. Saw a 27 year old Hermes delivery driver as a client, said he delivers to this address sometimes. Jesus. I live in mortal dread of my despicable secret being discovered by employers.

Moved three different flocks today with dogs; 400 ewes, 80 hoggets and 250 lambs. Took an hour and a half and was running late for a client. He rang me to say he was lost and was parked up by the National Trust tea shop on the moor, so as it was getting dark at this point, I drove out to rescue him. There he was in a canary yellow TR7, wearing sunglasses. I was in overalls and my canary yellow fisherman's coat and no makeup.

"Alright mate?!," I shouted over the wind and rain, leaning out of the pick up window.

"Hello Delilah, shall I follow you?,"

He did too. I was amazed, I fully expected him to hot foot it away in the opposite direction across the moors upon seeing me in my outdoor attire. He was very clingy once back at the hut and held my hand constantly, despite my trying to remove it without causing offence. Also kept telling me how 'wonderfully normal' I was. Not sure if that's a compliment or not.

January 14th 2006

Had to cut EID tags out of 20 shearlings today. Archie, bless him, had decided he was going to take an active role in his sheep flock and proudly announced he'd, 'tagged them all to help me out.' Sadly he'd put the wrong numbers in. Still, at least it's sunny today as I couldn't have done it in the rain due to the risk of causing ear infections.

Saw a train driver with bright ginger hair, engaged to be married,

"But why are you feeling the need to sleep around?," I asked, "do you love her?," long pause..

"I suppose so."

"Suppose so! Are you bonkers! She's not the one, don't do it, you'll live to regret it and so will she."

He left a whole lot happier, was hugely grateful for my honesty and said he would probably end it.

Was running very late for a client because I'd fallen asleep after my afternoon cup of tea. Lied and said a goat had got its head stuck in fence. He said,

"I'm here because my wife told me to go and sort myself out."

Blimey, a hell of a wife eh? He handed me the £100, politely asking,

"A pretty dress for a New Years party?,"

"Two tonnes of chalk to lay around lambing barn."

January 15th 2006

Made 48 jam tarts.

January 16th 2006

Jam tarts all gone.

January 17th 2006

Saw an older gentleman for 15 minutes, just a hand job, woo hoo. I do like the older clients; they are sensible, often cannot produce an erection and hence I am not obliged to bend my poor old legs into silly positions.

January 21st 2006

Cows bust the float on the water trough so had to get that fixed before anything else. Currently getting through about £100 worth of bird feed every month, I don't begrudge a penny of it.

Saw a guy with Parkinsons today. He had the serious shakes, so much so he couldn't hold his own willy. Sex was, shall we say, different.

Ok I agreed to do an overnight again. I swear to the Gods of sparkly dog collars, that I will never do it again. Thing is, it's a goodly chunk of money, and reasonably easily earned if I can get the man to fall asleep for as much of the night as possible. He was in his 70's and had me wear a diamante dog collar whilst I crawled around on all fours for hours, with him smacking my backside and croaking continuously,

"Bad girl, bad girl!."

Utterly weary with boredom I was, until eventually he went to bed.

"I'm just off to powder my nose," I lied.

Off with the collar and on with the woolly jumper, as I raided his fridge and ate three rounds of Shiphams meat paste sandwiches. I don't know which was worse, crawling around on all fours wearing a dog collar or the puréed cows intestines sandwiches.

Talking of outcalls, many months ago I agreed to see a man some 20 miles away who when I arrived was well on the way to being very drunk. It was a nice, clean modern apartment and he said his girlfriend was due home in two hours, not good. He was a very slender, Asian chap, but after another huge shot of whisky and water, his speech was slurring to the point that he was unable to form comprehensible words. At his request, I assumed the all fours position on the sitting room floor, awaiting his attention. Five minutes elapsed and nothing had happened. I looked behind me to find him crouched on the carpet, blind drunk, swaying left and right like Stevie Wonder, and wearing latex gloves. He had managed to get a condom on his unresponsive member, and was attempting to get a second one on over the top of the first. Twenty minutes passed and still he swayed to and fro, muttering unintelligible phrases; "must make it fit, can't get it over the top, mustn't get gonorrhoea, had a bit too much to drink." And all the while he crackled constantly; the crackling of latex gloves and condoms. The gloves were not the smooth fitting type, but the clear, crunchy plastic film such as fresh flowers are delivered in.

I wanted to scream, insensible with boredom and acutely aware of his girlfriend due home at any time. He continued to peer drunkenly down at his willy with intense concentration, condom in hand and crunching and crackling away.

"Do you mind if I get a book?," I asked.

I reached up from my position on the floor and read a Jamie Oliver cookbook.

After ten minutes I stood up,

"Ok! times up, gotta go!."

Holy mother of Jesus, I don't think I can take much more of this prostitution carry on.

January 23rd 2006

Was driving pickup through gateway with Nellie pushing sheep away for me, I grabbed phone with one hand and read text;

"Oh yeh is this Delilah? Ow much for the hour babe and do you do the 'ousewife experience?,"

"Sorry?," I texted back.

"Is it all inclusive? Do you do face-sitting?."

(What has face sitting to do with housewifely things such as hoovering and laundry?)

Earlier today, a hideous experience, thankfully short, with an elderly man who refused to pay the £70, I accepted £50. Oh dear God, I lay there whilst he suckled greedily on my nipples with rancid breath and brown, decaying teeth. I winced and scowled, a woman having her nipples salivated over by an octogenarian, just shoot me now.

Another bloke a couple of hours later was a typically stressed businessman, we had a good chat. He laid there, reluctant to leave and seemingly glad to have found someone to talk to about his marital problems, whilst I discreetly Googled shark attacks.

January 25th 2006

A guy I saw at 1pm, openly said he had a foot fetish and wanted to visit me today. I was honest about the appalling state of my feet but he insisted. So I duly sloshed them around in soapy water in the hand basin. He drove in at the appointed time, I laid down on the bed, fully clothed with bare feet and had a wonderful foot massage. It was sooo good, just the ticket for my swollen old plates. He toddled off half an hour later, £70 lighter and said he wanted to revisit. God I love my job. Not really.

January 27th 2006

Really bad black dog for a couple of days but finally snapped out of it. Was worming and dagging 35 of last years lambs that did the trick. Nothing like a bit of manual labour to sort your head out. Kipling summed it up perfectly; (not the cake man, the poet)

"The cure for this ill is not to sit still,
Or frowst with a book by the fire;
But to take a large hoe and a shovel also,
And dig till you gently perspire."

January 31st 2006

Up at 5am, first snow of year, hay to ewes in Tansy field, dead hogget, no idea as to cause of death, possibly fluke but unlikely. Cleaned two water troughs, need new tyre on quad.

Saw a married man in his 60's, brought a riding crop with him, I had to whip his backside until it was red. Every time I cracked whip, Bett the neurotic collie howled like a werewolf, nightmare.

The following text conversation is absolutely genuine, probably the craziest I've ever had, the Aunty Debra text:

"Will you smoke a fag while you suck my cock?,"

"I don't smoke."

"Please Aunty Debra, I love watching you smoke, you look so sexy. I want you to flick your fag ash on my bell-end again. I won't tell your kids. I'll pay you £150 for half an hour."

"I'm Delilah not Aunty Debra."

"I know I want you to pretend to be my Aunty Debra."

"I'm afraid I don't offer role play services."

"Please don't tell anyone Aunty Debra, you just make my dick so hard when I see a fag in your mouth. I'll let you use me as your ashtray while I lick you're asshole out."

(Blimey your Aunty Debra's a game old bird)

"Come on Aunty Debra I know you're a slut and love sucking big dicks. Come round and smoke a fag while I fuck your ass or I'll tell Maxi you gave me a blowjob in the toilet at her wedding."

"Are you ok? I mean, are you unwell?,"

"I'm wanking over pictures of you smoking a fag right now, you want a pic of my dick?,"

"No thanks, I'm having breakfast."

February 1st 2006

Oi oi here we go...

"Hi, (huge blubs and gulps) "wh..wh..whose this?," (much weeping and wailing..a woman's voice)

"I'm sorry?," (oops he's been busted, always have two phones guys)

Much louder and frantic now….

"wha..wha..what's your name?," (enormous gulps and blubs) "I..I..I found your name, oh my god, why why?!." (blub, gulp, cluck, sniff)

"This is Ellie, I'm a dentist from Nottingham, I think you have the wrong number."

That was good of me wasn't it? Let's hope it helped to save the relationship.

February 2nd 2006

Spent a horrible hour in town being ushered out of every shop like a pustule covered leper because my quiet collie was with me, on a lead. The sour faced old cow in the gift shop, greeted me with a, 'I'm afraid you can't bring..,' I left her to trail off as I hovered on the threshold, gesticulating towards the glass cabinet, indicating that I wished to purchase some handmade chocolates for my Aunty's birthday (not Debra, my real Aunty). Why couldn't I bring my dog in the shop? The likelihood of Nellie wrestling herself from the lead, climbing inside the chocolate cabinet, mounting the edible display contained therein and eating, peeing or pooing on them was, well, unlikely. Do these establishments actually question WHY they don't allow dogs in? I am forbidden to sit in any one of the several dozen coffee shops here because I have a dog. She has no more harmful bacteria on her paws than a brat has on the wheels of its 4x4 pram or smeared across its front.

'Beautiful, beautiful Nellie'

Ok, some emails now...

"Hello Delilah,

I found your profile quite by chance but I have to say I'm rather glad I did. Now I must admit to having a soft spot for your namesake, Delia Smith. You do seem to possess more than a passing resemblance to her which can only be a good thing. Your blog is one of the most amusing reads I have seen for quite a while. It had me laughing out loud in the way most alleged modern comedy can only dream of doing! Do keep it updated please.

Can I ask about your dogs? I'm actually allergic to dog and cat fur, shame as I really like them, and no, I'm not allergic to pussy. I must congratulate you on such a magnificent pair of breasts! They have such a lovely, even shape and delicious looking nipples. I could see myself playing with those for ages, head buried between them, my tongue skiing down that cleavage and laying entwined between your broad thighs. Oh madam!

Do you perform other services that are not listed upon your profile? as it seems a little spartan. Do you for example do deep throat? With the right enticement of your favourite Milk Tray chocolate at the base and a line of Cadbury's buttons laid along my cock, perhaps that would be an enticing treat for your mouth. How about a tie and tease? Ever fancied doing that? A voluptuous figure such as yours would look marvellous in some fully fashioned stockings and suspenders. I would have to remember my camera if you would kindly pose.

I see in your pictures there are some outdoor shots so perhaps once the weather improves there maybe the possibility of some alfresco fun on your rural retreat? What a truly delectable prospect! (for you matey I'm sure, it all sounds like hell to me.)

Anyway Delia. Hopefully speak to you soon.

Simon xx

"Hi babe, love your big tits and your big fat ars. Can't wait to fuck that ars and come on your hard tits." (he sounds an absolute charmer.)

"Hi Delia, lovely big fucking tits you have love to shoot my SPUNK ALL OVER THEM AND YOU LICK IT OFF. What do you say to that babe?." (I'd say you appear to be a close relative to the author of the previous monosyllabic warthog email.)

"Dear Delilah

As I love gracious, feminine ladies, I am very interested in your look and would like to spend some time with you..not necessarily venally (venally?) as i'm 63 years old and you may find it difficult to arouse me, although by God you can try! Yet I still have the mental desire to entertain ladies and spend a lovely fulfilling time with them.

Are you interested? I am.

Robert x."

"Dear Delilah,

I have recently seen your profile, you look very pretty and my what magnificent breasts you have. I have a day off work today to do with as I wish. The weather is fine, a relief from recent events and I would love to come and see you for an hour of fun (why do these men consistently refer to sexual activities as 'fun?.' A less fun-filled activity I cannot imagine: faked enjoyment with a stranger and the inspecting of his foreskin and testicles appeals as much as fell running to a 16 stone woman with a GG bust.)

I am a very long way away from you, between London and Cambridge, but I am at a loose end and your pictures have excited me somewhat. Would you consider £90 an hour? I am happy to do anything that would turn you on, like you sitting on my face.

I look forward to hearing from you, David xx."

"Hi Delia, (it's not bloody Delia)

A couple of quick questions before I book you, none of which are show stoppers:

Do you have any big granny pants or shaping knickers." (Loads)

Could you wear tights and heels as well?

Do you support cross dressing at all? It's something I would like to try.

Des x."

"Well Delia, I bet this line of work makes a change to cooking on the telly and writing cookery books or snorting cocaine. (wrong chef) Glad you are getting things back together and had the confidence to move away from what was an established career. My name's Ian and I'd love to meet you, please let me know if you're interested."

"Hello, I am in my 30's. First of all, BBW? You don't look that big to me. But I am more interested in how hairy the bush is! Looking for a Serena Grandi type. I do have a very fat cock/big head so I am told and I think so too. Do you prefer fat cocks to long thin ones?. Don't worry I'm a good 6 inches in length just a big girth.

Regards, look forward to response X."

February 5th 2006

Earnt £110 from a nice 50 year old prescribing pharmacist who discussed with me in great detail, the processes involved in post nasal drip. The down side was enduring doggie style for five minutes. He'd been married for four years, four years! What the devil is the point in marriage when you're resorting to paid sex after so short a time. Seems to me a lot of men, if not the majority, are pressured into marriage. Very few men I've spoken to, earnestly wished to have been married, it was usually always the female who craved the legal bond.

I put winter coats and blankets on all five of the bosses old goats tonight, looks like it's going to be damn cold.

Have noticed that quite a few of the emails I receive, when I click on them, read, 'the sender is no longer active on this website.' Maybe men cancel their profiles when either they get an attack of morality when the wife cooks their favourite supper or agrees to oral sex after a ten year abstinence. Or possibly when she finds their second mobile phone.

"Hello Delilah my name is Darren. I'm a 41 year old male with severe arthritis and I wanted to give you the courtesy of an email before I might call you. The last thing I want to do to such a beautiful lady is irritate you with requests or unwanted information. So as a courtesy I thought I would email you with my preferences to give you the chance to say no without having to talk to me. I am a cross dresser, and would like to request an hour of your time for straight sex, but I would be dressed accordingly in a skirt and heels. I would also like to bring an outfit for you to wear, nothing weird, just a cocktail dress, tights, camisole and slip. Hope they fit ok, they're a size 20. My final request is to be able to look through your underwear drawer in order to be able to buy an item or two from you. The sensation of looking through a lady's underwear drawer is very exciting for me.

With much respect,

Darren xx."

(I have six pairs of full brief cotton pants and two bras, my total underwear collection, it wouldn't take him long. I certainly don't recall an arthritic man rifling through my pants, so I assume it was a no to a meeting from me.)

February 10th 2006

What a hideous hideous shitty little bloke from Lancashire. He had already booked me yesterday then cancelled, texted today and booked for 3pm, then changed it to 1pm, then turned up at 1.45pm with no cash. Utter dickhead. He drove back into town to get cash, I wasn't expecting his return as he'd seen me in my, 'Mine's a pint o' cider please,' Wurzels teeshirt.

Surprisingly he did return, and having asked him to park discreetly just outside the farmyard, as Archibald had the vet out to one of his horses right in front of my gypsy hut, the bloody idiot drives up to the gate in a Wincanton articulated delivery lorry. Moron, nee, total spaz.

I just knew he was going to be horrid and I was right. Small, exceedingly common and full of himself, he obviously thought he was up for a thoroughly debauched hour (an hour, oh god, a whole bloody hour) of erotic fun. I stretched out conversation for as long as I could, before he grabbed my breasts and pummelled and pinched them like a ball of sourdough. Put a condom on his horrible Hartlepool willy and reached for the vibrating machine, hoping to hell I could relieve him ASAP, which he did but then proceeded to work himself up again. The second time went on forever. Eventually he removed the condom in order to masturbate himself. A whiff of fish propelled itself through the air and I gagged silently. Why do people do this sex thing? It's bad enough owning my own crotch, never mind pressing it up against someone else's. At last the hour was done with and as soon as he was gone, I was on with the boots and off across the hills with Nellie to blow the thoughts of the previous hour away.

February 12th 2006

A quiet day of mostly blue skies except for half an hour of freezing rain and bitter wind when I was up on the moor walking dogs. Came back for breakfast, then on with the hobnails and up hill to muck out cows. One of the Herdwicks is lame on its front left foot, probably scald as it generally is at this time of year, such a pain in the backside. With this in mind, I plan to vaccinate with Footvax when the lambs are weaned in August. Footvax is a vaccine for 'footrot,' an infection caused by a different bacteria but it does significantly reduce the incidence of scald as well, so will give it a try.

Had a Dorset Down ewe stuck in a badger hole today. Was checking them as usual and thought one was just lying down, but as I drew closer to her, I could see only her front two legs and head were above ground! There was no way I could pull her out as the suction was so great so called on a neighbour and he dug her out. Poor thing, she hobbled away none the worse though.

I can hear the kestrels in their box, high up in the sheep barn, it's so wonderful to have them here every year.

My ever tactful father pointed an enquiring finger at the 'beauty spot' on my upper lip area today, as we shared a pub lunch;

"Why is your mole green?,"

An explanation follows: I had my eyebrows defined with a permanent ink about ten years ago, back in the last Ice Age when I gave a dog's kahunnas about things such as eyebrows, and recall the dissappointment upon seeing the results of the beautician's ministrations; I looked like a bloody drag queen; huge, arched, semi circular jet black brows, like a set of mud-terrain tyres drawn on my forehead.

"Aren't they great! Are you pleased?," she had said, thrilled at her efforts, her face two inches from my Lily Savage monstrosities.

"Er, yes. They're um..quite dark," inwardly weeping at my stupidity at ever having considered the treatment. Anyway, ten years later, having faded into an odd shade of turmeric, they are now companions to my green beauty spot.

I'd had the spot tattooed in order to enlarge and darken it. What on earth was I thinking! A grand short cut to skin cancer I reckon. I can't believe the so called professional beautician agreed to do it. I asked her if it was a sensible idea, given that moles are susceptible to cell mutations. 'Yes of course it's fine,' she'd replied breezily, pocketing the £45. The mole has changed from its original natural nut brown before the girl burnt the buggary out of it and filled it with black ink, to an unattractive olive green these days which looks most ghoul-like in the light of day. So I just put up with orange eyebrows, a green mole, a pernicious beard that sprouts back like ground elder no matter how many times I tear it out by the roots, and thinning teeth owing to my compulsive grinding habit. The poor dentist, Mr Patel, is convinced I am on my way to a mouthful of teeth like Parmesan shavings. Speaking of battling age; before my brother's wedding, I was persuaded by my mother to have my hair trimmed and coloured. I have been chopping haphazardly away at it with sheep dagging shears a couple of times a year and gave up on colouring long ago, having decided to go officially grey. After studying at great length, various colour charts in the hairdressers, I decided on a basic all over dark brown, with random dark copper and caramel coloured highlights. I was very specific about what I wanted and had even been asked to bring a picture to illustrate my wishes, which I produced accordingly.

Well..for £120 I was rather expecting a result at least similar to the picture. It was nothing like it; bright gingery hair, with the only noticeable difference being the reduction in length and the absence of grey. I poked up with my hair for a couple of months, until unable to bear the Lucozade coloured apparition in the mirror every morning, I bought an off the shelf dark brown hair colourant for £4.99.

My transformation into the hair of Gollum had begun as I vowed to let nature follow her natural course thenceforth.

The day of the wedding arrived and I was feeling very pleased with myself for having been so organised; my outfit was all laid out ready for the transformation. I had bought the expensive, red ankle boots some months previously, and when they arrived in the post back in the summer I had opened the package, put on a left hand boot, which fitted perfectly, and replaced them in the box, not bothering to try the right boot on. What was I thinking? Who the hell tries just one on?! The taxi was due in ten minutes. The left one went on perfectly, luvvly jubbly. Right hand boot on..what the?!..I had been sold two left hand boots, unbebloodylievable. But I had no choice, it was Dunlop wellies, hobnail boots covered in cow shite, or a pair of whorehouse scarlet six inch heels that I'd only ever managed to squeeze my size 8's into once, for some escort profile photographs. They were agony and I'd never actually walked in them, so I wore two left hand boots to the wedding, which caused the best man much merriment, exclaiming;

"You'll be going round in left hand circles on the dance floor!."

So anyway, back to today, gotta go, a one hour booking with a bloke, fab, can now put diesel in truck.

February 13th 2006

The best thing for reducing the desire in mens' bellies is to mention their marriages, it helps me stall for time. Apparently I am helping to make up the deficit in their relationships and they are often very grateful for having found someone to off-load on, pun intended.

A chap I saw today worked as a contractor for BT putting optic fibre thingies underground. It certainly does 'pay to talk;' he gave me a bundle, free of charge, of enormous cable ties for use on the farm. One will be used to stop my new bread maker getting over enthusiastic during the kneading phase. It dances across the worktop and is in danger of clattering to the floor. Don't these poxy manufacturers carry out tests in real life situations before their products go on sale?

Text conversation:

"Hi I'm Andy, lovely pics. I'm 29, could we arrange £50 for cash?,"

"No sorry, prices are per my profile."

"Hmm, for £70 I'd wanna finish in you ars."

"Go away."

"Ok"

And another as I'm enjoying a coffee, the sunshine flooding into my gypsy caravan....

"OH MY DAYS!" I went on this adult site to see what the fuss was about and saw your pics. Never thought I'd say this to a 38 year old but you look amaaazing! You look better than most 28 year olds let alone 38. Shame you're an escort LOL."

"Many thanks for the age and escort comment."

"Didn't mean to offend, you gotta do what you gotta do, I just meant it's a shame for me,"

"Why?,"

"Because I'd have hit on you otherwise LOL."

"Shame for me too, I'd never hit on a guy that uses escorts. LOL."

February 15th 2006

Terrible wind due to two big cans of curried beans and two packs of diabetic sweets. Overdose of sorbitol and beans and I'm a walking talking biofuel plant trying like fuck to keep the flue shut and the fuel feed open for business. One client saw me for free today cos I talked for an hour last time, anyway he rolled on one of his own bollocks and was in agony!! Ha ha ha. I made him tea n toast and asked permission to break wind.

February 18th 2006

Got all the ewes and lambs in yesterday and carried out various treatments which will keep them safe from the perils and often fatal afflictions of intestinal worms, clostridial diseases and lameness. Had some neighbours pop round today, a husband and wife who have just moved up from Surrey, having purchased a small farmhouse with 20 acres. They asked if I would email them with sheepy advice, before they go about buying a small flock.

February 23rd 2006

Moved twenty lambs to stubble turnip field and foot-bathed hoggets. Rushed in, covered in sheep crap and sweat, washed fanny, sprayed armpits, eyeliner on, smile 'n go. Bloody builders everywhere as boss is having work done. Forestry guys in road dealing with fallen tree and I'm trying to sneak a client in. Hands stained bright yellow with the sulphur I've been using to treat the Shire horses feathered hooves. The smell isn't too good either.

February 24th 2006

The twenty Poll Dorset ewes have just started to lamb, walked dogs, fed twin-bearing ewes but only 0.5kg as in such good condition because of the free access feed blocks they are on. Just eaten a whole box of fudge. I deserve it, life is hard. Two ewes have retainers in for small vaginal prolapses, hope they do the job. Checked ewes, bedded up, hayed up, watered and fed. Castrated and tailed lambs, did feet on three ewes and numbered up and turned out the well-mothered singles. Took numerous calls and texts whilst doing that lot,

"Oh yeah, hi, is this Delilah?,"

"Yes how can I help you?,"

"Do you do rimming?,"

"What? Did you not read profile?," (assuming you can read. Musn't call him a fucking idiot, musn't, must be nice.)

"Is that sheep I can hear?,"

"Yes I'm lambing." He hung up.

Back down to cottage, directed Aga service man to main house. Arrange to see a man at 11.30am...

Very smart, professional looking man drives in punctually at 11.30am in enormous, black glossy Discovery. Sky is barking and unstoppable because the house alarm has gone off, a regular event as it's faulty. Wainthropps the knacker guys are here to shoot a Poll Dorset ewe who's prolapse is incurable and I'm hopping from foot to foot in growing panic as he's just stomped up the hill to the barn with a barrow to bring her corpse back in. Explained to glossy Discovery man would he mind waiting as I'd have to sign docket for the dead sheep. The grim reaper finally reappeared with his laden barrow and unloaded its grisly contents into the back of the truck, which now open, revealed a very dead, oozing Shire horse and a bloated calf. Mr Discovery gave a series of guttural coughs in short restrained bursts. Did my best to entertain him once inside but I don't think his heart was in it.

"Hi, you working?"

I know from these three simple words that here is a man who I would no more wish to see than Tony Blair cutting his toenails.

"Do you have black nylon suspenders and belt with a corset and big heels?,"

"No."

February 26th 2006

Well dang me if I haven't just invented a grey muffin, a full on, prison corridor, battleship grey muffin. They haven't risen either so they are flat and grey, but pretty tasty. True to form, not content with making an average number of muffins, I have made enough batter for 60. I simply can't do things on a normal scale. I began making soap a few years ago, from scratch, the real thing, using fat and caustic soda. I spent hundreds of hours concocting different scents and colours and the results were splendid. I must have made about 100kg of the stuff in total, but sadly had absolutely no interest in or aptitude for selling it. So to try to get rid of the stuff I gave soap to everybody, to people who didn't really want soap, because they used the liquid stuff.

Today has been bliss, not one man have I seen, spoken to or received a text from. Bad for the bank balance but marvellous for the mind and well being. Lumbering around Tesco this afternoon on my flat feet, watching carefree youths with their impossibly slim bodies and unlined faces, laden with wine and lager at the checkouts, a night of fun and flirting ahead of them, I couldn't help but feel a pang of longing to look pretty once more. It is a fact however that now I no longer consider myself to be physically attractive, I am vastly more content. Weight gain is the most effective barrier against wanted or unwanted male attention. No more do I cast furtive glances in the direction of attractive men, thinking, 'could he, would he?, if I have 20" hair extensions next week, lose another stone and find an extra strong glue so my eyelashes stay put during a snog.' As a heavily overweight nearly 40 something, I have become invisible to men on the look out for totty, and it is like being released from prison.

'Battleship Muffins'

February 27th 2006

Saw two blokes on their wives' birthdays, both of whom had young children. Christ these men must have a rich seams of lies to bombard their families with. One of them, a mountain of a man at about 20 plus stone, had only been married 18 months, was having an affair with his neighbour's wife and also saw escorts. The deceit involved must have been exhausting! Heaving a silent sigh when he replied with the answer 'both,' to my question of 'would you like intercourse or oral sex?,' he mounted me like the honey monster and was so heavy, I was having trouble breathing. Politely easing his bulk a little, he requested doggie style, a great relief as I would be free of his immense weight. I rotated myself like a frying sausage and he determinedly ploughed on whilst I rested my chin in my hand, planning supper while he poked around inside me, seemingly quite happy.

Was reminiscing over past jobs today whilst feeding the animals. A couple of years ago, I worked as a part time home help to a couple who had adopted two Chinese girls. Aged 11 and 14, both were sullen, and the parents, presumably riddled with guilt over working all hours in the city, spoilt them shamelessly when they eventually saw them. Meals were lovingly prepared with an extensive selection of food, and the girls, if they could be bothered to raise their heads, would grunt their choices. The youngest of the two, Pippa, affectionately known as Peepee to her adoring parents, had some sort of irritating, beeping, electronic thingie, a Tamagotchi was it? The pointless device enabled the user to take full care of an imaginary electronic dog; if you didn't feed, walk and medicate it regularly, it died. Two metres from the girl sat Penny, a beautiful golden retriever who had been alone all day and needed feeding and walking. Pippa had no interest in doing either.

The morning routine on a school day ran thus;

"Peepee like scramblies? (scrambled egg) or Peepee want toastee and jammie for brekkie?, or Mummy can make creamy porridge and honey?,"

(Peepee needed a sound cuff round the chops and made to eat what she was bloody well given or it's back to the orphanage on boiled rice)

I saw a chap a few days ago. He was pleasant enough but possessed an all pervading aura of depression and lack of personal hygiene. Vague wafts of unwashed hair, jumper and trousers that have never known a bio wash at 40 degrees. I may be a lot of dreadful things but stingy with the Persil Small and Mighty I am not. I chatted amiably away, silently gagging at the thought of being within six foot of his exposed penis. He didn't disappoint, turning over to release an odour of unwashed buttock crevice. GOD I HATE MY JOB!

March 1st 2006

Why am I only attracted to 30 something, attractive, successful men. It's a ridiculous notion. And as likely as Scarlett Johannsen dating Arthur, the yellow toothed, clinically obese gardener that works here.

There's over a foot of snow up here on Gallows farm and I'm stranded in my hut, my mud-terrain tyres can't get through the drifting gateways. Fortunately I always keep a tonne of flour for bread-making. No electricity either so it's candles and a wood burning stove tonight, which I love as the hut is even cosier without power and the stove chucks out so much heat I often open the window during the winter.

Having agreed to see a bloke today and affecting my 'damsel in distress' voice, I asked him to bring me industrial quantities of Dairy Milk. Such was my need for chocolate that I chose not to tell him the roads were treacherous,

"What are the roads like up by you?,"

"Oh they're fine! Bring your wellies just in case."

He arrived three hours later with a bag of chocolate and biscuits looking a little flustered, having walked the last half mile. Afterwards I took him back to his stranded car and towed him to the nearest road that was clear of snow, with the tractor, all heart me.

March 2nd 2006

Opened up my 'hooky' inbox today, dear dear me.

"Good morning Delilah, hope you are well. I'm a 24 year old, of average build, and a good looking guy. I have a foot fetish and I love watching women stand on balloons to burst them with bare feet. Would you be up for this? Will the balloons stand a chance under your bare feet? Xx"

This is a new one on me I have to confess. And it was a definite no.

"Dear Delilah, my name is Michael. I'm 53, very clean, reliable, submissive, confident and articulate. I've recently returned to the UK having spent the last 12 years in America. I wondered if you might have a lady that will be able to act as a key holder for me and to provide me with a weekly over the knee spanking. I work from home and everyday have the temptation to masturbate. There is nothing wrong with that of course, but I have so little self control and enjoy masturbation so much that uncontrolled I will wank for hours and hours. I have regularly spent 4/5 hours at my PC playing with myself. And so knowing this, I bought a CB-6000 chastity device and found myself a key holder in Chicago. It was an arrangement that worked wonderfully and we became great friends. My previous key holder was a beautician.

Now that I am here in the UK, I need to find a new key holder and am looking for exactly the same kind of thing; a long term, regular arrangement whereby I am held in chastity and disciplined regularly. I am very much a no drama, obedient kind of man. Very sane and sensible. But without a key holder I will simply masturbate the day away.

I sincerely hope this is something you feel you may be able to help me with.

Warm regards

Michael."

Bless you Michael, but it's a no.

As the ground is frozen, I've let the cattle out for a run around. There's nothing to graze of course but they love the exercise. Will bring them in again this afternoon.

March 4th 2006

Appalling half hour session with a window cleaner, though sadly, not spent cleaning windows. He had so much cheese on his penis that I could see it through the condom. It took all my concentration not to throw up. His teeth were thick with plaque and his breath could have felled a tree.

Jesus Christ, I saw a 30 stone bloke today for an hour. A mistaken glance in the mirror next to the bed, saw me crouched over an enormous pile of man flesh. I could hardly get hold of his willy it was so embedded in his belly.

March 10th 2006

I have spent the last week in deep thought and simply cannot continue with this ghastly business. I have enough savings now to be able to move my own sheep, cattle and equipment to rented land and just need a decent livestock job to support me.

March 29th 2006

Hurrah hurrah and thrice hurrah! I have been offered a job on a farm in Derbyshire, it sounds really good and they're happy to have me keep my livestock there. I start mid April.

HERE ENDETH THE YEAR OF THE COCK

www.ingramcontent.com/pod-product-compliance
Lightning Source LLC
Chambersburg PA
CBHW071724080526

44588CB00013B/1889